MEDIA WORLDS
IN THE POSTJOURNALISM ERA

David L. Altheide and Robert P. Snow

ALDINE DE GRUYTER
New York

ABOUT THE AUTHORS

David L. Altheide is a Regents Professor at Arizona State University (School of Justice Studies), where he has taught since receiving his Ph.D. in Sociology from the University of California, San Diego. A specialist in mass communication and qualitative research methods, his work has received national and international acclaim. *Creating Reality: How TV New Distorts Events,* was the first work by a non-Italian to receive the Premio Diego Fabbri Award. *Media Power,* another book, received the 1986 Charles Horton Cooley Award from the Society for the Study of Symbolic Interaction. He was selected as Arizona State University's Graduate College Distinguished Researcher for 1990–91.

Robert P. Snow is Professor of Sociology at Arizona State University in Tempe. He received his Ph.D. at the University of Minnesota and has been affiliated with the State University of New York at Buffalo.

ALDINE DE GRUYTER
A division of Walter de Gruyter, Inc.
200 Saw Mill River Road
Hawthorne, New York 10532

The paper used in this publication meets the minimum requirements of American National Standard for Information Sciences—Permanence of Paper for Printed Library Materials, ANSI Z39.48-1984. ♾

Library of Congress Cataloging-in-Publication Data
Altheide, David L.
  Media worlds : in the postjournalism era / David L. Altheide and Robert P. Snow.
    p. cm.—(Communication and social order)
  Includes bibliographical references and index.
  ISBN 0-202-30376-4 (cloth). ISBN: 0-202-30377-2 (paper).
  1. Mass media. I. Snow, Robert P. II. Title. III. Series.
  P90.A7285 1991
302.23—dc20   90-48033
                                                              CIP

Manufactured in the United States of America

10 9 8 7 6 5 4 3 2 1

For Carla, Suzanne and our television-age kids.

CONTENTS

PREFACE

Today all social institutions are media institutions. As more experiences are influenced by media logic and discourse, our worlds are totally media. The nature and impact of total media on social life are our topic. We are concerned with the impact of media perspectives on other domains of social life. *Media logic* consists of a form of communication, the process through which media present and transmit information. Elements of this form include the various media and the formats used by these media. Format consists, in part, of how material is organized, the style in which it is presented, the focus or emphasis on particular characteristics of behavior, and the grammar of media communication. Our focus is on the process and impact of this logic on other domains of social life. Our thesis is quite clear: Social order is increasingly a mediated order, and any serious attempt to understand contemporary life cannot avoid this fact and its implications.

Our approach represents another generation of media studies. McQuail's (1983:176ff) insightful demarcation of "phases of media effects" lists the following approximate dates and focus:

Phase 1. (1900 to late 1930s) The emphasis was on the nature and impact of the mass media to shape public opinion.

Phase 2. (1930s to 1960s) Attention turned to the role of film and other media for "active persuasion or information," including some of the unintended consequences of media messages (cf. Rosengren 1983).

Phase 3. (1960s to 1980s) Interest was in studies of media effects, but with a shift toward long-term social change, beliefs, ideologies, cultural patterns, and "even institutional forms." (Note: This was the period for the rise of "cultural studies" approaches (Williams 1982), interest in structural and rhetorical uses of the mass media, and also a renewed interest in semiotics, deconstruction, and critical literary criticism.)

With the exception of a few works represented in Phase 3, the overwhelming majority of significant works examined media as content, and tended to focus on individual effects, e.g., voting behavior, violence, prejudice, and susceptibility to messages. It was really in the latter part of Phase 3 that attention began to shift to cultural and especially institutional analyses, but even here—including some of our previous work—

the focus was on content, ideology, and how messages can be "biased." We add Phase 4.

Phase 4. (1990 to the present) The contemporary focus in on cultural logics, social institutions, and public discourse (cf. Ferrarotti 1988; Gronbeck 1988). This phase focuses on media and modes of representations as significant features of social life. Drawing on a breadth of theory and research, the latest phase of mass communication studies assumes that since all "messages" are constructed, there will be different interests represented in the content, including those made by social scientists about the biases of others! It is axiomatic that all statements contain and reflect some features of the cultural and ideological context and perspective in which they are offered. Although such pronouncements are useful to inform the lay public about, say, news programs, our understanding of media effects is hardly enhanced by spinning our conceptual wheels on such forms of bias. The reason, of course, is that the problem is not solved by merely altering the "content" or by having one news source replace another one. Rather, what is needed to move ahead in Phase 4 is a fresh approach to the nature of communication basics, especially cultural forms.

During this latest phase of media analysis, attention shifts decidedly away from the content of communication to the forms, formats and logic of order. Formats of communication and control are central elements of this phase; communication modes are no longer regarded merely as "resources" used by powerful elements, but rather communication formats become "topics" in their own right, significant for shaping the rhetoric, frames, and formats of all content, including power, ideology, and influence. In this period, significant social analysis is inseparable from media analysis. Here the key concept is "reflexivity," or how the technology and logic of communication forms shape the content, and how social institutions that are not thought of as "media arenas"—such as religion, sports, politics, the family—adopt the logic of media and are thereby transformed into second order media institutions. We are in this phase now. *Media Worlds in the Postjournalism Era* is one attempt to describe the communicative features of our situation.

In a media world, organized journalism is dead; we are postjournalists for two general reasons. First, journalistic practices, techniques, and approaches are now geared to media formats rather than merely directing their craft at topics; second, the topics, organizations, and issues that journalists report about are themselves products of media—journalistic formats and criteria. In a sense, it is as though journalists, and especially TV journalists, are reporting on another entity down the hall from the newsroom. Public life subscribes to the media logics and formats that have been spawned in our age of electronic information; the politicians and others who are covered use the same criteria the journalists do, and often more skillfully! These are worlds of media, built from standard communication procedures and formats borrowed from the journalistic enterprise. Journalism will not be reborn until information formats are recognized, evaluated, and altered with journalistic criteria in mind, rather than organizational and nonsubstantive mandates.

When we first examined the mass media's impact on culture and everyday life more than a decade ago, it was already clear to us that very few academics had adequately conceptualized the broader effects of the mass media. Indeed, it is no exaggeration to say that several "respected" professionals at the time discouraged these efforts, and at least one British researcher begged off the opportunity to write an Introduction to the earlier edition. Although the rationale for such academic caution remains unclear to us, one point was quite apparent: The innovative approach we proposed challenged several prevailing paradigms, including the most radical "ideological" accounts of mass media content and effects. Undaunted (perhaps foolishly!), we stayed with our perspective and developed the systematic cultural appraisal of mass media effects.

Our Preface to the initial publication of *Media Logic* began with, "Anyone not already convinced of the power of the mass media in contemporary social life may find the following chapters a bit strange." Now, some 12 years later, as we draw out further the examples and theoretical implications of media order, it is apparent that few serious social scientists find the power and significance of "media logic" to be strange (Real 1989). One indicator of the success of our efforts could be measured by book sales numbering in the thousands around the world. But that would be deceiving since many bad books do sell well. A fundamentally better way to gauge the impact of this perspective is to simply note how widespread the notion of "media logic" has become for media analysts. (Indeed, it has been used so pervasively that numerous researchers appear to have forgotten the origins of that term!) Consequently, a number of authors have "reinvented" our wheel during the last decade (cf. Lindlof 1987; Miller 1988). However, the important point is that the concept "media logic" is now part of the discourse used in any serious effort to understand the significance of the mass media for culture and social change (Ewen 1988).

Moreover, as shall be reiterated below, we are pleased that numerous scholars throughout the world now consider the mass media to be an important feature of any serious effort to understand, clarify, change, or even critique contemporary social orders (Carey 1987). Only recently has the study of media logic and its impact become more "legitimate" among students of popular culture and social change, largely as a result of the rediscovery by some intellectuals that objective truth is quite elusive, and that the methods we use to study something and the words and media we employ to carry our messages are really helping shape those messages. A variant of this "postmodern" period labeling—itself a feature of media logic—asserts that the product is hard to separate from the process. Of course, we agree and have argued for this position repeatedly. Fortunately, this understanding is now building on an approach to culture, media, and social control that we began several years ago. Unfortunately, the diverse lines of argumentation do not always converge around the central issues involving media logic and cultural transformation. For example, Miller's (1988) rendering of the culture of TV focuses on the content of the images, and like many chroniclers of the present who lack data about the technology, organizational processes, and audience behavior, they employ misunderstandings, questionable assumptions, and misleading metaphors from literature about social issues and processes. Thus it is now common for students of literary criticism, semiotics, and deconstructionism to consider the mass media. In this sense, we are pleased if our work has contributed to the rediscovery of the relevance of mass communication logic for social life.

In this expanded view of "media logic" we do not attempt to convince those readers who view the mass media as but another "variable" or "factor" (such as age, sex, and religion) in influencing social processes. Rather, we accept the premise that the mass media have had significant effects on social life, and then suggest some conceptually fruitful ways of discovering and understanding the role of media in our lives. We offer an analysis of social institutions transformed through media to illustrate not only how the logic and forms of media perspectives have transformed much of the social stock of knowledge we share, but also how any effort to single out particular "variables" of media impact is likely to miss the most fundamental reality of our social culture shaped by media.

Our perspective on media logic and its consequences for media culture has evolved through fundamental changes in theoretical and methodological issues in social science, our various research efforts, and a host of critical intellectual challenges we have faced as students, teachers, and colleagues.

Among the significant issues are the powerful and still emerging perspectives of symbolic interactionism, ethnomethodology, phenomenological and existentially informed sociological approaches (cf. Douglas & Johnson 1977) as well as related developments in field research methods oriented to describe, articulate, and then account for the multiperspectives that constitute social life. But over time the process of social life comes to be seen as fixed by many of the participants, who, in their subsequent routines and rhetoric, produce institutions. Thus we strive to show the congruency between perspectives and their institutional application; in this way field studies, combined with systematic qualitative content analysis and other research methods, cogently guide investigators to the "big picture" of modern life.

Like the origin of the concept "media logic," many of the basic assumptions underlying symbolic interactionism and phenomenology have been subtly appropriated by researchers throughout the world. The ideas are now taken-for-granted elements of competent social analysis, and, essentially, have been incorporated into diverse methodologically and ideologically informed approaches. For example, a number of approaches in education, communication, and even rhetoric are based on these perspectives, which essentially state that reality is socially constructed through a process of symbolic interaction.

Among those most directly responsible for our approach to the mass media are Jack D. Douglas, whose work on "news power" raised many of the issues we address; John Johnson and his valuable insights; Stanford M. Lyman and his work on the assumptions of everyday life; Arthur J. Vidich and his work on the crises of legitimacy; and Danny Jorgensen and his analysis of media treatments of the "occult." In addition to these contributors, Paul Rasmussen, the late Levi Kamel, Erdwin Pfuhl, Jr., Dennis Brissett, Gregory Stone, Beverley Cuthbertson, Noah Fritz, Carl Couch, and scholars with whom we have been fortunate to work throughout Canada, Scandinavia, Italy, England, Scotland, and France have added to the chaotic cauldron essential for any creative effort. We are especially grateful to the insights of Professors Luigi Spedicato, Henri Peretz, and Richard V. Ericson and his associates. David Maines' encouragement and insights, along with helpful suggestions from Bruce Gronbeck, helped us further explicate our ideas about how our perspective underlies many approaches in cultural studies and rhetoric. We are also grateful to Dion Dennis and selected former students, several of whom are cited in various chapters, for their interest in learning while doing, and having the patience to teach us a few things too!

Finally, although we offer a new conceptualization of the media's role in social life, it should be stressed that other scholars have provided important insights and examples to lead us in certain directions. Specifically, over the last decade, numerous works have appeared that examine the mass media's relationship to such substantive areas as crime, deviance, sex roles and family structure, energy and the environment, and social change. We not only find this trend encouraging, but suggest that it will continue as more researchers become aware of the theoretical import of joining media procedures and images to the tangled social phenomena they seek to unravel.

1

The Media as Culture

A TV Commercial: "General Motors . . . Official sponsor of America's Dreams."

The mass media are enigmatic for social scientists. As widespread and ingrained in daily living as any part of culture, the nature and impact of the mass media in social life are difficult to discern because they are so much a part of culture (De Fleur and Ball-Rokeach 1975). Our lives are so awash in media products, imagery, and, most importantly, media logic (cf. Comstock 1980; 1989). We have stressed in our previous work on media logic that the traditional distinctions between form and content were becoming blurred as the new mediation forms, and especially those of the electronic media, were altering the temporal and spatial formats of experience.

Our experience, and the way we think about that experience, increasingly is mass mediated (Davis and Baran 1981). Ours is a *folded culture* in which the content of the messages we rely on are influenced and shaped by forms of discourse (Carey 1987). It is as though the unique, single experience has vanished; now, more experiences are reflections of previous encounters shaped by formats that in turn direct future experience. Indeed, the ultimate indication of this folded condition is when standard formats are changed in favor of others, such as occurred in a recent play-that-isn't-a-play ("The Living Movie," *Tamara*), in which the audience was invited to join in the activities, to erase the line between the actors and audience (Lapham 1988). Despite the erudite interpretation of this play as a feature of postmodernism in which objective vantage point vanishes, and in which "text can be placed on top of text"— of course, it can—, it was hardly new, but was quite consistent with Music TV Videos (MTV) that have been airing for several years. Forget about the plays, imagine "real" plays on what we have been saying.

Imagine this. A posh English wedding, costing $35,000, was videotaped, but the wedding was reenacted because the mother of the bride

1

was dissatisfied with the footage, "The video was dreadful. . . . There were no shots of the reception, and the video man missed the bride going up the aisle" (Arizona *Republic* October 19, 1988).

Try this one, noting how quickly things change. In November 1988, a producer for "America's Most Wanted," one of the most popular "new" TV crime shows that dramatizes violent attacks and invites the audience to help capture the accused, stated, "We take precautions. One thing we never do is report rewards because if we were to put a price on a guy's head, our show would become essentially a game show" (Arizona *Republic* November 26, 1988).

In December 1988, about two weeks later, it was reported that a $100,000 reward was being offered for information leading to the conviction of a serial killer. Sixteen thousand calls were logged in by the police within a few days (Arizona *Republic* December 12, 1988). This is interesting not only because it was reported as "news," but also because it further suggests that audiences are meaningfully involved with the TV as medium and with the logic underlying programs.

Serious personal criminal attacks happen rarely, but they are regarded as typical and quite common by American citizens because virtually all mass media reports about crime focus on the most spectacular, dramatic, and violent. This is illustrated by the "America's Most Wanted" show noted above, and it has also been documented with an analysis of the "Missing Children" issue that stared at us in newspapers, TV movies, docudramas, news reports, milk cartons, posters, and "junk mail" (Fritz and Altheide 1987). Any discussion about crime and justice in the United States today must begin by correcting the audience member's assumptions about crime. With the images of blood, guns, psychopaths, and suffering in front of them, and inside their heads, it is quite difficult to offer programmatic criticisms of our current approach to crime and accompanying issues such as prisons, and other modes of dispute resolution, including restitution and negotiation. As long as crime and mayhem are presented in such familiar and "fun" formats, new information will not be forthcoming, but only a recycling of affirmations tied to previous popular culture. And in general as long as experience is enacted by human beings who participate in mass mediated imagery, and orient consumption toward markets and products that look like the status groups, personal identities and forms of conduct displayed through a host of mass media, media and culture will not only be electronically and technologically joined, they will be meaningfully united as well.

The mass media are significant for our lives because they are both form and content of cultural categories and experience. As form—which this book is mainly concerned with—the mass media provide the criteria, shape, rhythm, and style of an expanding array of activities, many of which are outside of the "communication" process. As content, the new ideas, fashion, vocabularies, and a myriad of types of information (e.g., politics) are acquired through the mass media.

Communication, Power, and Social Control

The mass media's transformation of our social world requires a new approach to understanding communication and social power. All official, unofficial, formal, and informal modes of social control involve communication formats (Altheide 1988; 1989). The mass media are merely one moment of such control, but they are the most powerful entities in the world today (cf. Noelle-Neumann 1973).

But, if these points are already known, why should we do this book? The problem is that all accounts of media effects have been flawed, including our previous efforts. There are three general problems with most theories about mass communications effects. First, their claims about the control of content and the effects on individuals are not supported by empirical examination, since most ad campaigns and new products fail. There are too many exceptions. For example, a number of scholars continue to look for overpowering effects on audience members of "the image," arguing that people are being duped and manipulated, and that these members of the audience—like teenagers—are not sophisticated enough to offset such efforts (cf. Ewen 1988; Miller 1988). These claims by "scholars," who are usually located in media centers such as New York and Los Angeles, continue to receive serious attention by both print and electronic news media, because of the continuing bias toward "content" as the explanation, rather than the form and logic of communication. Second, mass communication theories are focused on individual effects, and very significantly, the nature of these theories presumes that the individual audience members are passive and not active, incapable of interacting with the images to develop their own interpretations and meanings. This means that actors are regarded as "judgmental dopes," who are presumed to incorporate and accept certain messages as fact, rather than creatively sorting, redefining, and interpreting information and images within a specific context. Students in the "uses and gratifications" (cf. Levy and Windahl 1984) tradition have attempted to delineate this point, but the best work, in our view, remains that of Lull (1982, 1988). But the third problem is the most critical. Virtually all theories and models of media effects are based on content of messages rather than the communication form. It is the latter that occupies our attention. For example, despite a number of very significant insights into the impact of new electronic formats on political life, students of rhetoric continue to focus on the content of speeches, rather than the style, format, and logic, which makes something recognizable and credible as "a speech" (cf. Jamieson 1988; Hart 1987), these dimensions are not easily discussed or articulated by audience members because they are nondiscursive, but are taken for granted as essential elements of conversation and leadership. Ronald Reagan was a powerful "communicator" not because of what he said, but the look, rhythm, and format of how he appeared and was presented as a familiar TV character who looked like a "decisive and confident leader."

There are a few points to consider at the outset. Social order and communication are *reflexive*. They cannot be separated, either in terms of first cause or in terms of impact. One could argue that all social science has been based on this premise, although it has been mainly the symbolic interactionist, ethnomethodologists, and phenomenologists who articulated this relationship (cf. Schutz 1967; Luckmann 1989), which is now being rediscovered by students of postmodernism, semiotics, literary criticism, and cultural studies (cf. Fiske 1987; Newcomb 1974).

Power is about controlling the definition of the situation. Any person, agency, entity, and, as we will argue, format that controls social definitions, on the one hand, and can implement those while avoiding alternatives, on the other hand, will control the situation. Social order is about shared definitions, including the temporal and spatial configurations for realizing and enacting definitions (cf. Blumer 1969; Giddens 1984). Any theory of social order or social change implies a theory of social control, and a process through which meanings are established, negotiated, and sustained (Katz and Szecsko 1981). It is for this reason that we argue that any comprehensive social theory or perspective must articulate the relevance of communication, especially the mass media.

Another consideration is data or evidence. Any claim about a theory of social order must be subject to some kind of demonstration and test. As we noted above, it is this requirement that has set back most of the macrooriented theories of social order; there are too many exceptions. People simply do not cooperate with the theorists and behave as they should! For example, numerous studies that treat the media as hegemonic cannot stand up to even the most casual scrutiny; there are too many exceptions when, for example, the theory of "hegemonic control" predicts no coverage of certain topics from certain points of view (Altheide 1984a). Invariably, they do not hold up. This can be seen with some of best work to date on terrorism (cf. Schlesinger et al. 1983; Altheide 1985b, 1987c). The topics and emphases do not follow from what the hegemonic theories predict.

Our task, then, was to work with many of these other scholars, to reexamine the studies, and to develop a theoretical perspective about the media's impact that was not tautological, yet could be useful in understanding the media's impact on social life. That is what this book is about. We take it as basic that the mass media are the most powerful institutions in the world today, and that all forms of legitimacy and control pass through the logic and formats that distinguish the various media. We are very mindful of the differences between the mass media (cf. Ericson et al. 1989), and how certain content (programs) can have disproportionate effects. Nevertheless, what is needed is a major reformulation of the nature and consequences of communication forms, logic, and media for social order, which transcend conventional wisdom and practices of students of communication.

A Point of View

Our approach is intended to build on previous studies of mass media, while charting a different course into institutional and cultural analysis (Gronbeck 1990, Hall 1988). We pursue this other direction because the accumulation of findings, new theoretical developments, and major shifts in media effects demand it. Our cultural and institutional analysis focuses on the form and logic of mass communication within a social context.

Let us list a few things that we take for granted so that reviewers and others will not be misled. The mass media are irrevocably ideological, cultural, and, in many instances, hegemonic devices to serve a relatively small number of spokespersons, sources, and interests. This is so well established that it hardly needs stating, but we do so because the political and ideological climate of social science today requires it. Second, we support any and all efforts to make the media channels more accessible to a range of class, economic, and ideological interests. This would contribute greatly to the range of opinion, issues, and even news content. However, this would not be nearly enough.

As we have argued over the years, changing the "ownership and control" of the mass media would change some features of its operation, and some of its content, but its impact on social order would not be fundamentally altered. This is our point. Mass communication logic and discourse extends well beyond its content and information impact; that is relatively minor, compared to the discursive, temporal, and sense-making perspectives that have merged with media industries in the Western world—and, increasingly, throughout the world—over the last 50 years.

For several decades the scientific community and the general public have been asking how the various media affect our lives. Do media shape attitudes, sell political candidates, increase violence, dull one's senses, destroy culture, or even stop wars? Although huge sums of money have been spent and many volumes written seeking responses to these questions, there is still considerable doubt as to exactly how the media operate in society. We contend that the mass media have not been well understood because of two separate, but often related points of view guiding most inquiries. First, most media analysts have been oriented by a concern with the nature of messages and their origin. Specifically, the search has been for the instrinsic persuasive techniques in messages and the economic intersts that stand to gain by acceptance of those messages. With rare exception (McLuhan 1964; and Gronbeck on electronic rhetoric, 1990), media analysts have not considered that media may be significant in their own right in the process of affecting cultural change. Rather, the media are conceived of as but another element of the economic equation. Second, most studies of mass media effects have emphasized individual effects in order to be guided by rather narrow questions that have been formulated to be consistent with very limited positivistic research methods to generate statistical findings.

During the 1980s, more media analysts adopted the position we have been articulating for nearly 20 years that meanings in a mass communication context are the result of negotiation between medium and audience and are tied to the context in which they occur. Recent work by Kubey and Csikszentmihalya (Arizona *Republic* April 4, 1990) seem to agree with this position, namely that television offers people another alternative for making sense of their lives, to alleviate frustration, and to accompany other activities with which they are involved. Of course the essential insight about the contextual feature of meaning was not ours, but rather the work of major symbolic interactionists who have systematically developed how social order is meaningfully constructed, negotiated, and challenged through a process of symbolic interaction.

It is in this same tradition that John Fiske's elaborate and provocative "negotiative" theory (1987) articulates how audiences gain as opposed to lose a feeling of empowerment in the process of wrestling with interpretations of media experience. Anderson and Meyer's "accommodation" theory (1988) takes essentially the same position in arguing that individuals interpret mediated texts within the routines of social action, and in any social action context there is always room for maneuvering and accommodation (p. 308). We agree, and acknowledge the intellectual debt in symbolic interaction in general and the dramaturgical model in particular (Brissett and Edgley 1990). Given these works, and many others over the past decade, the research direction has finally shifted from the messenger as ideologue and propagandist to the self-involved audience member. The new question concerns the kinds of situational factors that audience members use to make sense of media experience.

Although the work of Fiske, Anderson and Meyer, Gronbeck, (1990) and others makes these exciting times in media theory and research, everyone would agree that we must press for conceptual clarity and distinguish clearly among the various factors (or variables if statistical analysis is being used) that are being examined. Our concern has always been to determine the most fundamental set of rules that a person follows in constructing meaning. All of the previously cited works begin with the Sapir/Whorf hypothesis that cultural meanings are consistent with the grammatical structure (logic) of a language. And everyone in this group seems to accept the general approach of Georg Simmel (1950) that culture emerges through the process of using social forms (problem-solving strategies that are independent of content). However, differences emerge between our media logic approach and the work of Fiske, Anderson and Meyer, and everyone doing semiotics analysis.

Our theoretic concern is with the identification and description of social forms, and we try to articulate how content emerges through those forms. Even though we illustrate the power of these forms with "content" examples, our emphasis is on the way in which forms and their logics shapes the content. Other approaches obscure the distinction between form and content, such as Fiske's concept of "discourse," which he defines as "both a topic and a coded set of signs through which that topic is organized, understood, and made expressible" (1984:169). We think this distinction is important for several very fundamental reasons. First, form is prior to content in the temporal process of constructing meaning. Second, since form is abstractly independent of content, any contamination of form in conceptualization and analysis obscures how form operates in the process of constructing and changing such cultural constructs as discourses. Third, and most important for the 1990s, people are more concerned with maintaining proper form than with substance or content! If this strikes a responsive chord, then let us get on with it.

We begin with a much different assumption. Although no social scientist would deny that economic considerations play a major role in social life, it is the way such influences interact with other elements of culture and social structure that is important. For more than 50 years we have known that mass media in every society tend to stress images and messages that reflect dominant beliefs and ideologies of that culture, and are less favorable to others. Our perspective is much different. We examine mass media influences in terms of the logic, rationale, and taken for granted assumptions that individuals collectively share as a result of media logic. We include the way social institutions operate and reinforce how situations are defined.

Everyone knows media are important influences; in fact, it is difficult to imagine getting through the day without at least one—from clock radios to miniradios with headsets to newspapers to television to video recorders to curling up with a good book. It is our contention that media are so pervasive and influential that they are the dominant institutions in contemporary society.

Contemporary life cannot be understood without acknowledging the role of various communication media in the temporal and spatial organization and coordination of everyday life. The important work of Harold Innis and Marshall McLuhan not only directed attention to the contribution of the technology of media for any message, but further argued that it is the technology that is most important in altering information and social relationships. However, it has remained for others to examine their thesis and incorporate the surviving corpus within an awareness of culture and especially popular culture, commonly associated with mass production, including mass media programming and other information.

Our approach to understanding media as a social force in society is to treat them as a form of communication that has a particular logic of its own (Elliott 1972). Media logic becomes a way of "seeing" and of interpreting social affairs. As logic they also involve an implicit trust that we can communicate the events of our daily lives through the various formats of media. People take for granted that information can be transmitted, ideas presented, moods of joy and sadness expressed, major decisions made, and business conducted through media. But, at the same time, there is a lingering fear that media can and will distort what they present. This fear of media has been defined by some as a conspiracy in which powerful media moguls willfully set out to determine the character of behavior: how people vote, what they buy, what is learned, and what is believed. No doubt there is an intent to shape attitudes and "sell soap," but we contend that what the controlling agents of media intend to accomplish is not the critical factor in understanding media. Rather, we see mass communication as an interactive process between media communication as interpreted and acted on by audiences. Technological developments now permit explicit interaction with TV programs, as viewers of videotext can select additional information, as children (and some adults!) participate in TV action games, as "smart sets" enable video participants to draw on rudimentary microprocessors to project images of how one would appear in various clothing styles, and increasingly select programs and media usage to suit their needs (which may also be a commercial enterprise, of course). Forecasters project TV programming will fundamentally change from a logic of "broadcasting," or offering a few options to a broad socioeconomic audience, to "narrowcasting," or providing essentially personally selected contents and images.

Apparently, even though researchers have persisted in disagreements about whether the audience is "passive" or "active," media programmers and managers are convinced that they are active. Of course, there is no necessary cause and effect between what goes into media communication and how that communication is interpreted and acted on by audiences. Studies of children and television have already shown that children use television content in ways totally different from those intended by program producers (Noble 1975; Greenberg 1976; Greenfield 1984). People do not always vote for the candidate with the most exposure, and well-publicized movies are sometimes box-office flops. This evidence indicates that it is misleading to interpret media as stimulus–response conditioning. In place of a conspiracy or conditioning model, we propose that both communicator and audience member employ a particular logic—a media logic—that is used to present and interpret various phenomena.

In general terms, *media logic* consists of a form of communication, the process through which media present and transmit information. Elements of this form include the various media and the formats used by these media. Format consists, in part, of how material is organized, the style in which it is presented, the focus or emphasis on particular characteristics of behavior, and the grammar of media communication. Format becomes a framework or a perspective that is used to present as well as interpret phenomena. For a major medium such as television, audiences have become so familiar with different formats that they automatically know when something on television is news, comedy, or fictional drama. In a like manner, radio, newspaper, and magazine formats have become second nature to listeners and readers. Thus the logic of media formats has become so taken for granted by both communicator and receiver that until recently it has been overlooked as an important factor in understanding media. Analysis of media logic in terms of form and subform elements (format) is in part what we hope to accomplish in this book.

An equally important task is an examination of the consequences that arise from the form of media logic. The consequences may be described as *"media culture"* (Elliott 1972; Monaco 1978; Snow 1983). In a broad sense, media culture refers to the character of such institutions as religion, politics, or sports that develops through the use of media. Specifically, when a media logic is employed to present and interpret institutional phenomena, the form and content of those institutions are altered. The changes may be minor, as in the case of how political candidates dress and groom themselves; or they may be major, such as the entire process of present-day political campaigning in which political rhetoric says very little but shows much concern. In contemporary society, every major institution has become part of media culture: Changes have occurred in every major institution that are a result of the adoption of media logic in presenting and interpreting activity in those institutions. Religion, for example, has adopted a television entertainment perspective to reach the people. In sports, rule changes, styles of play, and the amount of money earned by players are directly related to the application of a television format. In the chapters that follow, we will describe some of the characteristics of this new media culture and show how it relates to the form of media logic.

A *medium* is any social or technological procedure or device that is used for the selection, transmission, and reception of information. Every civilization has developed various types of media, transmitted through social elements such as territory, dwelling units, dress and fashion (Kroeber 1919), language, clocks and calendars (Zerubavel 1977), dance (cf. Sachs 1963), and other rituals (cf. Couch 1984). But in the modern world, these types of media have been overshadowed by newspapers, radio, and television. Although social scientists tend to focus on the latter when discussing "media," we could expand this application to show how other types of media may be regarded as basic features of social life. It is valuable to examine how media differ from one epoch to another and from one culture to another; every historical period is marked by the dominance of some media over others, and the dominance affects other areas of social life. Groups aspiring to power seek to gain leverage and legitimacy through media. In addition, select media promote a public portrayal of everyday life and political power according to the logic of the dominant institutions.

However, although each of the foregoing may be regarded as propositions worthy of separate investigation, the thesis we propose is that *social reality is constituted, recognized, and celebrated with media.* This is by no means news; social scientists have known for some time that people share a sense of reality that sustains a sense of what is "normal" about everyday affairs (Gunter and Wober 1983). Our claim is that in contemporary society the logic of media provides the form for shared "normalized" social life. Indeed, Meyrowitz (1985) has argued provocatively that social hierarchies are communication hierarchies, and that access to the codes of various media varies inversely with support for social hierarchies. This has been shown with our previous analyses (Altheide and Snow 1979) of media such as the calendar (Zerubavel 1977), fashion

(Bell 1978), and dance (Katz 1978). Those who could use such media to define the time, place, and manner of certain activities, including the knowledge to participate in them, controlled significant features of social order. Thus, Meyrowitz suggests, because TV is so widely available and exposes audience members to the same information, TV tends to reduce social hierarchies. As the dominant medium in our age, TV becomes even more important than print because of the visual nature of the information being transmitted, as well as the capacity of TV experience to transcend temporal locations of experience. Thus young people can learn at an early age how to be older. Our aim, then, is to view social life from a "mediacentric" perspective, seeking first to discover as well as clarify how media logic operates, and then to describe what media culture follows.

From Modern to Postmodern Media

Our contemporary scene is said to be "without standards" and clear points of reference. Continental literary critics have referred to this moment as "postmodern," or beyond the rational guidelines and models that have underscored several hundred years of thought (cf. Featherstone 1988). The postmodern age is said to be one in which distinctions are blurred between reality and appearance. The appropriate attitude, according to some writers, is that of skepticism, if not cynicism. If we can have no, or much less confidence in anything, then everything is one equal footing (except, of course, the claims of the postmodernist writers—their claims are expected to be honored by all others!) Although all of the largely anarchistic implications of "doing away with all reference points" need not be accepted, it is clear that part of the impetus for this reflection is the realization that our lives, work, and claims about reality are "reflexive," meaning that we cannot easily separate our biographies, cultural contexts, and modes of analyses from our activities and research findings. Nowhere is this more evident than in the media logic and forms with which we are concerned in this work. Indeed, we argue that it is the communication order that is partly responsible—and holds the key to opening fresh perspectives—for our postmodern condition.

The present-day dominance of media has been achieved through a process in which the general form and specific formats of media have become adopted throughout society so that cultural content is basically organized and defined in terms of media logic. It is not a case of media dictating terms to the rest of society, but an interaction between organized institutional behavior and media. In this interaction, the form of media logic has come to be accepted as the perspective through which various institutional problems are interpreted and solved.

To understand media logic, it is worthwhile to consult the works of Georg Simmel (1950). Simmel argued that form is a process through which reality is rendered intelligible. Form is not structure per se, but a processual framework *through which* social action occurs. Media logic constitutes such a form. Although this form is difficult to define in concrete measurable terms, several general characteristics should be mentioned. Modern communications media are a technology and as such carry a connotation of rationality. Consequently, both communicator and audience are oriented toward a rational means–end type of communication—rapid dissemination of vital information at relatively low cost. This practical approach to communication is a logic in itself. An audience also expects the information received to be accurate and current. In turn, media producers strive to at least give the impression of being accurate and topical. This rational/practical character of media logic further leads to dependability—in other words, audiences want information that is relevant to their desires. In total, these characteristics become a form of communication that is consistent with the modern scientific manner in which contemporary society operates.

But there is much more than a scientific rational logic to modern communications media. The style in which the technology is used may promote affective mood response, as in entertainment. Traditionally, media have been a source of enjoyment, as is the case with dance, theater, and music. Audiences have come to expect that media technology will produce entertainment, and every type of medium has done exactly that. Combining the rational/practical logic of media communication with entertainment yields a new form of communication, one that is unique to modern urban society.

Our approach to understanding media logic as a general form will consist of dealing with the subproperties of selected media—media formats. By examining various media formats and their adoption by various institutions in society, we hope to gain an understanding of the interaction between media and nonmedia sectors of society. In focusing our attempts at understanding media logic on the specific formats of selected media, we intend to avoid abstract theorizing and deal with more concrete interactive processes. Therefore, we shall focus less on the abstract nature of media logic and more on the description of how media culture emerges through specific media formats. In short, we will examine the specific elements of media logic (that is, media formats) and demonstrate how they connect with specific institutional activity to produce a media culture.

As a final note is this introduction, we feel it is not too pretentious to claim that our approach to media analysis is relevant for the sociology of knowledge (analysis of the conditions and processes that yield knowledge, cf. Mannheim 1936; Nisbet 1976). We feel that through adopting a media logic people have, in effect, developed a consciousness that affects how they perceive, define, and deal with their environment. What emerges as knowledge in contemporary society is, to a significant extent, the result of this media consciousness. What we shall describe as media culture should constitute strong evidence for this argument.

Plan of the Book

In the following chapters we will examine entertainment, news, politics, religion, and sports as institutions in American society that have adopted a media logic and specific media formats as their own institutional strategies and thus have become part of the total media culture.

Chapter 2, "Media Entertainment," presents the elements of the entertainment perspective now present in prime-time television and suggests effects this has had on other media also concerned with entertainment. Chapter 3, "Media News," applies the logic of television format to the rational efforts to profitably coordinate and produce entertaining coverage of a variety of events. It also covers how this effort, on the one hand, has spawned new approaches to journalism and new epistemologies to legitimize what is really being done in the pursuit of ratings while, on the other hand, the ratings logic has had to adjust to technological breakthroughs that give local affiliate TV stations more freedom to do their own programming. Together, these changes have prompted programming changes that will permit "narrowcasting" to a "grazing" audience in search of ever more dramatic programming, a remarkable change from the "broadcasting" mode when the audience we regarded as more stable and more homogeneous.

Chapter 4 examines the impact of the "news perspective" on politics in general, and especially the coverage by selected print and electronic media of the 1976–1988 presidential campaigns. The interplay between formats in different media is also discussed. The role of image makers who are at home in both the media world and the political environment suggests a more than coincidental occurrence. Chapter 5 shows what happens when government agencies become imbued with the contexts and purposes of mass TV news considerations. Examining the first "post-Watergate" enforcement by the news media—the Bert Lance case—illustrates how the publicity effect of simply being named and cast in a bad light by the major media can cancel out other impressions and

evidence contained in conversations and hearings. Chapter 6, "A Political Kaleidoscope," examines how political behavior and the unfolding of
major events such as the Iranian hostage crisis and the Iran/Contra
affairs, make it clear that the mass media have taken hold of journalism
and fundamentally transformed it into the third, and perhaps the second, estate rather than the press's traditional "fourth estate." The interactive relationship between media logic, TV programming, viewer–
voters perspectives, and politics permits us to offer a novel look at the
1988 election of George Bush and Dan Quayle, and the subsequent
invasion of Panama. Chapters 7 and 8, dealing with religion and sports,
further document how the coverage and presentation of these activities
have changed, and with them, the inducements to significantly alter the
very nature of religion and professional sports. As TV evangelists have
become more like sports and movie "stars," their fortunes have sky-
rocketed, but as the cases of Jim Bakker and Jimmy Swaggert illustrate,
they also have farther to fall. The implications of these findings and
predictions for the future are presented in the concluding chapter.

2

Media Entertainment

"Life imitates art."

Oscar Wilde

It takes little more than a casual glance to discover that entertainment is one of the most pervasive characteristics of American culture, and, most people do not seem terribly bothered by this. In fact, the extent to which people argue over the merit of entertainment, even in church services, campaign speeches, or the classroom, seems to hinge on matters of taste and performance criteria. In short, it is either good or poor. And yet, when the war on drugs turns to Saturday morning cartoons to carry its message to preadolescent children, when the U.S. military uses Rock'n'roll music as a weapon (against General Noriega in Panama, 1989), and when a President develops enormous personal popularity but receives low marks for leadership and policy (Ronald Reagan), then something more is going on than simple entertainment. In other words, it is becoming increasingly difficult to draw the line between entertainment and nonentertainment. As satirist Ian Sholes says (tongue in cheek), "It's all rock'n'roll." ABC Honchos must agree since they are launching a new show in 1990 called "Cop Rock."

In 1967, sociologist William Stephenson anticipated this cultural movement in America when he stated that most mass media audience behavior could best be understood as an entertainment or play experience. He did not mean that the content mass media was trivial, nor was he casting entertainment in a negative light. Rather, he was simply looking at media experience from the audience's frame of mind, and the subsequent meanings that audience members attribute to their media experience. In brief, he found that people often used media for what he called "pleasure-communication," and claimed that audience members can derive significant personal social and psychological benefits from using a play orientation in interacting with mass media. John Fiske

(1987) drew a similar conclusion in looking at the power relationship between television and viewer. He argues that when viewers resist being controlled by the messenger, they can derive pleasurable meaning from their television experience (p. 19). In other words, Stephenson and Fisk are saying that television popularity is due in large part to the fact that viewers use the experience for enjoyment and self-enhancement. This should not be a big surprise, but the substance of this argument and its implications seem to have eluded a great many students and critics of television. We accept Stephenson's and Fiske's position, and go on to analyze the properties of entertainment as a format, and how this format interacts with other formats.

The Entertainment Perspective

Entertainment follows a general set of criteria that, although largely taken for granted by everyone, can be identified by contrasting it to the mundane or routine (cf. Reeves 1978). In juxtaposing entertainment and the mundane most people would probably agree that a continuum could be constructed with the mundane at one end and entertainment at the other. The content along this continuum may not change, but the meanings attributed to that content certainly do change. Simply put, two people can witness the same event and one will see it as entertaining and the other will not. Form, such as the entertainment criteria, is used to shape content. A good example is provided by comedian George Carlin who constantly takes material from everyday life and turns it into hilarious comedy sketches.

In contrasting entertainment with the mundane, the most obvious difference is the absence of the ordinary in entertainment. Following Georg Simmel's (Levine 1971) ideas, entertainment would qualify as an "adventure." In general terms this means that entertainment is outside the expected boundaries of continuous routine behavior. It can be unusual as a rare or bizarre event, unusual in terms of the talent required to perform the act, unusual in terms of the perfect flow or rhythm and tempo of the act, and unusual as something spectacular or larger than life. And, in each case, the audience member must be willing to suspend disbelief and accept the extraordinary as plausible for the moment. Certainly there are phenomena that meet some of these criteria and are definitely not entertaining, such as a grizzly auto accident. Therefore, we hasten to add that although the extraordinary character may be necessary, it is not sufficient by itself to ensure that onlookers will perceive the event as entertaining. At least one or two additional criteria must be present. The experience must have an element of spontaneous enjoyment and/or have the potential for vicarious involvement.

Enjoyment, or satisfaction, is not merely a measure of the quality of entertainment, it is a test of whether the activity was indeed entertainment. To achieve this status, the event or experience must stand alone. In Simmel's terms, the event has a definite beginning and end. It does not blend into the continuous on-going routines of the day. As a discrete event it is also felt, or imbued with emotion. Emotions during the event may range from sorrow to exultation, but the feeling is one of satisfaction for a performance well done. In rare situations, the event may become a "magical moment"—that kind of moment that seems suspended in time. Through dramatics the entire scene becomes breathtaking, and we are awe-struck by the sheer enormity of it all. Although these are difficult terms to make rationally precise, we all know a show-stopper when we see one.

Spontaneity goes hand-in-hand with emotional satisfaction. We laugh hysterically, cry real tears, feel pride, love, hate, and even shame, and if these are "legitimately" felt emotions they will be instantaneous. This is what performers look for—the spontaneous outburst—the stunned silence. No time to think, just gut reaction. Although psychologists may raise questions about what is occurring physiologically and cognitively, it all boils down to an "after-the-fact" definition of the experience, and people are most apt to use the appearance of spontaneous emotional states as proof that the experience was entertainment.

With respect to vicarious involvement, we have long recognized the fantasy/escape character of the stage performance, Hollywood film (cf. Ryan and Kellner 1988), and television (cf. Cantor 1980). Escape is perhaps an unfortunate term, as it implies a dereliction of duty or a failure to confront real problems. Work ethic norms still cast an onerous character on play and flights of fancy. Nevertheless, we all engage in vicarious involvements, and they are just as social in our minds as overt interpersonal interactions are in "real" life. Vicarious behavior is simply acting internally without the restrictions and responsibilities that emerge in overt relationships. One can identify with a parent in a sitcom, imagine making love to a sexy film star, or take the field in sports without being hindered by personal limitations. Through vicarious behavior we have nothing to lose, however transitory the situation may be. Why else do Bogart films continue to draw large audiences? Why do people see the same film six or more times? Why do television reruns such as "Star Trek" have such faithful followings, and why are glamorous award show spectacles always popular? The vicarious character of entertainment and the pure fun of this involvement are a powerful inducement to buying the theater ticket or turning on the television.

Whatever else entertainment is, and our list of criteria is not exhaustive, it is commonly understood that entertainers use the criteria of entertainment to elicit audience response, and hope that audiences will use the same criteria to evaluate the performance. But we all know that in human interaction there are no guarantees, and audiences may use entertainment criteria inappropriately, such as frequently happened to Vice President Dan Quayle. More to the point, most media experience (through American mass media) occurs through an entertainment perspective. The question is, how is this accomplished, and what are the implications.

Media Format

Fundamentally, a format is a media strategy for presenting particular subject matter. For example, stand-up comedy is a type of entertainment that may be presented through a typical television format of the night-time talk show, or a situation comedy format of one-liners followed by the artificial laughtrack. As we have said, format functions as a logic that guides and defines more general experience. As with any language or communication system, format rules become part of the taken-for-granted character of communicating and are largely unnoticed by media professionals and audiences in day-to-day media use. Consequently, the form, in the sense that form "informs" content, often is ignored or over-looked both in scholarly analysis and in casual observation. Audience members claim to know instinctively when they see and hear something that can be defined as entertainment, news, historical documentary, and other frameworks, but they commonly explain these definitions as a function of content rather than form. Our position is just the op-posite. People draw upon various forms to make sense of various kinds of experience. People interpret or make sense of phenomena through familiar forms. At that point content is established. It follows that our concern is to ascertain the various standardized features of these forms.

Although our approach appears to be an exercise in ethnomethods (uncovering taken-for-granted norms), we do not assume that any nor-mative framework in media strategy or media experience is chiseled in stone. Nor do we assume, as is often the case in semiotics, that strategies, signs, symbols, or other media productions *necessarily* produce particular interpretations or behavioral consequences. Despite the appearance of embedded meanings and strategy in modern media, these are nothing more than examples of a fragile consensus between media and audience that may change rapidly. The fact that high percentages of people see sexual connotations in many advertisements implies more about eco-nomic affluence and leisure time than it does about the so-called innate power of sexual symbols. On the other hand, since we live in a culture with these characteristics, it is wise and prudent to determine the format characteristics that are effective regardless of the content.

The standardized procedures of any media format consist most fundamentally in grammatical rules covering syntax (organization) and inflection (rhythm and tempo). In electronic media these translate into scenes, acts, edits, lighting, sound effects, and so on. Over time, media professionals and audiences have come to accept specific rules regarding editing, lighting, music, and even prose, as these rules are associated with various genre, such as sitcoms, MTV, Top-40 radio, or romance novels. In turn, these genre take on historical significance as they become associated with particular media eras, such as the "film noir" of the 1940s or the TV sitcoms or the 1950s. In this fashion, the genre as era becomes instantly recognizable as a temporal dimension of culture. And these genre/formats function as fashion when they become the "in" or popular format of the day, such as the music video montage formula so common in TV advertising in 1990. To illustrate further, examine the format norms of radio and television.

Radio

Radio's continued popularity rests on its ability to serve a number of important functions simultaneously. It can be practical, playful, rational, emotional, and social all without restricting or immobilizing the listener. In what seems to be the definitive description of the functions of radio, Harold Mendelsohn (1964:239) stated that in addition to presenting news, time, and temperature, radio brings the outside world into the home or car, becomes a reference for organizing daily routines, and serves as a forum for interpersonal activity. It wakes us in the morning, gets us to work, and provides moods on demand, topics to talk about with others, and we may interact vicariously with the radio personality, or sing along with the music. As such, radio is ubiquitous in everyday life. We scarcely notice how often it is on or in what context it is used. But remove it, and many of us panic. At the very least we must substitute for its absence. Surely, not only the content is missed.

The Grammar of Radio

The grammar of radio consists of ways in which the use of time, the organization of content, and conversation make this a very personalized medium. Briefly, time follows the listener's pace through daily routine, content is organized into segments that meet music subculture requirements as well as daily routine activities, and radio talk augments the time and organizational factors of grammar (keeping in mind that entertainment is the underlying interpretive framework for this grammar).

Uses of Time.   Unlike television, the temporal syntax of radio follows "normal" everyday routine. Whereas television alters time in drama, news, and comedy programs, radio follows an exact linear progression of time, maintaining pace with the listener's sense of real time throughout the day. Listeners may use radio as a clock and a metronome. As a clock, radio gives the time and serves as a time reference through the knowledge of when various segments occur during the program. As a metronome, radio programs maintain a pace in the program that meshes with listener's demands as they change from the frantic morning drive-time to more relaxed periods during the day or evening. This variation in rhythm and tempo also can be used as an inflection device to cue the listener for appropriate action or activity. At 6:30 A.M. an announcer in Minneapolis would talk softly to his working girl audience telling them "it was time to move the body." By 7:00 his rapid fire voice was commanding "get a move on," and by 7:30 he was into "40 MPH traffic music."

In today's commercial radio format, the most obvious and common element of inflection is music. Most listeners are thoroughly acquainted with variation from Top-40, light rock, to new age, and so on, and they can dial in and out of predictable changes in rhythm and pace. Listeners are also aware of the standardized practice of varying tempo from one selection to the next, a practice that has become standardized to the point that computer software makes the selections. Furthermore, rec ord companies tailor music in a "made for commercial radio" to "made for MTV" versions of the same tune, and listeners are aware that beginnings and endings of records are deliberately extended with repeating phrases to provide background for DJ voice-over. Overall, stations strive for *a sound,* which translates as the temporal dimension of the format.

Disk jockeys become an integral part of *the sound* with appropriate conversational tone and pace. A point to keep in mind in this discussion is that most radio listening occurs in automobiles. For drive-time periods, people listening to Top-40 stations want the DJ to be absurdly crazy and keep everything at a fast pace, whereas new age music audiences desire rush-hour stress reduction. At midday periods, the general tone and pace of most stations are more relaxed, although that strategy began to change as urban life became less patterned. Today the city at night is alive with a daytime pace. Store shelves are being stocked, cleaning and construction workers labor under halogen lights, and people do their banking at automated tellers with headsets tuned to their favorite music.

Consequently, some radio stations are beginning to sound the same regardless of the time of day.

By and large, the conversational tone and pace of the "deejay" correspond to the music tempo and listener routines to the extent that they can be predicted. Looking at this another way, radio conversation is integrated into the music rhythm and tempo without altering the mood of the music. When stations claim to have "more music; less talk," they are marketing according to the mood/pace factor. On the other hand, stations need to sell products and keep an attentive listener. Here the interruption of talk in the flow of music can accomplish two things at once. Talk attempts to prevent monotony while making advertising dollars at the same time. Adept use of this strategy is particularly important for the occasional listener, as these listeners may perceive a great deal of repetition in a particular music genre. In other words, people who do not particularly like rock, or jazz, or classical usually claim that "it all sounds the same." The "boredom quotient" is particularly acute for these listeners.

To summarize, radio time corresponds to how listeners carry out their daily routines. In this sense, radio time is subordinate to listener time, with radio facilitating and helping to establish the sense of time a listener wants to achieve. For many listeners, using radio to establish and sustain their uses of time has become a routine in itself. Ask yourself if you can wash the car, clean house, study or read, or engage in a myriad of other activities without background radio noise? In these instances, radio is an integral part of the flow of the event. Indeed, without radio, some activity, such as driving, would become awkward at best, and perhaps impossible.

Organization and Scheduling. The organization of content in radio programs has become a sophisticated procedure in the past 30 years. During the mass-audience period of the 1930s and early 1940s, radio used the time-block formula that is currently in television. Quarter, half, or hour-long programs featuring the music of a particular orchestra or artist were supported by one or two advertisers. As the record industry expanded (with nonbreakable 45s and LPs), and affluence increased, the hit parade was born, and radio scheduled music according to sales/popularity. With the baby boom and the explosion of youth-oriented rock'n'roll, record profits soared and companies began pressuring radio stations to create and play hits. Suddenly radio was in a position to exercise considerable influence over the music industry. The vehicle was "format" radio.

Over the past three decades, the most successful format, sometimes called the Drake Format (after its originator), spread from rock music throughout all popular music genre. The all-to-familiar format consisted of organizing time periods into three or four units with each unit further segmented into categories based on degree of current popularity or rhythm and tempo. With this syntax a station could use a few as 30 records for an entire broadcast day, and rotate the top ten to repeat within two to three hours. It was this strategy that enabled a station to standardize its "sound" throughout the broadcast day and throughout a music genre. And through this strategy program directors replaced DJs as the geniuses behind successful ratings. It was the PD who achieved the "sound," and hence the identity of a station, and it was the PD who took the credit or the blame.

Throughout the 1980s this practice evolved to the point that formats within formats were created, patented, and trade marked, and marketed under innocuous but meaningful (to listeners) terms, such as "Power _____FM," "The Wave," and "Pirate Radio." More common was the development of subgenre, which radio professionals call "fractionalization." Recent examples of fractionalized Top-40 include Dance Party, Rock, and Mainstream. Three types of Album rock include Traditional, Classic, and New, and three types of Nostalgia are broken into the time periods of 50s/60s, 60s/70s, and Golden Oldies. The list seems to go on endlessly in groups or three or more. Even religion radio is divided among Gospel, Inspirational, Christian, and Family Life. Are differences in all of these categories discernible? Listeners and program directors say yes (Jackson 1990).

Given the apparent success of what is now called "format" radio, the only stations that do not follow rigid format rules are those in isolated rural areas that must serve a variety of utilitarian community interests. Even these are difficult to find, as today's radio audience has become accustomed to the grammatical character of popular large market formats, and demand that level of performance. Consequently, medium and small markets across the country are moving to satellite feeds from various music services. The Hi Tech sound of Unistar, Format 41 (soft rock) can now be heard on the remote deserts of West Texas.

Special Features of Vocal Communication.   An intriguing feature of radio throughout its history has been the loyalty and appearance of intimacy that can be acheived between listener and radio stations and personalities. This may partially be explained by the necessity within subcultures of developing a sense of shared experience among a dispersed membership. In fact, a medium, such as radio or a magazine, may be the primary integrating agent within a subculture. In urban areas, radio stations make a major effort to become the symbol and focus of attention for

specific music and age-specific subcultures. In turn listeners form loyalt-
ies as displayed through T-shirts and bumper stickers. To maintain listener loyalty, station personalities must literally speak the subculture
language in terms of jargon, rhythm, pitch, and phrasings. Examples
are abundant, and a good actor can move from one subculture to another. In Phoenix, Arizona one of the more popular DJs over the past
20 years is W. Steve Martin. He began his career as Steve Martin on a
bubblegum top-40 station talking staccato teen slang to 12 year olds during the early 1970s. A decade later he became W. Steve Martin speaking
with a slight drawl on a country station. As that station became more
"uptown," so did Martin's voice and speech. Martin's career is not unusual. DJs grow older and become less able and willing to meet the subculture demands of audiences outside their own life-style. Examine the
biography of an announcer at a easy listening station or an all news station and you will find a rock jock earlier in life.

Another feature of radio talk, one explored extensively by Erving
Goffman in his last major book *Forms of Talk* (1981), is the extraordinary
vocal precision of radio announcers. Typically, radio communication is
clear, crisp, pleasing to the ear, and devoid of long (dead air) pauses.
The talk of radio professionals appears articulate and polished, and it is
these criteria that listeners use in judging whether a station is major or
minor league. In this respect the radio announcer represents an ideal
and a standard for measuring articulation in general. In other words,
articulation has come to mean spontaneity (form) more so than the substance of verbal discourse. Riding the crest of this category are talk show
hosts such as Larry King.

Overall, the various features of radio grammar result in a low degree
of ambiguity with respect to both format and subsequent content. Anyone who is at all familiar with radio can turn on a set at any time and
instantly recognize the format and predict subsequent content. In turn,
this predictability facilitates establishing or maintaining particular
moods. From up-temp pop rock for commuter traffic to late-night easy
listening for romance or winding down, listeners may dial in and out
of moods at will. Almost every mood imaginable can be brought to the
foreground or moved to the background through the dependable formats of radio.

Combining the timing and organizational properties of radio leads to
the conclusion that radio time is subordinate to listener time, with radio
facilitating and helping to establish temporal dimensions of a listener's
everyday life. In the process, radio listening has become a routinized
part of completing routine tasks in everyday life. Moreover, when these
mundane activities become difficult if not impossible without the back-

ground provided by radio, then radio becomes an integral part of the
flow of the event.

The Radio Personality

The most enduring umbrella format of radio over the years has been
labeled "personality radio." This may seem all too obvious or even re-
dundant, but when automated stations began appearing during the late
1960s, some experts believed that live talent behind the mike might be
outmoded. After a decade of experimenting, the 1980s saw a return to
personalities. Although stars of the magnitude of Arthur Godfrey or
even Wolfman Jack are absent in today's spectrum, top rated stations in
most markets hold those high ratings by virtue of one or more popular
DJs, particularly for the morning drive-time period.

The key to success with all radio personalities is that listeners feel the
person on the radio is talking to them. To use a well worn sociological
concept, the radio communicator becomes a significant other. The listener may feel part of a unique club or group, as demonstrated by Murray the K and his Beatlemania fans during the early 1960s, Jonathon
Brandmier's "loons" in Phoenix during the early 1980s, and the current
new rock format fad "the Morning Zoo," which features a team of two
or more (often co-ed) wild and crazy people laughing it up over inane
jokes, quips, stunts, and an otherwise cynical approach to everything.
The traditional solo personality is still found on m.o.r. stations and talk
shows, and this person's popularity rests on becoming a companion or
friend to the listener. Among the most popular in this category is Larry
King, who helps many lonely folks through the small hours until television can take over.

One sociological explanation for the success of personality radio is
that the on-the-air personality encourages listeners to take on a recipro-
cal role, such as being an insider in the DJ's loyal group, to whom the
DJ provides validation on a daily basis. In turn, the station and radio
personalities are dependable and their friendship is unconditional. Indeed, the increase in personality radio and talk shows during the 1980s
underscores the demand for friendly or agreeable voices. Increasingly,
that friendly voice is female, although as yet women do not anchor the
plumb drive-time periods nor are they heard on Country stations. This
will change during the 1990s.

The basic technique or approach used by all successful radio communicators is speaking one-on-one to the listener. In their words (Snow
1983), it consists of visualizing a person on the other side of the micro-
phone and speaking to that person on their level. Sociologically, the process is simply one of role-taking and role-making. To obtain a measure

of audience response, they invite call-ins, play call-in games, ask others to evaluate their performance, and listen to themselves on tape. Although it might appear that radio would be a relatively impersonal medium, it is just the opposite. Since the relationship between speaker and listener is so fragile and temporary, the speaker must put constant and intense effort into developing and maintaining the relationship. Their do their homework on the audience, and gather material for spontaneous appearing small talk that will hit home with the listener. Over time, the degree of familiarity between medium and listener may result in the feeling that radio personalities can anticipate listener needs. At that point, a significant sense of intimacy has developed. When Larry King suffered a heart attack, the outpouring of sympathy and support was immense. When he subsequently quit smoking he was a new hero. In sociological terms, he had become a significant other, and who knows how many others may tried to quit along with him.

Implications

Over a decade ago, we claimed (Altheide and Snow 1979) that radio had created a culture of its own through its formats. Illustrations included the fact that record companies began tailoring records to fit radio format. DJs such as Wolfman Jack became legitmators for music scenes and listeners rallied around stations for a sense of belonging to a music subculture. We do not wish to retract anything said then, but we would like to add several observations that were not foreseen.

The most important consequence of media logic that we underestimated was the extent to which form would actually replace content as the focus of attention. In other words, during the past decade, the means (form) has become the end in itself. An example is the use of radio as what some have called background noise. In contrast to television, which often captivates audiences within program content, people use radio to facilitate other activities, such as getting to work, eating, reading, and making love. Even when radio is being listened to attentively, the listener is often engaged in some other activity. Consequently, listeners employ radio to facilitate activity in other social contexts. This is not to say that radio fails to be involved in social affairs, for it serves as a guideline, reference point, and legitimizer for numerous fairly specialized social worlds. However, as a so-called background, the grammatical features of radio may become important, particularly in the temporal character of these external social affairs, such as driving, shopping, eating, and studying. When a person cannot wash the car without turning the radio on, that person may be setting the temporal parameters or the beat and pace for washing the car as well as maintaining some social contact with a music subculture. Life without radio is not just social isolation or cultural deprivation, it is a loss of a temporal framework. Stretching this idea, it may be the loss of a physiological pattern that impacts on emotional well-being. If this seems absurd, why do some people need their stereo headset to jog? Or ask anyone under 40 what they do to prevent boredom while riding in their car or waiting for a traffic light to change. Invariably the answer is, "I turn on the radio." Usually the radio is always turned on, but the point is that at the moment of perceiving boredom, the person looks for something to establish or change the rhythm and tempo. Format radio guarantees relief.

At this point, anyone who has gown up in the age of rock'n'roll is probably saying that it is obvious that radio provides a beat and pace. We not only acknowledge that observation, but add that radio has become indispendible in the lives of many people for exactly that—radio is one of the more significant drums of modern urban life (Denisoff 1975). The fact that radio has not only survived in the age of television, but has become more profitable than ever indicates that radio must be a powerful and socially viable medium. Despite the fact that television is the medium of choice (music video), and magazines provide a behind the scenes peek at these subcultures, what is left for radio is by no means trivial. At the very least, radio serves the important temporal function in present day American culture of maintaining the appearance of a background flow or motion to everyday life. Radio seems to "keep things moving," although in no particular direction.

Another change that surprised even close observers of radio was the switch from AM to FM (Jackson 1990). In 1970 AM stations were the large audience m.o.r. stations with big budgets and price tags, and FM stations were either simulcasting AM or doing highly specialized small audience service. By 1979, FM audiences equaled AM and advertisers took notice. By 1990 the AM/FM difference had completely reversed, and AM stations were simulcasting and doing the specialized material. The trend for the 1990s is that FM will continue to roll, and AM will present talk, sports, business, minority and ethnic culture, and experimentation. This might reverse again if the FCC adopted a standard for stereo AM broadcast that improves sound quality. Regardless, we can expect talk radio to continue expanding its total audience through specialized topical formats, such as sports, financial, political, religious, and health. As urban life becomes more privatized and socially fragmented, talk radio will function both as an opportunity for vicarious and overt social participation, and as a source of information on issues as well as gossip and soap opera style drama in everyday life. This is not simply a matter of finding a remedy for loneliness. Rather, as reported in *U.S. News and World Report* (Rosellini 1990), today's talk format audience includes well-informed people who lack a satisfying intellectual forum to discuss the issues of the day (p. 51). For most people, this discussion, or more accurately involvement, consists of listening as they work, drive, or jog in order to feel mentally and socially active in vital issues of the day. In turn, this knowledge can be used as a form of small talk with friends and co-workers. For example, the custodian on the floor of our office building, affectionately known as "Grizzly," constantly bounces ideas and tidbits of information off the secretarial and academic staff that he hears while listening to local news/talk stations as he works. The extent to which this practice exists may make talk radio one of the more powerful sources of information on social issues in American culture today.

As talk radio expanded, news on radio declined. News reports have all but disappeared on commercial music stations, and they are difficult to find anywhere after 10 A.M. except at all-news stations. Many program directors now claim that television and all-news radio make it unnecessary for music stations to present factual news broadcasts (Jackson 1990). In place of factual news, these stations have turned to service-oriented or utilitarian information, such as traffic, weather, and community bulletin boards. Although a strong case can be made for this type of "service news," we would add that format considerations seem to be a strong reason for abandoning factual news. In short, news does not fit into many of the rock formats, especially when these stations advertise "less talk; more rock." To maintain consistency, these stations usually reduce stories to one sentence headlines. Another news of sorts is being presented by some of these stations as part of the "morning zoo" format. The zoo comedy team takes the familiar cartoon type statistical graphics from *USA TODAY* and makes cynical comedy. Until recently, news as entertainment was found primarily in the tabloid press, television, and magazines. (Note the increase pop culture material in weekly news magazines during the past decades.) With the popularity of *USA TODAY* and the traditional practice in radio of "rip and read" (taking news from the wire service or clipping from the newspaper), it was a logical move to bring news as entertainment into radio.

Television

Robert Nisbet has said: "We live in a world of ideas, and ideas, stereotypes, and images have far greater directive forces in our lives, generally, than do the conditions they are supposed to reflect" (1976:76). The question for contemporary society is: What happens when those ideas, stereotypes, and images are obtained through television? TV has become so inextricably woven into contemporary daily routines, institutional strategies, and leisure activity that American society appears to be adopting a television logic and problem-solving perspective. Societies have always used some central institutional framework and form of communication through which they "made sense" of their environment and solved community problems. From primitive cultures to the preelectronic age, the form of communication basically has been the same—verbal, face-to-face communication augmented by print. With the advent of television, the nature of communication changed. As Marshall McLuhan (1964) and others have argued, the nature of electronic media has a particular bias that emphasizes certain characteristics of communication over others. McLuhan emphatically claimed that seeing the world through television is significantly different than seeing it through print. In concluding that "the medium is the message," McLuhan meant that the medium affects how people experience the world through the medium. Regardless of whether one takes McLuhan literally, the inescapable conclusion is that communication through television has been significantly different than through other media.

The Grammar of Television

To argue that the central characteristic of television is entertainment might seem obvious to the point of absurdity. But an error is made when that observation simply treats entertainment as a noun instead of a verb. This is illustrated in the new televisionese term "info-tainment," which refers to superimposing an entertainment framework on traditional information or news media. News and information specialists have come to recognize what comedians have always known, that it is not the content of their routines that make people laugh, it is how that content is presented. The more familiar elements of how content is presented are as follows.

Syntax. To the typical viewer, program scheduling would be the most conspicuous example of syntax in media logic. All viewers are aware of homogeneous program units and how they are positioned throughout the day, such as morning shows, games, soaps, talk, news, sitcoms, drama, news, and more talk. Viewers are also familiar with the network strategy of using popular programs to pull newcomers into the fold, such as "Different World" following "Cosby," and then moving newcomers that are solid hits to evenings that need a ratings boost. Of course, the strategy fails sometimes, as happened with "Chicken Soup" following "Roseanne." In short, viewers are savvy about scheduling norms. They know they are being manipulated, but they also know they can depend on the fact that sitcoms, adult material, games, and so on will appear only during particular times during the evening and day of the week. And it is understood that the big three networks share the same rules.

The stability of network scheduling strategies enables viewers to schedule their own daily routines around the television. This is slightly different than the situation with radio, in which radio caters to the needs of listeners. Although network television also attempts to mesh with viewer schedules, they also attempt to schedule the viewer, and have done so with moderate success. And yet, the real point is that television serves as a means for achieving temporal sequence in everyday life, particularly during the prime time hours. With television, the evening hours progress through half-hour and hour segments to a routinized bedtime that coincides with a specific program feature (e.g., Carson's monologue) or end of a particular program. Therefore the television schedule becomes the organizational logic for a viewer's evening.

A more subtle characteristic of television syntax is the subordination of verbal dialogue to visual information. In large part this means that visual information is more important than auditory information. CBS correspondent Lesley Stahl discovered this when she aired what she thought would be an uncomplimentary piece on Ronald Reagan. To her surprise, the White House loved the piece because the visuals were positive. As a White House spokesperson told Stahl, "The public doesn't pay any attention to what you say, they just look at the pictures" (*Time*, March 30, 1987:35). Another implication is that viewers notice visuals first, and then use the visual material to inform the overall experience. Dialogue may be used to interpret the visuals, as was the case in Hollywood film prior to television's dominance (Snow 1983), but the visuals may also be used to make sense of events independent of verbal explanation. This certainly is the case in MTV, montage advertising, and recent cartoon genre of Hollywood films. It might be called the Nintendo syndrome, since the syntax is to anticipate visual information rather than verbal interpretation. We feel this is a fairly new dimension in the logic of viewing television, and is the result of recent changes in presenting news, editing in sitcoms and dramas, as well as MTV. However, a distinction must be made between the anticipation of another visual image and the anticipation of specific content. With respect to content, music video and a great deal of news video is nonlinear. In music video everything is in perpetual motion: change for the sake of change. Television news is similar in that images would continuously blend into each other were it not for cutting back to the anchor periodically. Dennis Miller of **"Saturday Night Live"** does a parody on this when he shuffles papers at the end of each story.

A more mundane example of syntax is the linear development of storylines through a series of shifts or "takes" from one camera to another. Although viewers are forced to follow what is designed by the director, they are also spared any problem in figuring out what is going on. Never is the viewer's attention allowed to wander to extraneous stimuli as is the case in everyday-life situations. Another consequence of this organization is the appearance of interaction that flows smoothly. Characters never speak out of turn, they always have a ready answer, and the viewer is always in a privileged position.

It is often difficult to illustrate syntax without overlapping with inflection, as is the case in discussing timing. Everyone is aware that comedians describe successful comedy largely as a sense of timing—the effective pause before a punch line, a pause for laughter, and the roll (three or four punch lines delivered in rapid succession). For television, timing involves adherence to this principle, but within a context that approximates the reality of everyday life. Most television drama and situation comedy scenes are fairly natural, that is, they are situations in which the viewer can readily identify the real-life characters, even though they are slightly exaggerated. Within these somewhat natural settings, the performers use timing to intensify the drama or humor and at the same time draw the audience into the action. Timing is personalized and neutralized for the audience while at the same time intensifying and exaggerating the dramatic experience or one-liner humor.

Inflection.   Distinct from the timing of interaction is the way in which time is compressed on television. Specifically, the pauses and delays that characterize everyday life are removed through editing, and new accents are added—namely, a laugh track. The familiar result is a compressed event in which action flows with rapid ease, compacting hours or even days into minutes, and minutes into seconds or "sound bites." Audiences are spared the waiting common to everyday life. Although this use of time may appear unnatural in the abstract, the television audience has come to expect it, and critics demand it. More important, television performers, or people who depend on television, such as politicians, are evaluated by viewers (voters) on their ability to meet time compression requirements, such as the one sentence graphic statement or metaphor to capture the moment. It is the statement that is in bold print or the boxed insert in newspaper and magazine articles. As such, compression techniques accentuate another important temporal dimension of television—rhythm and tempo.

As an important feature of television grammar, the internal rhythm and tempo of television programs establish a sense of movement and interest in the mind of the viewer. The content of a program may peak a viewer's curiosity, but staying tuned is usually achieved through accent and movement, as is illustrated so well in most advertisements. Rhythm is the most difficult to identify, although some experiences, such as music, poetry, riding a train, or working on an assembly line have rhythms that are unmistakable. In television, as with other media, rhythm may be far more subtle. And yet, in comparing an afternoon soap opera to a situation comedy, the difference in beat or rhythm is readily apparent. But by and large the internal rhythm of a TV program is a subtle pattern or series of patterns that viewers become accustomed to and expect. For example, in viewing an afternoon soap opera the knowledgeable viewer knows how long a particular camera shot will last before the camera slowly zooms into a tight close up and then pulls back slightly as the scene ends. Other examples include the time duration of camera shots in a sequence. The first shot may be moderately short, followed by a longer shot, several short shots, and end with a lingering shot. Viewers have become so familiar with the timing of commercial breaks in prime-time entertainment that the beginning, ending, and climax of a program is associated with advertisements. Consequently, the flow of commercial television entertainment is achieved through a rhythm of advertisements, with a current duration of 11 minutes between breaks. Directors now talk of being forced to think in terms of two or three 11-minute acts to a program.

Whereas rhythm refers to the beat, tempo is the pace of an event. In fact, tempo is often confused with rhythm simply because it is the most obvious. Everyone can tell how fast or slow they are moving, but the internal rhythm may escape notice. Most television programs appear to move at a fairly rapid pace, and this is primarily due to the editing of visual material and the tempo of background music. Although the actual tempo of speech and body gestures by television performers is rather slow or deliberate (to avoid ambiguity), the pace of nearly all types of programs has increased over the past two decades. In a comparison of sitcoms before and after 1970, Denise Rejent-Lee (1990) found that tempo almost tripled through edit changes. In reading postmortums of the annual Hollywood Academy shows each Spring, the critique of whether it was a good or bad show usually hinges on its tempo.

One additional aspect of television's temporal character that deserves brief mention is the manner in which program schedules serve as brackets or parameters for organizing other (nonmedia) activity. It has become almost commonplace for people to schedule meals and other domestic activity, such as waking up and going to bed, around particular television programs. People have also become accustomed to half-hour and hour schedules for particular activities, such as eating, studying, writing letters, or anything else that can be done while watching television. The fact that some cookbooks specify one-hour preparation times for evening meals may be another illustration. Among homebound individuals, such as the elderly, rigid TV viewing schedules become routines that can be used to achieve a sense of movement or progress through the day. In turn, these routines also give the viewer a sense of stability and control as they move from program to program. Similar to radio, television can easily become both a clock and calendar with implications for social rhythms. Consequently, when TV networks change the schedule for a popular program, they run the risk of losing viewers who are ensconced in their own day-to-day rhythmic schedule.

A related example of this same process is the visual rhythm of new rock music. Specifically, the most recent popular rock of the early 1990s is danced more than sung or acted. Groups, such as Milli Vanilli, Bobby Brown, and The New Kids on the Block perform highly intricate and tightly choreographed rapid tempo routines. Although listening to these groups offers nothing unusual or even interesting, their visual routines are high-energy synchronized dances that are rather fun to watch. Whereas Elvis and Chuck Berry may have been the first to put a rudimentary dance to performing popular rock music, the dance did not become the dominant characteristic of the performance until television took hold of rock. With legitimation from television, through leaders such as Ed Sullivan, white kids could imitate what black kids were doing with rhythm and blues. In 1990 it all came together on the highly aclaimed television program "Living Color," on the Fox Network.

A final point on television and temporality in everyday life is the suggestion that while watching TV, time itself can seem suspended as a "time-out." Future concerns are placed on hold and the moment is enjoyed as a play activity much like a daydream. This may help explain why some people can easily go into an alpha brain wave state as they watch TV, or fall asleep almost instantly. Television may be the only major mass medium that can function as a biofeedback technique or sleeping pill. Stretching this notion, the success of the arts and crafts street fairs over the past decade suggests that people are looking for activities in which the progression of time or the clock is irrelevant. In street fairs, individuals can wander through a maize of visually interesting displays and feel a sense of mellow involvement. As with television viewing, these street fairs are safe social affairs, and the hurried urban life-style is momentarily abandoned. We are not suggesting that television has caused the popularity of street fairs, but the social psychological dimensions of these events are not unlike a television experience. And the format character of the street fair is similar in visual inflection characteristics to the editing of entertainment television programs—a collage of close up shots with fairly rapid editing.

Another feature of the grammar of entertainment television, one that illustrates both inflection and specialized vocabulary, is the nonverbal dimension of interpersonal interaction through television. One illustration is the talking head. Facial features and gestures are, without question, paramount in television grammar. But here an interesting irony in television emerges. American culture has strict rules about observing others in close interpersonal encounters, and one of the more stringent rules involves eye contact. Although everyone in daily life uses nonverbal cues for anticipating another's intentions and making sense out of talk, we seldom maintain intensive eye contact in real-life situation. With television the viewer is allowed the anonymity to read faces intently, and from the viewer's perspective television can be highly interpersonal and intimate, or impersonal and detached, depending on the viewer's desire.

Accenting the nonverbal features of televised interaction has become a very sophisticated technology. Lighting, makeup, camera angles, and background sound are factors that can make or break a performance. Lighting may be the most critical factor, as present day screen resolution in America does not allow the picture quality that is attainable with film. Heavy use of close-up shots in television requires lighting that prevents distortion. Consequently, characters literally appear "in their best light." This factor aids in the development of the extraordinary "star" quality of many television performers. Obviously, if lighting can enhance appearance, it can also accent negative features, as former President Richard Nixon learned so painfully.

Lighting is always determined with the camera angle in mind. These angles can help establish the heroic stature of a character, the importance of a character in a scene, the physical features of a character, the "glitzy" effect, and many other elements that add emphasis to the dialogue and action. A dramatic example occurred on a televised birthday tribute to Sammy Davis Jr. in February 1990. From the view of a low angle camera, Michael Jackson's musical number began unannounced with him standing alone as a black and silver silhouette shrouded in smoke. The initial response from many in the audience was not a cheer or applause, but a gasp. Clearly, through techniques such as these, Michael maintains a God-like status among his fans, or faithful followers.

One conclusion that may be drawn from this is that television aims for a high degree of clarity that is achieved instantly. There is no abstract symbolism, and no need to turn up the volume. Plots, characters, dialogue, and action are clear and concise. A typical illustration occurred in a review of an NBC special in 1990 of Ernest Hemingway's *The Old Man and the Sea*. The reviewer commented that the television special was a "simplification of the already simple" (Joseph 1990). Then again, given the necessity of mass audience appeal, television cannot afford too much ambiguity, especially when modern technology makes it is so easy to change the channel. The typical viewing situation also has considerable potential for distraction: chattering kids, pestering pets, the telephone, unexpected guests—the list is endless. Consequently, television communicates so that viewers can predict and comprehend with a fair degree of accuracy immediately after the set is turned on or after parts of a program have been missed. After all, the object is to get the viewer to the next commercial. Television does not peddle surprise or deferred gratification. When the experimental program **"Twin Peaks"** was aired during the Spring of 1990, viewers became so bored waiting to discover who the killer was that T-shirts appeared saying "I killed Laura Palmer!"

Content Standards

The recurring criticism of television is its tiresome repetition and banality. One equally tiresome explanation is that television presents material according to the lowest common denominator. Although the notion of common denominator is accurate, the term "lowest" is quite misleading (and elitist). Although more than enough sex and violence can be found on television, the same holds true for other art forms. In fact, close examination of television reveals that the prime-time period is probably the most conservative form of pop culture in American society. The reason is partially economics. Since the strategy in network television is to capture the largest number of viewers, in order to charge high advertising rates, the last thing networks want is controversy and inactive television sets (McDonald 1990). They discovered that the best plan was to follow a line of least resistance, or "least objectionable program." As coined by Paul Klein (1975), the concept of least objectionable program (LOP) is not based on a principle of attracting the viewer, but in keeping the viewer from turning off the set in anger or disgust and complaining to the networks and advertisers. Pragmatically, many viewers are creatures of habit, and they watch until they are offended or bored, and then they change channels. But when they are offended, the history of television (as well as radio during its mass audience days) shows that viewers will take the trouble to complain in writing and take consumer action. Looking at this sociologically, prime-time television viewers can appear to act as a public, similar to voting in a national election. And, at the public level, the norms and values that people espouse are the cultural ideals.

Ideal Norms

Ideal norms refer to those rules and strategies we all uphold as the best possible way to live. Honesty, modesty, fidelity, and hard work are examples of ideals that people will agree to at the public level, even though deviation from those ideals is quite common in everyday life. Most everyone understands this as common sense, even though few of us ever attempt to explain why this apparent contradiction exists. But no politician, priest, or school teacher would dare disavow an ideal norm in a public arena. To publicly suggest that an ideal norm is not worthy of our respect challenges the very fabric that people believe holds society. This was discovered by members of the heavy metal rock group Guns N'Roses when they uttered profanities while accepting an award at the American Music Awards presentation carried by ABC (January 1990). The band was cut off in mid sentence and ABC apologized after receiving a barrage of viewer complaints. When "60 Minutes" personality Andy Rooney allegedly made negative remarks in a newspaper interview about several minority groups, CBS reacted quickly and fired him from the highly rated program (apparently believing that Rooney's alleged remarks would reflect on CBS). But these two examples are quite different. The award show profanity was a television (public forum/mass audience) experience. Rooney's alleged crime was committed in a small newspaper (private/specialized audience). Viewers of "60 Minutes" had no reason to object to Rooney and they demanded his return. This was graphically represented in the Nielsen ratings through a five point loss and regain (the day Rooney returned).

Network television applies the ideal-norm format to most prime-time offerings, including the news and some daytime programs. Viewers may object to specific acts of violence or scenes and dialogue that emphasize sex, but the ideal of justice and family that form the heart of the program are rarely challenged. A quick scan of *TV Guide* indicates how the ideal-norm format operates. In comparing the 1977–1978 television season to the 1989–1990 prime-time schedule, sitcoms dominated both periods. In the late 1970s, the ratings winners were "Happy Days," "Barney Miller," "Welcome Back Kotter," "Laverne and Shirley," "M*A*S*H*," and "One Day at a Time." Although some of these shows were social issue oriented, the issues were rarely discussed in any sociological detail: issues such as homosexuality, premarital sex, prejudice, and women's rights were topics of discussion, but the way in which issues were defined and the solutions reached were all achieved through ideal norms, or traditional ideals. In "One Day at a Time," the eldest daughter left home with her boyfriend only to eventually return full of sorrow, admitting that she had a lot to learn. Policemen were portrayed as humanitarians, even though they occasionally bent the law to achieve justice. Bigoted Archie Bunker was a lovable father and a good provider husband. In "M*A*S*H*" everyone but Frank Burns hated the war, but managed to have fun being hard-working, dedicated doctors and

nurses. Although every major issue that confronted the family in contemporary society was used as a plot, the issues were solved with the
traditional ideal solutions and/or laughed away through zany, burlesque
characters.

By the late 1980s little had changed. The five top rated shows were
sitcoms, and the first two featured modern day family life. Bill Cosby
was the contemporary father, and both he and his wife constantly reaffirmed time-honored traditions when their children wanted to spend
money they had not earned, become adults too fast, or treated friends
in a callous manner. "Roseanne" gave an apparent realistic view of blue-
collar life, but when kids or parents deviated from the norms, the same
old lessons came into play. Other consistent rating favorites, such as
"Cheers," "Golden Girls," and "The Wonder Years" provide delightful
characters, who also did the "right" thing. And then there is the curious
case of "Beauty and Beast." Although this show was consistently a ratings failure, it had one of the most intensely loyal audiences since "Star
Trek," and it promises to have a syndication potential on the order of
the "Treky" phenomenon. When rumors of cancellation emerged in
May 1989, loyal fans from 50 fan clubs with an estimated membership
of 350,000 mobilized to save the program. CBS received over 7,300 telegrams, and after putting it back on the air in mid season, the fans went
to work posting flyers in supermarkets, and libraries, and laundromats
in order to boost the ratings (Carlson 1990). Although only modest rating gains were made, fans remained loyal and even created a B&B inspired subculture of fiction, poetry, editorials, and fan mail in fan club
newsletters. According to one fan the core of all this was primarily the
ideals of love, integrity, and compassion (p. 5). Even religious organizations claimed the B&B message served a religious (ideal norms and values) purpose. As such, "B&B" became a quasireligious, philosophical,
and gothic romance experience especially for women viewers. Although
the ideal norms did not ensure mass appeal, they became the rallying
point for a number of loyal prime-time viewers.

An interesting twist on the "B&B" phenomenon is provided by Melodye Lehnerer (1990) in an unpublished paper. She argues that Vincent
(the Beast) symbolizes the best possible romantic relationship for the
modern woman. Vincent is not only a loving, caring, and superb protector, he also is not constantly underfoot, demanding, or controlling. Perhaps his robust appearance does not hurt either.

The best example of the ideal norms framework may be the beauty
pageant, particularly the Miss America Pageant. In fact, everything
about the Pageant and the television program is "lily white." Contestants
are screened to ensure that none is tarnished with past transgressions
from America's ideals, and during the publicity week prior to the big

show pageant officials see to it that contestants get kid glove treatment from the press. The show itself is a model of class, but with a touch of youthful naivete and a heavy dose of morality, as exhibited during the questions posed to the final group of contestants. Each of these questions is designed to reaffirm the fact that our Miss America upholds what we hold sacred regarding family and country. Although this event masquerades as a beauty contest, the criteria are more consistent with homespun and classic beauty than is typical of other beauty contests. These women should not appear sexy, provocative, alluring, mysterious, or even mature. They are most definitely not the Tina Turner type. They are a mother's daughter who looks chaste, humble, and wants to do what is right (traditional), and as the winner tours the country during her reign, she symbolizes what is most idealized about America. Although the Pageant predates television, it was an instant hit during the during TV's early years, and as such helped mold the LOP formula for prime-time.

By 1990, the ideal-norm format for prime-time had become a routinized, taken-for-granted policy. Plots, settings, and characters may change, but the basic strategy of using traditional ideals has remained the same since the early days of **"I Love Lucy."** Even daytime programs, such as soap operas, talk shows, courtroom shows, and game shows support traditional values and are highly moralistic in the solving problems (Cantor 1980). Given the longevity of this strategy, it may be hypothesized that mass audience media strategy works to maintain the value/norm status quo. This does not mean that TV can get away with being inane or banal to the extreme, as was discovered with tacky attempts, such as "USA Today On TV." Although the newspaper *USA TODAY* was a successful application of television format to print media, the reverse was even too dumb for television.

A potential exception to the ideal norms rule arose through the ensemble/serial dramatic program, such as "Hill Street Blues," "St. Elsewhere," "L.A. Law," "Thirtysomething," and the video realism programs, such as "COPS" and "Reporters." These urban life dramas often expressed the cynicism, materialism, and short-run outlook that characterized urban life in the 1980s. And yet, in the final scenes of many episodes, the proper emotions (shame and guilt) usually reestablished the importance of basic ideals. The message may be subtle, but evil and flagrant deviance never triumphs on prime-time television. Even "bad-boy" teams in professional sports get verbal reprimands from sportscasters.

On the other hand, there are periodic ventures into voyeurism that at the very least stretch the limits of good taste. At the extreme, slow motion replays of injuries (even death) on the football and basketball court make the issue of cartoon violence appear absurd by comparison. Although voyeurism will be addressed later in the chapter, the point here is that on occasion the camera and television crew are as stunned as the onlooker at a traffic accident. The scene is captivating by its similarity to the format characteristics of entertainment, but it is existentially quite different in its implications for the viewer. Given the stark juxtaposition of entertainment as an exhilarating expression of life, and the instant loss of that feeling when a performer is severely and graphically injured or even killed, the viewer is frozen in a moment of paralyzing ambivalence. Television can be excused for replaying the event within that context, but when it becomes entertainment, or even entertainment news, it violates the LOP formula and viewers have and will most certainly object.

Television Personalities

One of the more telling consequences of television over the past several decades is the emergence of the media, or more accurately, the television personality. These are people who, by virtue of their talent and media logic abilities and characteristics, have emerged as popular and in some cases well-respected individuals. Arthur Godfrey may have been the first, and both Walter Cronkite and Johnny Carson may tie for the longest tenure. Certainly Ronald Reagan qualifies for the Hall of Fame in this category, as well as Milton Berle, Jackie Gleason, Jack Paar, Phil, Oprah, Sally, and the list goes on. In most cases the media personality has legitimate talent that transcends TV, such as stage performance, sports, politics, education, and religion. However, what distinguishes the television personality from the talented person who never emerges on television is the ability to meet television format criteria. Television news is one of the clearest examples of this, as there are many radio and print journalists who have or would fail in television despite impeccable journalism credentials. In fact, the cart is before the horse in broadcasting television news. Meeting television format criteria comes first; journalism expertise is second, at best. A rather dramatic illustration of this process is found in the meteoric rise to stardom of Jane Pauley as co-anchor of the NBC *Today Show*. Although Jane was relatively inexperienced in broadcast journalism, the test-marketing of her audition tape showed that people preferred "waking up to her" over all the other women tested for the position. When she left the show after a highly successful 13 years, audience demand for her return was so great that it promoted this PR style reply from NBC President Robert C. Wright:

We have to figure out what to do with her. . . . We have never seen Jane in any other role than the morning show where she was a star. Now she's a superstar, a bigger-than-life star, a virtuoso. (Goldman 1990)

This logic holds true for every sector of culture, from entertainment to religion. What makes Johnny Carson television's "top banana" is a combination of factors that follow from the discussion of ideal norms. Carson's overall appeal is "Middle America" in nearly every respect. Born and raised in the Midwest, Carson constantly reminds the audience of his Nebraska roots and homespun heritage. Honesty and boyish charm innocence make him every mother's son, despite silver hair and several failed marriages. He is handsome, physically fit, and awkwardly debonair. Quick witted, he elects to make himself appear to be a comic on the edge of failure, and audiences love it. He represents the middle-American ideal of hard work and success tempered with modesty, humility, and sensitivity. He is the John Wayne of urbane television, and here again is the ideal norms formula at work. Consequently, just as the heartland has always symbolized the ideal norms of American society, all TV personalities who are associated with the Midwest should be symbols of morality. Most of these individuals, such as Carson, take this duty seriously and make moral statements at critical times, especially times of crisis for the country at large. In part, this is a major feature in the talk show format—moral (ideal norms) statements by media personalities.

More subtle and yet more significant in understanding Carson's prestige is the fact that he speaks for his audience. He asks the questions of performers, politicians, and experts that his viewers would ask. That these questions seldom go beyond the superficial is beside the point. Observing through an entertainment format, the public does not want its heroes put on the spot and embarrassed. They want just enough behind-the-scenes information to make folks on the small screen seem more intimate and personable. Carson responds by teasing out anecdotes, embarrassing moments, fears, and phobias, while adding a touch of glamour. Consequently, the audience places trust in Carson to define for them what is important in the relationship between viewer and performer. The result is that Carson, as well as any media personality, becomes both an agent of legitimation and a symbol of morality.

In extreme cases, personalities may extend their power of legitimation beyond the cultural sector in which their fame initially emerged, such as Ronald Reagan. Other common examples include advertisement testimonials, social issue advocates, and talk shows in which media personalities become instant experts on everything from marital relations and parenting to the ecology, education, and even mystic knowledge. The logic in this phenomenon is simply that television viewers are likely to pay attention to people who are "good" at television regardless of the context. Again, form not only precedes content, it shapes and even becomes content.

Supporting evidence for the legitimation power of media personalities is most dramatic in the case of individuals who establish their media ability prior to establishing their talent or skill in a particular activity, such as the TV or sports star who becomes a best selling author (e.g., Bill Cosby), and the talk show favorite who graduates to sitcoms or sports announcing (e.g., Bob Uecker). Reverend Jesse Jackson is a rather dazzling example of the process. By 1990 his roots as a religious leader were all but irrelevant, and his political prowess and diplomacy seem largely the result of his television ability. This is not to deny Jackson's considerable charisma when he appears in person, but many people would not accord him viability in political or diplomacy circles were it not for his television IQ and exposure. By the late 1980s, television viewers expected Jesse to appear at all big social issue gatherings. Furthermore, it is not a question of whether Jackson attracts the camera or the camera attracts Jackson. Rather, they follow each other, as they are interdependent elements of media culture, each conferring legitimation on the other. The same is true for the other Jackson—Michael. When President Bush announced (on April 6, 1990) that a summit conference between the superpowers would be held late in May of that year, Michael was at his side on the steps of the White House. Michael, with his ever-present dark glasses and gloves, was dressed in a black and red toy soldier uniform festooned with ornate chest medals. While thanking Michael for dropping by on this occasion, the President said that Michael was one of our "thousand points of light." One should wonder who was using whom to ensure a front page photograph in newspapers across the country.

Other Implications

In discussing various implications of media logic in American culture, it is essential to recognize that this is a sociology of knowledge argument. Stated emphatically, by the 1990s the primary cultural symbol system that informs people's various experience in any and every institutionalized sphere *is* television. In 1978, television critic Charlie Haas stated "The images that surround you in any event are more and more television images. Peoples' minds are working according to television rhythms" (*New Times*, July 24). A decade later this notion was all but taken for granted, as people commonly referred to "Spin Doctors" and "sound bites" in describing TV-created reality.

In our minds the critical phrase in that last sentence is "taken for granted." It is our belief that for most viewers, TV just is! As a reality, television is no longer thought of as unusual or fantastic. TV is a world, or worlds, that have been made commonplace. However, we are not saying that television renders television experience mundane. Quite the contrary. Television, as entertainmentized information, is extraordinary, and that quality in itself has become expected. Furthermore, the fame that comes from extraordinary performance has become an important dimension of establishing legitimacy. Fame confers legitimacy, and just appearing on television is often enough to achieve fame. What is commonplace is that people have come to expect the extraordinary, and they confer legitimacy and value on the basis of television exposure.

Although the illusion of the extraordinary is a difficult phenomenon to describe much less measure, it makes intuitive sense to anyone who has ever had a hero or fantasized about anything. Fictional TV series have produced characters that have become an indelible part of our collective history. The Cartwrights of Bonanzaland represent the Old West, while the Ewings of Dallas are the modern counterparts. J.R.'s ten gallon hat hangs in the Smithsonian. For people too young to have experienced Elvis, The Fonz became the essence of the 1950s. "Roots" rewrote slave history, and WWII became "The Winds of War." As such, television has become a significant culture machine in its own right, and most any event presented on TV is redefined for TV and magnified beyond the dimensions of first hand experience. This certainly is true for the award show spectacles that must be relatively boring to watch in person, but are magical on the screen. By contrast, the new genre of visual rock music and concerts, such as "glam rock" and "theme concerts," are rather awesome spectacles when witnessed live, but there again giant TV screens hang above the stage to enlarge the visual impact.

As an illustration, consider the San Francisco earthquake that delayed the third game of the 1989 World Series. With electric power disrupted in the Bay area, natives were literally in the dark about the extent of damage, injury, and so forth. Meanwhile, the rest of the country watched network television attempt to construct a totality of the situation and make prognostications of what the next few hours and days might hold for the region. While people in Phoenix, Denver, Buffalo, and Boston sat glued to their sets watching a major disaster in progress, people in the Bay area were forced to call friends outside the area to find out what was happening. Natives somewhat accustomed to earthquake activity went about the business of helping, cleaning up, or waiting it out. Their reality was highly localized, and without television it was rather unexciting (with the exception of people in high destruction areas).

Outside the Bay area, the event promised to be of colossal proportions, one that kept many awake all night. To meet those format demands (the extraordinary), television searched frantically for physical and emotional evidence of disaster, but without electricity and mobility they were hard-pressed to fill the bill. Viewers stayed tuned with the belief that extraordinary evidence would appear, changing channels back and forth to see if the competition somehow had (uncovered) new information. The point is, that as a disaster, the earthquake was a television event. It was understood through the news-gathering machinery of television and television formats (primarily news). The extent to which anyone obtained a "whole" picture of the disaster was made possible through television. Meanwhile, on the streets of San Francisco people helped evacuate those trapped in the rubble, sat inconvenienced in traffic jams, searched for flashlight batteries, tried to obtain safe drinking water, partied in bars telling personal experience stories of where they were when the ground turned to jelly, and called friends in Phoenix to find out what the "real" story was (from television).

The dove-tail matter of legitimacy through fame rests most commonly on the fact that anything that is reported or dramatized on TV becomes significant simply by virtue of getting air time. As stated earlier, TV establishes reality. Therefore, news is what TV says is news, malfeasance is what "60 Minutes" says is malfeasance, and Ted Kopple turns news events into confrontational issues. On a more subtle and individual level, television can temporarily elevate the importance of anyone lucky enough to be caught in the camera's lens in a news event or human interest story on a local newscast. As stated (tongue in cheek) in a *Newsweek* article, our most basic biological urge is to "get on TV" (p. 54). The television screen not only legitimizes events and ideas, it validates self. For Jane or John Doe, this usually means being the butt of humor, as in stupid pet and human tricks on the "David Letterman Show," and doing a prat fall on a home video for "America's Funniest Home Videos." If none of this gets you on TV there is always a game show, a talk show audience, or a protest movement. During the Spring semester of 1990, students on the Arizona State University campus protested tuition increases by strapping themselves to palm trees to form a living bar graph depicting increases over the past decade. It became a traffic stopper and a guaranteed TV news item. Although our approach here may seem cynical, we hasten to emphasize that participants in this process would surely claim that it is all done for fun. And that is our point. Getting on television is an existential expression that also earns admiration from others, but to get on TV requires doing something in a entertainment framework. More specifically, it requires entertainment within current television formats. "America's Funniest Home Videos" provides a good illustration.

As the hit of the second (Spring) season in 1990, "America's Funniest Home Videos" caters strictly to amateur video productions that are short and funny. But, what kind of funny? According to a *Newsweek* article (March 5, 1990, pp. 51–56), the categories used to reject entries included "it can't be funny only to the family (too esoteric), and it can't be contrived (it must meet the criterion of spontaneity)." In other words, the video must meet the criteria of entertainment discussed earlier, and be visually interesting. Apparently, viewers have learned what gets selected or rejected, and they may go to great lengths to make a hit video. A recent winner (the studio audience selects a winner each week from three selections) showed a woman who got her hair caught in a dishwasher while trying to retrieve a fork. As reported in the *Newsweek* article, her husband Bill "obeyed his most natural instinct. He raced for his camcorder, set it on a tripod, and taped his trapped wife for a full five minutes—periodically tickling her for maximum hilarity." [*Newsweek* suggested that perhaps that entry should have been categorized as "OFTDRADL—Only Funny to Dishwasher Repairmen and Divorce Lawyers" (p. 55).]

Not too many years ago the legitimation of what and who was funny came from Las Vegas rather than television. As people who watch television variety programs during the 1950s will recall, Ed Sullivan and Steve Allen would preface their introductions of a comic or variety entertainer with the phrase "Direct from the Sahara in Las Vegas, Nevada." Perhaps it was Elvis who started the change, but today Las Vegas acts are television acts. Rodney Dangerfield, Jay Leno, Rich Little, and so on all started in television and became headliners in Las Vegas on the strength of TV popularity, and the content of their acts is essentially television material. Gone are the days of headliners, such as Redd Foxx and Shecky Green, who performed Las Vegas acts that would be unsuitable for television. Now, Las Vegas is prime-time television. In fact, George Carlin (another TV comic) tells of being fired in Las Vegas for using a profanity in a major hotel-casino. Not too many years ago the use of profanity in major Las Vegas shows was standard operating procedure. Ironically, Carlin and others find that today they can raunch it up on cable TV, but not in Las Vegas.

Additional discussion of the expectation of the extraordinary and conferring legitimacy on the basis of fame will be dealt with in subsequent chapters. Another matter that deserves at least brief attention is the social psychological dimension of intimacy in television experience, and establishing and maintaining a sense of self and self-worth through their television experience.

There is no lack of evidence for the contention that TV viewers can and have achieved the feeling of intimacy with characters and personalities on television. Starting with the fictional character relationship, viewers who immerse themselves in a program, particularly a serial program, such as a soap opera, can easily develop a vicarious relationship with one or more of the characters. For example, during the 1970s the public related to Archie Bunker, the Fonz, J.R. Ewing, and so on to the point that any attempt to change or kill off the character was met with passionate public objection. J.R. became the object of an intense loved/hate relation with women viewers, and femme fatales, just as Alexis on "Dynasty" became an object of lust to male viewers. More recently, Vincent (the "Beast") has become the ideal protector and object of affection for women, while men join Sam at "Cheers" in pursuing Rebecca. Every daytime soap opera provides considerable vicarious potential, particularly in the kinds of problematic situations that viewers can or would like to have. In the case of daytime soaps, viewers would like to be in situations where they are forced to wrestle with these dilemmas, or see parallels with their own lives. Nighttime soaps are the same, only more glamorous, whereas ensemble shows, such as "St Elsewhere," "L.A. Law," and particularly "Thirtysomething" deal with the struggle for intimacy among singles and young married in contemporary society.

Joshua Meyrowitz (1985) points out that this process has resulted in depriving people in public view of any private retreat. They are not safe from public scrutiny anywhere, as Presidential aspirant Gary Hart learned so painfully. In turn, Meyrowitz argues that the destruction of public/private boundaries has changed the way people interact with each other. Through television entertainment, children have gained access to the backstage of their parent's lives, and men and women have peered into each other's secret worlds.

The process of establishing self and self-worth through television should surprise no one familiar with this medium. The range of potential sources and measures of self-worth are extensive, including advertisements, sports, talk and commentary programs, game shows, beauty pageants, and award shows. Everything on television has potential for comparison of self to TV portrayal, and much of it validates and legitimates. But one type of program deserves special attention. The daytime women-oriented talk shows hosted by Sally Jesse Raphael, Oprah Winfrey, Geraldo Rivera, and Phil Donahue are engaging for the range of social and psychological dimensions that can be elicited from audiences. Although their common denominator is "voices from the margin," they do not appear to have the voyeurism appeal of prime-time counterparts, such as Geraldo's special on evil (ABC 1989). Instead, these daily shows invite interaction between curious onlookers and subjects, much like a classroom, although at times they may appear similar to carnival freak shows, or invite hostile audience response for the sake of entertainment value. One day Donahue will feature a demonstration and discussion of anal cleft bathing suits, and the next day he will interview Winnie Mandela. Although entertainment is the central framework, there is also an invitation for intellectual curiosity that enables viewers to get involved in discussions and come to decisions regrading their own feelings, beliefs, and proposed problems. Most important, viewers are able to make comparisons among members of the live studio audience and between themselves and people very much like themselves in that same studio audience. Aided by the safety of anonymity, viewers have time for self-reflection and evaluation without fear of overt commitments. As is the case with the radio talk format, we expect this television counterpart to increase in popularity.

Another aspect to the afternoon programs that may also serve identity and self-esteem concerns is their potential as gossip. It has been observed that soap operas have become an institutionalized form of gossip on the order of a self-contained communication system (Chesebro and Glenn 1982). Indeed, much of what goes on in entertainment TV is identical to interpersonal gossip, and gossip is directly concerned with the moral fabric of society. Everyone gossips to some degree, and in doing so comparisons are made between self and others on the rules and values that matter in society.

In contrast to the daytime potential for self-reflection and critical evaluation, television also offers a considerable potential for what John Fiske (1987) calls "voyeuristic pleasure" (p. 226), particularly during primetime. He goes on to argue that when these experiences are defined as a play, they may be empowering; "the power to . . . insert oneself into the process of representation so that one is not subjected by it, but conversely, is empowered by it" (p. 236). Similarly, *People* magazine, or tabloid journalism, offers voyeurism through a peek behind the closed doors of the rich and famous or infamous. We need not get into motives, but the process seems similar to gossip in that secrets or backstage life are being uncovered, enabling comparison and a feeling of power. Popular examples include Barbara Walters' informal and psychologically revealing interviews, Brian Leach's foray into the lives of "The Rich and Famous," and, in a similar fashion, the humorous faux pas on "America's Funniest Home Videos." By contrast, there is always the sleazy or seamy side of life, as may be seen on the "tabloid" programs ("Cops," "Reporters," "Missing/Reward").

Through the marriage of entertainment and news, lightweight and low-light cameras and satellite transmission, and the acceptance of visual montage as pioneered in music videos, this tabloid video has been redefined as video realism. Ironically, this is not realism, as real life is far too boring to be acceptable on television. The main feature of video realism is the attempt to position the viewer in the action, particularly action that occurs at night. To facilitate this, both the visual and audio work lack the rhythmic flow and articulation that is characteristic of familiar commercial television. These deliberate amateurish techniques produce a drama that is raw, unsophisticated, and in many cases vulgar. As an alternative to typical prime-time fare, the Fox network in 1990 devoted two and one-half hours of Saturday night to these programs, beginning with "COPS," followed by "Totally Hidden Video," "Reporters," and ending with "Missing/Reward." Unlike the ensemble program, such as "Hill Street Blues," the video verite approach in "COPS" does not promote an identification with the characters in an on-going serial manner. Rather, video realism maintains a detachment and a "for-the-moment" type of emotional involvement. Video realism places the viewer in the scene to see it as a perpetrator, as a victim, and as a witness, but without any overlying sense of value or justice. Put another way, there is little attempt to provide an explanation or framework that would make it socially redeeming. Viewers can keep a safe emotional distance from the social activity while still being privy to the action. Therefore, the voyeuristic component of video realism may also be understood as another example of the primacy of form over content, or, in this case, the importance of realistically appearing action that is made more dramatic and exciting by night scenes.

Entertainment in Nonentertainment Subjects

It should come as no surprise to anyone who acknowledges the power of television that the entertainment perspective is by no means limited to entertainment programming. Unabashedly the entertainment perspective pervades news, talk shows, sports, religion, education and science, and the new docudramas as TV's answer to presenting history. It may be referred to through euphemisms, such as "visual appeal," "flair," "production values," "network quality," and even "good television," but it all reduces to the entertainment perspective, and nobody in the business seriously attempts to deny this, much less attempt to change it. More important, viewers have come to expect and demand it.

Network news may be the most extreme example of the pervasiveness of entertainment in television. The days of Edward R. Murrow are long gone. Today, news is action-packed drama narrated by superstar journalists—it is show business, and the profit stakes are too high to leave the programming to journalists. This was clearly demonstrated when ABC moved sports producer Roone Arledge to head the news department. He and other sports producers understand that the main characteristic of TV news is the visual impact that surrounds a story. The word "story" is important here, as that is exactly what news has become—a story or scenario that is constructed to fit the entertainment perspective.

As former president of NBC news Reuven Frank said: "Every news story should, without any sacrifice of probity or responsibility, display the attributes of fiction, of drama. It should have structure and conflict, problem and denouement, rising action and falling action, a beginning, a middle, and an end" (Epstein 1974:4). Enough said; more in Chapter 3.

Whereas the network news is a slick and somewhat conservative entertainment program, the happy-talk "Action News" program of the local community is either burlesque or trivial drama. Well-coiffeured men and women with matching blazers engage in repartee as they cover the latest stories on sexual fantasies, UFOs, celebrities, fires, spectacular auto accidents, and promos for local businesses. It seems the local news producers learned a great lesson from the late 1960s hit comedy show "Laugh-In." Every story is brief and visual whether it makes sense or not. Again, sense follows form, not content. To ensure the entertainment value of the news, a top banana is provided in the name of the weather reporter. To borrow one of their descriptive terms, the weather report is "breezy." In fact, sports may be the only serious coverage left on local news, although even here the sportscaster plays the fair-weather fan who makes side bets with the anchorperson. And like the superstars of network news, the local people become celebrities in their own right. The authors once witnessed a minor league baseball game at which a local weatherman played a pregame softball match. The weatherman signed more autographs than any of the professional ballplayers.

The latest wrinkle in entertainment news is Channel 1, the video weekly reader for adolescent school kids broadcast to schoolrooms throughout the country. The format is similar to pop radio with background music and trivia contests, and several minutes of advertising accompany each broadcast. Both California and New York have banned Channel 1 in the classroom, but it is not clear if the objection is to advertising or entertainment. Our guess is the former, as the latter is well established in education.

Another form of television entertainment that has gained in popularity is the fictionalized documentary, or "docudrama." Blockbusters over recent years include "Roots," the history of a black slave family in America, the fall of Richard Nixon in "Watergate," the private lives of Martin Luther King, Lee Harvey Oswald, General George Custer, and the entire family of Joe Kennedy. The implication in these docudramas is that history is being recreated and that critical questions concerning these subjects ought to be reexamined. Was King really a saint, was Custer insane, Nixon a conspirator, and all the Kennedys overachievers from the bedroom to the boardroom? Although these questions may be legitimate (certainly within the entertainment perspective), they have not been treated in a manner that provides rational analysis and conclusions. Rather, the viewer is being set up for a vicarious identification with the main character(s) in order to experience conflict, tension, persecution, and so on. This may be likened to a Hollywood film in which the underdog hero is pitted against overwhelming odds. Docudrama panders to our emotional fantasies as entertainment, not to our scientific interest as historians.

The phenomenon of docudrama is a clear example of how media logic operates. In viewing these fictional accounts, viewers may think they are getting a behind-the-scenes look at factual accounts of the past. It is the same approach that is used in programming and viewing the news: the "you are there" phenomenon is captivating. American people love to romanticize the past and be privy to inside information, and news and docudrama satisfy these desires rather well. There are little or no factual accounts of behind-the-scenes conversation for such stories as "Roots," "General Custer's Trial," or "The Kennedys," and yet viewers seem willing to accept the scenario as presented in the television script. Since the scenario television presents appears real, since we rely on television as an authority, since the format of television enables the viewer to become vicariously involved, and since the viewer enjoys the entertainment perspective in television, it is plausible that viewers have accepted a media logic that enables docudrama to become history. Perhaps this is how viewers want history to be presented—in ways dramatic, entertaining, and personal. As such, the docudrama represents what television viewers will accept as history, and how it should be presented.

Sports is another category that has become entertainmentized through television, and in the process a new type of fan has been created—the viewer fan. In turn, sporting contests are television programs with all the trappings and restrictions of prime-time entertainment. The tempo, the excitement, the visual aspects of the game, and the commentary and explanation are all the result of television. Even going to the stadium is like sitting at home and watching the game on the tube. As will be discussed later, it is difficult to find an aspect of sports that has escaped the influence of television.

Conclusion

To argue that mass media in general and television in particular have developed formats infused with entertainment criteria is certainly not novel, nor is it necessarily insightful. However, to suggest that specific aspects of those formats have impacted on other institutions, and have become a taken-for-granted interpretation scheme by audiences, is important in the task of developing theory to explain such matters as personal identity or cultural change. This is not trivial, as Neil Postman (1985) has observed, but the implications are also not as obvious as they might seem (Fiske, 1987). This also strikes at the heart of the so-called TV addiction problem. We feel there is nothing mysterious or sinister about the soap opera habit or any other TV viewing routine. It may simply be a social activity that is perceived as safer and far more interesting than "real" life. Or, as media scholar David Littlejohn states: "TV has become a reality for many people because it is more tolerable than any other. Real reality is too impossibly complex to deal with . . . television we can bear" (1975:79).

A decade ago, media critics, including ourselves, were optimistic that specialization in television would eliminate, or at least alleviate some of the problems that we and others had identified. By the late 1970s cable had increased the variety of television programs available at any given moment, and it seemed reasonable to predict that the industry would become more decentralized. In 1980 insiders were even predicting the death of the networks as entertainment monopolies. In part this was based on Alvin Toffler's prediction (1970) that the new technology would produce an overall "demassification," and change the major media from broadcasting to narrowcasting. Norman Lear viewed the new technology as a vehicle for experimentation that would result in a "video off-off Broadway." He stated: "The poverty [of cable TV] will force innovation. There may be 11 million viewers who are interested in opera on TV and there may be 11,000 people who want to see a show about polishing skis. In time channels will exist for all of that" (*Newsweek* August 3, 1978).

It has been 20 years since Toffler's prediction of demassification, and a decade since Lear's vision of "Video off Broadway," and very little has changed. In late 1989 NBC was the ratings leader with a Nielsen figure of 14.3 compared to all of cable with an 8.2. Although cable has been chipping away at the networks, and Fox (a fourth network) making gains (2.3), the percentage loss by the networks has not forced any major changes in policy or strategy. The big three networks still rule the business and rake in huge profits. Even with VCRs in over 50 percent of all TV homes, and exotics such as fiber optics, inexpensive satellite dishes, and the reception potential for well over one hundred channels per set, people still watch what they watched 30 years ago. Television is still the mass medium of American culture, although within the television industry there is a significant degree of diversity. In other words, television is both mass and specialized. Should we have expected anything else?

Another bit of optimism that we and others were guilty of in the late 1970s was the assumption that critiques of TV would increase viewer awareness and stimulate greater viewer involvement in shaping television programming. Obviously this has not happened. The public may own the airwaves, but it chooses to remain mute and simply turn to alternative sources. Again, this should not be a big surprise, as television has become a routine part of everyday life as opposed to tasks that we must complete or a duty that we must perform. TV is just there—a media environment within a larger environment. The fact that it has a logic that permeates the overall fabric and institutional structure of American (and elsewhere) society has gone relatively unnoticed by nearly everyone except a a few movers and shakers in these institutions and in media itself. On the other hand, it is a mistake to argue that we are addicted to media, or that we are victims of a conspiracy. Rather, we are participants in producing a media culture that is dominated by formats of entertainment.

3

Postjournalism Media News

Organized journalism is dead. It was killed by news organizations that developed formats to constitute symbolic reproductions of events in the world (cf. Mickelson 1980). These formats have been adopted by other social organizations, which in turn package their messages according to news formats. The journalism enterprise, especially TV news, essentially is reporting on itself; it addresses events that are cast in its own formats and frames of relevance, rather than attempting to understand the events in their own terms, and then trying to communicate the complexities and ambiguities of "real world" conditions.

From Journalism to Media Mechanics

The social construction of news—and especially TV news—is significant for how our lives, experiences, discourse, and worlds are being constructed (Desmond 1978). In the Preface, we noted that Phase 4 of media analysis focuses on the role of communication forms in shaping content, and guiding media workers to comply with media-generated criteria. The minimal requirement for *journalism* was that the thing, topic, entity, or phenomenon to be represented and given a reality within an author's medium (e.g., newspapers or TV) was *independent of the journalist, that it had a status independently of the journalist's craft and perspective*. This has now changed as the journalistic criteria and perspectives on the world and events have now been adapted by the very sources (of events and activities) the journalists seek to report. These criteria have been spawned by decades of "recipes for success," "ratings," "on the air presentations," and especially the format features, which in the case of TV news are, drama, action, visual quality, thematic emphasis, and audience relevance. In short, the communicative foundations of the events and activities are now increasingly reflections of the process and procedures for "doing journalism." This is mechanics and packaging; it is predictible and unambiguous; it is an organizational product that

51

sources, event-makers, and news mechanics now share. It is homogeneous metacommunication, but it does not represent anything other
than itself.

Our two decades of work following trends in journalism have convinced us that we are now in a fundamentally different age: Journalism
is so thoroughly limited by the mass media formats that for all practical
purposes it has been recast as *information mechanics.* We are postjournalism, and very much in the age of media "talent," "performers," and
"actors" who play caricatures of journalists. With some exceptions, it is
no longer the individual creative work of journalists that gives us "news
of the world," but rather, standard templates, routines, and typical
courses of action *dedicated to on the air performance and dominant visuals
and thematic emphases* that prevails (Altheide 1985). The constraint of organizations and their communication formats are more significant than
individual creativity and talent (cf. Schneider 1985). What we have today
is about as far from creative "existential journalism" (Merrill 1977) as
one could imagine.

Indeed, even awards for superior talent, e.g., Pulitzers, RTNDA
awards, are subject to routinized expectations, technical criteria, and
standards that can be easily faked and presented as competent work. As
our prior work has demonstrated, today the camera operators are more
significant for news reporting than the "correspondents" (Altheide
1985). The focus in this chapter is on the relationship between media-
as-form and news-as-content. We do not have "news" to study, but
rather "media news."

News is constructed and constituted through the various media (Hall
1973; Gans 1979). Media are critical because they make ideas and other
things visible by giving them a temporal and spatial arrangement, e.g.,
a letter as a symbol, a page, or a TV screen. However, the nature of
media is so taken for granted by most people that they do not regard
their essential form-giving character as integral to the content; most
people only think of the "content" of information, forgetting that the
form, as Simmel argued, is embedded in content (cf. Goffman 1974).
This means that one cannot understand "news" without having an
awareness of "media."

Youth and News

This problem of confusing the "content" of news with the "media" of
news can be illustrated by examining how numerous critics respond to
viewing differences. For one thing, people choose their messages and
images (cf. Graber 1984). They tend to select those with which they are
familiar and comfortable. As we argued in the previous chapters, *message
involvement is predicated on media involvement,* including familiarity with

and preference for certain formats. Such preferences are informed by the age, experience, and immediate relevance of a message for the viewer. What we watch, what we attend to, and what we recall are emotional and interactional phenomena: an infant will stop in the middle of a busy intersection to watch two butterflies mate, while a wall-street executive will furrow his/her brow over the latest stock reports, while still another person—a white-collar government employee—will pay close attention to the CBS evening news. And young people, especially teenagers, seldom will read a newspaper or watch an entire newscast. When opinion poll results are published in newspapers to indicate that young people are not as "news literate" as they used to be, and adult interpreters claim that the "media" and "information revolution" have failed to inform youth, we should be more cautious in our interpretations (Associated Press and Arizona *Republic* "Poll Says Youth Are Less Aware," July 1, 1990, p. A15).

Information and media use is a social phenomenon that is influenced by expectations, prior experiences, familiarity with formats, and emotional and identity preferences. First, from the perspective of most young people, TV news is not entertaining enough, partly because it is too slow; it is increasingly visual as we have argued over the years—and this has intrigued more adults—but it is quite slow, and linear, relying on words to flesh out visuals. Also, most news material is about adults dealing with adults, that have no perceived relevance to the younger viewers. News, in short, has a rational and future bias to it that is simply not shared by most younger viewers. Moreover, since adults share this view, and often the topics of conversation with co-workers and others who engage in public discourse, it is more imperative to be familiar with this material. It is a question of competence: As adults, especially adults who work in a university, we are continually making fun of individuals who do not know where certain world capitals are located, or which world leader has most recently been insulted by the President of the United States.

Children will become interested in news reports when it is socially consequential to do so. If, for example, parents and their children routinely discuss current events and translate the news of the "adult world" to the children's perspective and interests, then most children will listen. Or if a favorite teacher is focusing on key issues, e.g., nuclear war or ecological disasters, and locates examples within the evening newscast or newspaper reports, then young people will tend to follow such reports, and indeed, will even clip articles to show their teacher. It is the interactional character of this presentation of media materials that matters.

Our idea of media logic is not simply that news agencies use certain perspectives and techniques in helping them to define, select, and produce news. Of course they do, but this is hardly news. Media logic refers to the way in which those organizing features are incorporated into the perspective and activities of the audience members themselves, and are in turn taken for granted as reality.

From News Content to News Form

This chapter turns the usual question raised by an earlier generation of media scholars (and those who are still using a much earlier perspective) of "what is news?" into the more fundamental question, "what are news media?" As we stressed in the Preface, the former question was asked during the second and third phases of research on mass communication, while our current Phase 4 stresses the form of information and its impact on content. Recall, that this phase recognizes how news reports reflect ideology, but more fundamentally, this phase stresses how the formats of news messages themselves serve to shape ideological statements (cf. Golding and Murdock 1979). Our general argument, then, is quite straightforward: "News" is often referred to as "content," while "media" provide the form and logic through which content is organized and presented. Thus the medium for anything always shapes and limits content. However, as people attempt to make a better fit between media requirements and the content they hope to present through the media, the process of producing the content will itself change. This has happened to news, and this is what we mean by media logic.

During the last decade, the mass media in general, and TV news in particular, have been "conceptually rediscovered" by students of social control, cultural change, and political consciousness. Whether the approach is referred to as "cultural studies," "semiotics," "deconstruction," or "postmodernism," scholars throughout the world, and across disciplines ranging from education to sociology to literary criticism, are embroiled in controversies about the "true" meaning of "news," and its implications for "symbol systems" and social order in general (Carey 1987). Although not all voices are unified in the news choir, it is apparent that no competent analysis of politics, culture, social problems, and social change can proceed without an awareness of the nature, origins, and consequences of mass media news (cf. Kinsella 1990). The space limitations of this chapter do not permit a review of the findings of the best studies of newswork during the last decade, although we will refer to several of these. Our aim is to explicate the logic of contemporary newswork, especially TV news, in order to understand how definitions of situations are arrived at, publicly presented, and acted on. Although our focus is mainly on the United States, many of the issues and developments we consider are relevant throughout the Western world as more societies adopt the formats and perspective of U.S. news practices.

Several decades of research have shown that the news of the world reflects the logic of news production and the medium through which it is organized and presented (cf. Bennett 1983; Bensman and Lillienfeld 1973). The focus of much of this work has been on the news perspective and the cultural context of news, news organization and culture, news sources, and formats for the selection, organization, and presentation of news that join the message to an audience via a medium. With some exceptions, news has been studied as content and messages rather than as inextricably joined to the medium—including technology—that "mediates" and constitutes news (cf. Adams and Schreibman 1978; Adams 1981). Our work has covered all facets of news production, interpretation and "use," including several case studies in which we have engaged in what has been called "start to finish" news (cf. Cohen and Bantz 1989). It has been the tendency to see news content and the media formats and channels as distinctive, which motivates this chapter. In a sense, we are less interested in the idea of news than we are in the "medianess" of news, and how one shapes the former.

Despite the significant increase in the quantity and quality of news research during the last decade, it continues to fascinate us how many students of the news and especially the mass media seem to have come on it very late in their work, and often their careers. Moreover, most news researchers continue to focus on the traditional conception of news as content, rather than news as a part of culture that is mediated and transformed through changes in the media themselves. The main concern of most of these people who are steeped in a much earlier tradition of "communication research" is to look at the "biases of news content," especially its political biases or ideology. This is important, although it is not surprising, because many of these people are already committed to certain theoretical positions, so that when they recognize the significance of the mass media for social order, they must accommodate the two, but the joining usually is accomplished by making the news and communication issues subservient to the dominant perspective with which the theorist is most familiar (cf. Herman and Chomsky 1988; Mitroff and Bennis 1990). Very few scholars have been able to expand their theoretical acumen to integrate what may seem to be conceptual contradictions between a theory of social order informed by the communication process, on the one hand, and a position mired in fixed social structural variables such as "economic power." Rather than creatively negotiating the complex interfaces between the two, the favored option seems to be to quickly adapt the media work to the prevailing—and usually more popular—"macrotheoretical" perspective that blames some structural "defect" like capitalism, or its "hegemonic" control over an entire culture. In general, such analyses wind up pointing the finger at culture to explain culture, and are quite circular in their reasoning. Invariably, these works look at only part of the data, and often greatly misconstrue findings of actual news practices, the interaction between news sources and journalists, and the complex array of audience effects, especially the widely documented point that audience members are not "passive" recipients of messages, but are, in fact, "active" interpreters and constructors of the meaning of mass mediated imagery and information.

Accordingly, we will not embarrass the intelligence of the reader by picking out one "boogey man" to blame (e.g., capitalism, the rich, Jews, liberals, or conservatives). Any experienced reader of mass communication literature will recognize that numerous works tend to single out one or more of these "groups" or "causes" of the "problem," which, if corrected, can improve the media and content. Our work with these materials over a 20 year period has convinced us that although such pointing of the finger does win favor with key cliquish membership groups—and can do wonders for your career!—it does little for two things in short supply among academics—intellectual honesty and theoretical innovation (cf. Vidich and Lyman 1984).

News and Public Order

Public order is increasingly the news order; the logic of one is implicated in the other (cf. Seeger 1983). We do not deny that the major routine sources for news organizations are "self-interested" and serve their own definitions, perspectives, and constituents. Indeed, we have argued that much of what is transmitted throughout the news channels qualifies as "propaganda," and in particular, "bureaucratic propaganda" (Altheide and Johnson 1980). Furthermore, we accept that most news agencies tend to be ethnocentric, with content and perspectives that reflect many of their taken-for-granted assumptions and interests about culture, patriotism, and morality. We also take it as basic that most students of the news are also cultural critics who often engage in what anthropologists refer to as "negative ethnocentrism," or defining what is yours as bad. Although we do not regard our work as "neutral" in any sense, we do attempt to expand the argument about the nature and impact of mass media news to take us beyond "blaming" a particular economic or political order, in favor of developing theoretically sound perspectives for understanding the unique and still misunderstood contributions of communication technologies and their employment through various logics. Although such logics and formats are clearly tied to the historical context of their development, our assessments of possible targets for "blame" lead us to conclude that culture and its communication forms are reflexive.

Ironically, the impact of media logic on the content of programming is apparent in television news (Adams and Schreibman 1978)—ironic because, as a source of public information, television enjoyed the greatest potential of all forms of communication to enlighten people about themselves and others the world over. That potential was looked to with hope by those who felt that more detailed information could reduce the great misunderstandings that had for so long widened cultural and territorial gaps between peoples. And television's capacity to blend visual with aural information was believed to provide a sort of window on the world that would illuminate varieties of experience. Indeed, Marshall McLuhan (1962, 1964) felt that the capacity of TV to provide viewers with such engulfing experience would start the process of breaking down national barriers, as the world was transformed into a "global village." Although researchers continue to debate the long-term effects of TV on people throughout the world, a body of knowledge is rapidly accumulating that suggests that the ultimate impact of TV on our lives will—at least to some extent—depend on the organizational constraints through which all programming, both entertainment and news, now flows. How this organization works on TV news is our present focus; it will become apparent that this concern is not unrelated to the question of TV's impact on our lives and certain situations.

The advent of television news, and the direction it has taken, cannot be completely separated from the rise of the medium itself. Whereas "news" as a form of knowledge (Park 1940) has been around as oral communication for thousands of years (cf. Couch 1984) and printed news for several hundred, electronic news forms—beginning with radio in the early 1900s and continuing with television in the 1940s—are not only the most recent arrivals on the news scene, but have fundamentally altered it as well.

Accomplishing Television

The major modern media of communication—print, radio, and electronic—are woven together in terms of their history, technological development, audience considerations, and purposes (Freund 1978). When it comes to news, the very idea of news is associated with certain media that have not only "carried" the news to us, but have also shaped its content, logic, and our very idea of it. News is contextual and embedded in prior media and people's expectations. Previous accounts of the history of news media, from newspapers to radio and TV, show how each medium developed by adjusting to various events, e.g., the Civil

War, WW I, WW II, new technologies, and organizational shifts (cf. Schudson 1978; Altheide and Snow 1979). These factors contributed to the changing character and image of the audience, which in turn gradually acquired the "media competence" and expectations about formats.

Images of the Audience

It was the commitment to reach a mass audience, which in turn would produce the highest possible advertising revenue, that led programmers to define their "target audience" to include a heterogeneous audience, and especially women between the ages of 18 and 49.

It was the purpose of TV programming to make great profits that led to the definition of the audience, and not conversely. That is, the target audience does not exist as some objective entity, but is instead a social construction of the media agents. Contrasting the notion of TV audiences as a mass with the views of a widely diversified medium such as radio illustrates this point. Radio, partly because of competition from television and partly because of the advent of frequency modulation (FM), faced the problem of numerous radio stations within the same market area. Television, at least initially, did not have this problem because the signal wavelength prevented more than a few limited "senders" to be in the same geographic area; otherwise, signal interference would occur. In recognizing this physical difference between the two media, the FCC restricted the number of senders of broadcasting power. But, most importantly, radio was in a more competitive situation than was television; the latter usually consisted of three, four, or five stations all competing for the same audience, whereas often as many as 35 radio stations competed in the same market area! Clearly, the ground rules each medium used would have to reflect this physical fact of life, and they did.

Radio has engaged in "narrowcasting" to appeal to an array of different listener tastes for which there are popular, classical, and jazz music and even all-news stations. Radio benefits economically by recognizing its listeners' different preferences and levels of sophistication. Ironically, whereas TV programmers used to "broadcast" in keeping with their view of the homogeneous audience, recent changes in cable and satellite TV programmers have had to adjust their conception of the audience as a homogeneous mass because the advent of the cable and satellite technologies has expanded the viewers' options. All indications are that TV viewers will be perceived by TV programmers as highly selective throughout the 1990s.

This emphasis on views of the audience is central to the basic issues surrounding the nature and quality of public information on television today. It is part of the understanding of most media workers that "you have to play to the numbers," and this includes both entertainment programmers as well as news directors. Another way of stating this is that *programmers regard entertainment programs as commercials for the commercials,* since the number of people watching the ads is what really counts. The pervasiveness of the entertainment format in all TV programming is also evident in the BBC, often regarded as being powered by the highest values and standards of journalism and programming. As Tom Burns (1977:156–157) states:

> It is well to remind ourselves, at this point, that in terms of programme expenditure, and audience size, the provision of entertainment is still broadcasting's primary role in the life of the nation. . . . Nowadays, programmes of all kinds have to "capture" their audience; if they do not, they are relegated to off-peak times, when most people are either at work or in bed.

Over the years, much the same reasoning has been applied to newscasts. One reporter in Phoenix, Arizona, made the following comment after challenging the wisdom of programming for ratings:

> You have to have some formula to achieve what you're after, and what we're after is higher ratings, and you have to get the combination of people on the air that the people, the viewers, want to see or feel most comfortable with. (Taped interview, November 1978)

One result of the now-institutionalized legitimacy of audience research in general and ratings in particular is that serious efforts to understand the interests of the audience have been abandoned; it is as though the producers have a "workable" measure of the audience in terms of their commitments to commercialism. Burns (1977:136) has cogently described the impact of this development on the BBC, an organization originally intended to serve the public interest through educational and quality programming:

> There is little that any audience research could have added to the sensitivities with which people who write for a large public and speak to large audiences are ordinarily credited. Given the resources of social research and the money available for audience research during the fifties . . . and given the increasing preoccupation of broadcasters with ratings, *it is fairly safe to say that audience research, and the information it has produced, proved to be more of a barrier than a bridge between the broadcaster and his public* [italics added].

News as Entertainment

Television news evolved as another kind of entertainment programming committed to pulling in the viewers even at the expense of doing
deeper, more complete, and accurate reports. Erik Barnouw's
(1975:169) comparison of radio and TV news is instructive:

> A favorite pronouncement of the day was that television had added a "new
> dimension" to newscasting. The truth of this concealed a more serious
> fact: the camera, as arbiter of news value, had introduced a drastic curtail-
> ment of the scope of news. . . . Analysis, a staple of radio news in its finest
> days, was being shunted aside as non-visual.

The association of "visualness" with "entertainment" virtually sealed the
fate of the early stages of television news; TV news would be used first to
entertain and then inform. Since the broader context of entertainment
already had been wedded to commercialism, it was logical within this
context to develop news formats more compatible with—and more directly influenced by—rules for attracting the largest number of viewers,
than epistemological concerns regarding the best way to obtain the information and understanding. Burns' study of the logic and functioning
of various departments within the BBC suggests the same.

Within this media logic, efforts to improve newscasts are defined and
then implemented. For example, at local affiliate stations, efforts at im-
provement stress modes of presentations, which include visuals and
smooth discussions. Delivery becomes more important than content; the
form of presentation *becomes* the significant content.

Form includes several dimensions. First, there is the matter of the
length of the report about each item or event. In keeping with the commercial consideration to capture the largest share of the audience, there
is the related assumption that members of this mass audience are igno-
rant, uninterested in details, and even incapable of following any complex situation unless it is reported in the simplest of terms. This view
was expressed by one of Altheide's (1976:49) informants:

> [If] we can spark his interest, if I can start off with a flashy lead that will
> at least keep him there chewing his TV dinner and sipping his beer, til the
> next bigger news story, we will have succeeded.

That such sentiments are not lost to British media workers is illustrated
by Burns' comment (1977:133):

> It was a successful television dramatist who pictured the "typical television
> audience" as "mum sitting in the best armchair drinking cocoa with a teen-
> age son on the sofa trying to get his hand up his girl's skirt." And a televi-

sion audience of million had, it seems, to be seen as "moronic" by a distinguished radio producer.

Such views lead newsworkers to not only select events for coverage that are highly visual and filled with human interest elements such as drama, conflict, and even violence, but also to keep the reports as short as possible—seldom longer than 30 seconds, and most, only 15 seconds. Expensive media consultants provide the formula to media managers. According to news logic, the brevity of reports takes the viewer from one story to the next at a fast pace. The reports are then interspersed with witty comments by anchorpersons, banter back and forth between reporters, some exciting music, colorful sets, and, of course, the ubiquitous ads that may take up as much as one-third of a half-hour newscast. This standardization suggests that a kind of template or format is being followed.

News Format

Format refers to the way information is selected, organized, and presented (cf Goffman 1974). Many newsworkers do not fully accept the practical logic within which they must work, but they are stuck with it, partly because of the sporting rhetoric of "being number one" through "competition." In fact, current ratings practices—and the "help" of consultants—do not provide a thorough-going type of competition, but instead enable news operations to mimic each other. Also, the notion that all a news operation must do to "be good" is to "catch up to" or "beat" the opposition makes newswork in general, and news directing in particular, quite easy: New directions and options need not be pursued. Moreover, the power of this perspective on information has been diffused throughout the world, and it is increasingly coming to be seen as the "way to do TV." As stated by Burns (1977:56):

> What we now have is the BBC and ITV pacing each other rather than competing with each other. This is less mentally taxing, makes scheduling easier, is some kind of insurance against being driven into extravagance, and provides a very simple criterion for comparison in ratings.

Similarly, in a study of the Quebec referendum, Robinson (1984:213) found that interviews with the leaders displayed the personal emphasis TV formats found in the United States:

> More important, however, is the fact that the poll is immediately reinserted into the private lives of the party leaders. In doing so the television news discourse is merely following a narrative paradigm that personalizes

important events. This is what has been called the Americanization of the Canadian and Quebec political discourse.

The U.S. networks that have long denied their entertainment orientation—preferring to distinguish "news" from "entertainment"—are now embracing the concept of "entertaining news." This is all being done, of course, to obtain ratings. In the early 1990s the networks expanded on CBS' much heralded "60 Minutes," to add "West 57th," "48 Hours," "20/20," and others. The formats of these shows are remarkably similar, and as we argue in a later chapter on sports, involve sports-reporting-like commentaries and "late inning" recaps. These shows, along with the increasing array of "docudramas," have smashed the sacred claimed (although seldom realized) distinction between entertainment and news (cf. Altheide 1985c).

Stations within the same market area routinely present essentially the same news reports night after night because they share a common format. This is due in part to the use of common news sources that are transformed through certain cultural myths shared by many journalists. More importantly, however, is the logic and perspective that underlie news practices. This logic includes awareness of how news formats have emerged from reliance on routine news sources, and the "magic" of themes and angles to help produce a visual narrative account with a beginning, middle, and end.

Themes and Angles

Journalists begin with predefined notions about the *form* of their report which in turn leads them to shape the *content* of the message. The content, in turn, is often derived from a simple story line, organized around a theme or angle. Newspapers and electronic media rely on themes and angles. As we stress below, the big differences rest in the linear orientations of the former and the visual and aural bases of the latter. Consider an example about how two newspapers reported on some information about, ironically, the impact of news procedures on leadership! Working with a number of colleagues, (Hall and Altheide 1990) has tried over two decades to put the theoretical insights we have developed into practice. This usually means providing different interpretations of mass mediated messages, on the one hand, while making suggestions for less distorted coverage on the other hand. During 1989–1990, a group of social scientists at Arizona State University were enlisted to report on problems of "Leadership," in a state which routinely experiences budget shortfalls as government officials act in ways that have made them targets of derision, anger, and more commonly laughter. The form of this effort would be a "Townhall" report, divided into different chapters about various dimensions of leadership and authority. The usual mode of operation was for a team of researchers, who were familiar with the academic as well as actual practices and situations in Arizona, to use a variety of local data sources for additional information, including interviews with a theoretical sample of persons who were knowledgeable about the Arizona scene.

Altheide worked on the impact of the media in Arizona. In a chapter of approximately 25 pages, a number of issues were set forth, along with some scholarly literature on the nature and impact of media logic, formats and sources on public behavior, and social perceptions of issues, problems, and decision-making. The resulting newspaper coverage of this report, however, was predictably distorted in stressing certain features along format lines. That is, a series of complex events were reduced to one controversy, namely, as one headline screamed: "Media Blamed for Arizona Leadership Void." First, we present excerpts from the concluding section of our chapter on "media and leadership," and then we will compare what the newspapers stressed in order to illustrate the power of format and thematic emphasis.

A number of suggestions for improving press coverage of issues and concerns relevant to leadership and decision-making are implied in our foregoing analysis as well as explicit comments by some of the Arizona government leaders who we interviewed. *While none of the interviewees blamed the press for a "leadership crisis" or for less than admirable political decision-making,* most of these people contended that the news media could do a better job of being accurate, giving more complete information in context, and informing people about various facets of the decision-making process—including the legislature . . .

The mass media set the nature, tone and grammar of public discourse. What will be discussed and how such discussions will take place is critical in understanding any question about leadership . . .

One of the goals should be to evaluate current reporting and programming practices in order to improve the quantity and the quality of coverage about issues which will inform our citizens and leaders for the decades to come. Students of the mass media as well as informed journalists are becoming more aware that the traditional relationship between the news media, sources and formats must be scrutinized . . . (Altheide 1976, 1985e; Ericson et al. 1989)

A key, of course, is avoiding "media frenzy," or the wholesale pursuit of a single angle or theme for topics.

Many of these considerations are relevant for leaders, media managers and front-line journalists. *An overriding caveat for all elected and informal leaders was echoed by most of our sample of leaders to become more familiar with media logic and formats.* Suggestions for the media managers and workers would also be relevant for decision makers. First, journalists can become better informed. *Several people commented that on more than one occasion they*

have had reporters freely admit to them that they did not have the foggiest awareness
about the topic on which they were about to conduct an interview! . . .

We should not cease to be concerned with malfeasance, misfeasance and nonfeasance
in public office, but we must also address systematically those issues on which we
expect our elected and appointed officials to act. (italics added)

When contacted by a telephone call from one reported who had just received, but not read, the Townhall report, Altheide pointed out the irony to the reporter, noting that this lack of preparation by a journalist was one of the major points of the report under discussions. Altheide asked that the journalist read the report. The next day, the following p. 1 headline appeared in The Phoenix *Gazette* (April 11, 1990): **NEWSPA-PERS HURT STATE LEADERSHIP, TOWN HALL CLAIMS.** The major focus of this report was on the news media's scrutiny of individual decision-makers. This angle permitted newspaper executives, and ironically (double irony?) some university professors to proclaim that freedom of the press was important, and that we must investigate politicians. One statement from the telephone interview with Altheide was used: "While there's nothing wrong with dealing with sensational or dramatic things, it's very important that the issue is not lost. Right now the issue is increasingly getting lost."

Arizona's major newspaper, The Arizona *Republic,* carried the following p. 1 headline and emphases the next day (April 12, 1990): **MEDIA BLAMED FOR ARIZONA LEADERSHIP VOID.** The reader may note that one of the statements emphasized in the conclusion presented above explicitly stated that no one solely "blamed" the media for these problems! The second paragraph of the newspaper article plays to the predefined theme: "scrutiny of candidates by newspapers, radio and television is one of the top obstacles to better leadership."

TV journalists, like their newspaper colleagues before them, have developed routine ways of getting the job done (Epstein, 1974, 1975; Altheide 1976). Specifically, as TV journalists learn their craft from those with more experience, they learn to see the world in certain ways (cf. Altheide 1985c; Ericson et al. 1987). They acquire a sophisticated stock of knowledge about what is relevant and they learn how to treat the production of events into news stories through the application of cognitive and evaluative criteria that are more firmly embedded in the organizational context of newswork than the reality of the events themselves or consistent interpretations of epistemological concerns, including the problems of objectivity (Epstein 1974; Altheide, 1976, 1977, 1985c; Ericson et al. 1987, 1989; Tuchman, 1972, 1974, 1976, 1978; Fishman 1980; Phillips 1977; Schudson 1978). This way of "seeing" the world in general and events in particular has been referred to as the "news perspective," the view that holds that, for practical reasons, any event can be summarily covered and presented as a narrative account with a beginning, middle, and end (Weaver 1972; Altheide 1976). This orientation is quite useful given the time pressure to cover an event, especially a complex one involving various facets and numerous possible interpretations.

The foundation of this practical epistemology newsworkers to approach most events with an established framework or format; just as the entire newscast has a format, so too do most news reports. When journalists receive assignments that may know little about substantively, it is conventional occupational wisdom to realize that one does not really have to know a great deal, since only a few of the basic questions will be asked on film—and that film will be edited to fit what is often a predefined story line tying the various elements together. The origin of this story line may be a predefined "angle" or statement of what it all means; it also may be a "theme," a generalizing motif that shows this particular report to be related to other "facts" that in turn are selected to fit the dominant theme. Thus the selection of themes and angles is of major importance in providing substance to the news report and defining the practical and organizational context in which the report will fit; this includes the format of the newscast referred to above.

Routine use of angles and themes solves certain problems, but it can create others for the viewers who may accept the facts and interpretations presented. Although analysis has shown that not all news reports are equally problematic (Altheide, 1976), it is nevertheless important to be aware of the potentially distorting way that news procedures can shape the presentation of reality. To put the matter somewhat differently, events with all their complexities are *decontextualized* from their shared meanings by members and *recontextualized* within the news format.[1] The consequences for certain reports and the impact they may have can be extreme (Rosengren et al. 1978). One way mistakes can occur is when certain generalizing themes are emphasized and then events are sought to support those themes. Previous studies have shown the consequences of the routine use of themes and angels for individuals (U.S. Senator Thomas Eagleton, Altheide 1976), and the Vietnam War (Braestrup 1978). We believe that newswork will not be improved and will not make a richer contribution to our lives until this systematic disjunction between news formats and world events is realized, reflected on, and finally improved. In short, we are suggesting that most TV news agencies—and certain other news media as well—are making mistakes that are unrecognized, and the criteria for observing them fall outside of the epistemology and dominant criteria of "good work" now employed by most newsworkers. An important part of the perspective of TV newsworkers that has been virtually neglected is the role of visuals, and especially "film" or "tape." When combined with the use of themes and angles, visuals provide a way to "prove" or demonstrate the journalists' reality.

The Problem with Film

When Louis Daguerre and Joseph Niece developed the photographic process in 1839, no one realized that this invention not only would be the foundation for the visual media such as television, but also would be put to good use by politicians and others interested in presenting particular views of reality. Since very little TV coverage is live, film (or videotape) is the content transmitted over television; without film, and derivatives from this process, there could not be permanent images to present—TV would have to make do with "live" occurrences. Despite the importance of film for all news media, surprisingly little attention has been given to either the actual use of film in TV newswork (Altheide 1976; Tuchman 1978; Rosenblum 1978) or its essential foundation in the meanings of viewers.

Film and videotape are used in TV news because they are the essentials of this particular medium; they are what distinguish it from newspapers and radio. Most importantly, TV news tells time with visuals and especially videotape. This means that time will be allotted to a story on the basis of the availability of visuals. This can be stated in a very simple formula: Significance = Time = Visuals. Film is used in television news to illustrate and show the facts and emphasis of the reporter's creative application of the news perspective. This is done according to certain established patterns of "perspectives" and formats, including a variety of angles and focuses to distinguish private from public time and space, personalities from common people, and the like (Tuchman 1978:104–132). Our fresh understanding of the relationship between visuals and text requires that the following statement by the Glasgow Media Group be amended:

> In most newsfilm the shots do not directly relate to one another in the ways we are used to from the feature cinema. Rather they are used to illustrate the audio-text, and rules governing their juxtapositioning come not from the visual but from the audio-track—indeed largely from the commentary. (Glasgow Media Group 1976:29)

These researchers erred in making text the primary orienting logic of TV news, when their own work suggested that visuals contributed significantly. Their entire analysis could have benefited from a statement they made a bit later in their text:

> A lack of film material does not necessarily mean that an item lasts less than half a minute. On the other hand, if film material is used, the item

is almost certain to be longer than half a minute. (Glasgow Media Group 1976:91)

As noted previously, time constraints prevent showing too much detail about certain events, yet the production must look as complete as possible and be presented in an entertaining way. All this requires editing, which, if done properly, will not be detected by the uninformed viewer. Film editors follow the narrative sequence of a beginning, middle, and end, which presents a plausible view of the event, although the event actually may not have occurred that way. For example, if an interviewee states in his opening comments what the interviewer regards as a good close (to the reporters' story), the editor adjusts the sequences to achieve the preferred order, the one most useful for the news format. A story on atomic power plants illustrates this process (Altheide 1976:92).

> *Cameraman:* We talked to a guy in an orange grove. We edit him twice; the hard thing about him is that [the reporter] wanted to take the last thing he said—well, he said it earlier—but then again, in conforming to the minute and forty some seconds that they're allowing these, it had to run. He said, "Well, all we want as farmers is clean air, clean water, and good land." [The reporter] wanted to use that 16 seconds so I had to take that and put it in the last 16 seconds of film, so that meant that I had to have B-roll [silent film] going over the last 16 seconds. . . . I put in a 20 second B-roll about 35 seconds in and brought in this last 16 seconds and had them turn and kind of walking off camera, and then we cut to the statement about "clean air" but God, I am thankful now that I went ahead and shot all that wide stuff or we wouldn't have anything to cover all these frigging edits we made.

Although it comes as no surprise that TV news is constructed in a manner compatible with the organizational constraints of time and entertainment, it is less obvious why the grammar of film shooting and film editing has not been described by TV people themselves (Fang 1968). Certainly one reason is to perpetuate the audience's assumption that what they are seeing is what happened. Tuchman (1978:109–110) describes the misleading aspects:

> News film casts an aura of representation by its explicit refusal to give the appearance of manipulating time and space. Instead, its use of time and space announces that the tempo of events and spatial arrangements have *not* been tampered with to tell this story. By seeming *not* to arrange time and space, news film claims to present facts, not interpretations.

A basic reason why such practices can continue, including the selective choice of newspaper photos, is that newsworkers have simply carried to its logical end a widespread belief among readers that "a picture is worth

a thousand words." As we have seen, pictures also can be quite misleading unless they are placed in some context. Anyone who has ever
glanced at a newspaper photo without reading the caption knows that
pictures by themselves are either vague or, at best, incomplete; only
when background information is provided does the photo take on its
contextual meaning. Nevertheless, most readers and TV viewers continue to be symbolically exploited by the respective news organizations
that do not reveal their routine procedures for constructing visual messages. In addressing the various constraints that help shape any TV production, Burns (1977:206) has critically examined the potential
distorting influence of the "viewability" of news reports:

> Yet because television news and current affairs programmes convey ac-
> tion, movement, facial expression and demeanour, scenes and actors, as
> well as verbal, messages, they seem *more* satisfactory than any account pro-
> vided by newspapers. "Viewability" is easily construed as reliability because
> any intervention by broadcasters is largely invisible, and because the dra-
> matic intensity of film and video recording carries conviction and guaran-
> tees authenticity in ways which words cannot. And the constant striving
> for "viewability" sets its own traps.

A theory of visuals must be articulated in order to fully appreciate
the nature and impact of current journalistic practices. Although all the
details of such a theory cannot be presented in this work, the beginnings
can be suggested.[2] Photos have meaning for many readers and viewers
because, in their own lives, they are accustomed to events they see occurring in a context that they understand. For example, when people view
their own photo albums or home movies, the significance of these photos and films is not simply confined to the album page or screen, but
includes placing the events and actions in a scenario that the observer
immediately recalls—the item simply calls forth these memories and
background understandings. Relatedly, when in the course of daily life
we interact with people, visual messages are an important part of human
interaction, and people have developed highly sophisticated ways of
placing a given act in the context of the interaction. This is why many
people can tell if someone is "putting them on," lying to them, or trying
to take advantage of them. But it is the context of the act—a used car
lot, a passionate embrace at a lover's apartment—that enables us to interpret this visual information. Moreover, we intuitively make this transition from a specific act to its broader context. *This tendency to merge what
is given with what is not given is the essential symbolic and cognitive foundation
for the belief in photos as reality.* We simply assume that certain "obvious"
and "naturally inherent" features of an event must have preceded the
photo and that other equally "natural" developments succeeded it; this

is the way the logic of everyday life provides typifications without which we would have trouble negotiating the multitude of situations confronted in daily life (Schutz 1967).

With these changes have emerged some major ethical and professional considerations that turn less on questions of "right and wrong," and more on the appearance of reality and truth. The ability to "digitalize" or "pixelize" photos—still and videotape—now permits editors to adjust the visuals to their perception of what viewers anticipate, believe, and prefer. This has taken two forms. One is with the expanded usage of "graphics" in newspapers and magazines, which are products of TV imagery. This is especially significant because the skill and expertise of the "graphics" editor has altered the balance of power in newspaper production, and increasingly journalists are being "edited" according to graphics considerations, including stressing certain visual themes (cf. Gentry and Zang 1989).

News Sources

The events selected for inclusion in the newscast are defined according to the same occupational logic. Not *any* event qualifies; only those acquired from a handful of institutional news sources that tend to have incorporated many of the practical considerations of scheduling, visual interest, and conciseness that news people look for. The sources for local news differ from the networks', whose larger budgets follow up on international events reported by the wire services. So important are these services that Jeremy Tunstall (1977:45) and others have suggested that the routine use of these sources (Braestrup 1978), combined with the formats they have inspired, influence not only local and national news but world news as well:

> These agencies have largely shaped the presentation of international news in all countries around the world; these agencies do not merely play a major part in establishing the international political agenda, but they have done so now for a hundred years. And for a hundred years, they have been the main definers of world "news values," of what sort of things become news.

But local operations tend to rely more on local press reports, self-serving press releases dispensed by various organizations and institutions, competing stations, fire and police radio monitors, and occasionally a reporter's personal "tip." Few topics not included within these sources will ever be covered on the evening newscast, a fact that has prompted some groups to form organizations that give themselves titles, print letterhead stationery, generally appear to represent a body of people, and therefore be more legitimate vis-à-vis newsworkers' criteria of proper news (Roshco 1975). For this reason, most news that is presented is quite familiar to the reporters who cover it (Altheide 1978b). At the same time, however, most news that is reported is either old or staged for news purposes. Both considerations are due to the scheduling problems of television. For the "desk" to assign crews to events in order to have enough material for the day's newscast, they must know hours—if not days—in advance what will be occurring (Fishman 1980). A lot of the "desk's" time is spent filling an accordion-like "future-file" with newspaper clippings, press releases, slips of paper with telephone messages, and suggestions from the producer or news director. This mode of organization enables chief organizers in the newsroom to have a good idea on, for example, Friday what is likely to appear on Monday's newscast. Good news sources are those that recognize and supply this need for advanced warning.

Still another major problem with using institutionalized news sources is a gradual blending of self-serving interests with "facts." The capacity for organizations to generate self-serving reports couched in even the most scientific terms has been shown to occur with alarming regularity and efficiency (Altheide and Johnson 1980). This emerging mode of what may be termed "bureaucratic propaganda" has been tied to the expansion of the news media and their respective needs to fill "news holes" created by an ever-blossoming array of advertisements.

A number of studies of newswork and news organization have documented the close relationship between the perspective and interests of news sources and news organizations (cf. Ericson et al. 1989). Interest implies two things here: first, is the purpose or intent of a news organization, like the police department, to promote its own point of view about the state of crime, the need for more resources, etc. If a news organization simply accepts such information without analyzing or scrutinizing it, then a news report becomes a form of propaganda (cf. Herman and O'Sullivan 1989). There is another form of news-source relationship that is more subtle, yet perhaps more significant. We refer to the way in which certain kinds of sources that offer a view of social order and social control may be preferred by news organizations because of the tendency for news organizations to treat stories about disorder as the ideal type of what news is. If the quest for stories about disorder, threats to order, and the efforts of certain agencies to enact and repair order in their own image come to dominate news content, then we must ask what it is about the news perspective that gives rise to such acceptance? *This is an important question because it implies that the agencies and the organizations are doing the same work.* Although both could be said to "use each other," the implication is much greater: nonnews agencies and news agencies share a view of order that is realized through the logic and criteria of news, on the one hand, and an organizational accomplishment, on the other hand. If so, then we would state that the newsworkers and other agency perspectives are *reflexive,* or the view of one is circularly based on the views of the other.

Some of the best work on this issue is by Richard Ericson and his colleagues at the University of Toronto in a series of three important works: *Visualizing Deviance* (1987), *Negotiating Control* (1989), and *Acknowledging Order* (1990). Based on ethnographic and content analyses of news reports from "quality" and "popular" media outlets—two TV stations, two radio stations, and two newspapers—these studies document how media logic and formats have infused the control ideologies of formal agents of control—the police, prosecutors, and courts—that frame their activities in discourse compatible with the various mass media outlets. Thus not only do the reporters and sources within the various organizations work together, they also come to speak the same language, and often see as significant the same things. In simpler, but somewhat distorting terms, the journalists have incorportated the source criteria and perspective, while the sources have learned to select, develop, and pursue certain tasks that are compatible with the themes and angles routinely employed by the journalists!

> As we saw in the relationship of some parts of the police organization to some journalists and news organizations, the news media do function as a conduit pipe for the bureaucratic propaganda or preferred sources. Just the same, there is a hierarchy of relatively powerful and influential journalists and news outlets from whom everyone else takes their lead. At their disposal are powerful resources that have to be respected if one wishes to have a position of authority in public life. Moreover, all news outlets have some fundamental assets that put them in a powerful position: the power to deny a source any access; the power to sustain coverage that contextualizes the source negatively; the power of the last word; and, the power of translation of specialized and particular knowledge into common sense. (Ericson et al. 1989:378)

The influx of media logic into the way sources are selected for news reports has tremendous implications for the *contextual embeddedness* of news, formats, and propaganda. Several studies show, for example, that reports about drama and conflict are shaped by news criteria and procedures, on the one hand, and by sources and processes that anticipate, promote, and often take advantage of these criteria and formats, on the other hand (Altheide 1985c). One example is the coverage of major social changes in our electronic era.

Researchers' and journalists' accounts are now available of media coverage of conflicts in Vietnam, the Falkland Islands, Honduras, Nicaragua, Cuba, Brazil, Argentina, Iran, China, and the bloc of East European countries that have thrown off totalitarian oppression (Glasgow media Group 1985). These were—and remain—exciting times. The coverage of Iran will be examined within the thematic context of American politics and especially the Carter administration in a later chapter. The events of China during the summer of 1989, and Eastern Europe during 1989–1990, illustrate the significance of sources within the context of news procedures (cf. Weschler 1990).

We take two things as basic: the major dramatic political changes that occurred throughout the world during 1988–1990 were influenced by the nature and extent of public information, especially TV news and the routine use of satellite technology. We include the political actors who interactively negotiate their future actions on the readings of news coverage, opinions, and reactions of various publics. However, to illustrate our points about news sources, we will take a brief look at some of the news overage of the significant demonstrations in China in 1989, the U.S. invasion of Panama in December 1989, and the successful marketing of a "problem with apples."

China.   During the spring of 1989, a "pro-democracy" movement was underway in Beijing. The key symbolic and media-focused location came to be Tiananmen square, the scene of numerous demonstrations, which, by all accounts, were oriented to change in China by a range of groups, including students (cf. Schidlovsky 1989; Reiss 1989). For several weeks students had gathered in the square, taken up residence, engaged in numerous politically symbolic acts, and erected their own version of the Statute of Liberty! Throughout this period, there were numerous news reports about the "pro-democracy" movement, including the routine journalistic quest for "spokespersons" and leaders. The morale of this vignette is quite simple: The Chinese students were cast by themselves—and the Western reporters who covered them—as extensions of the U.S. student movement during the 1960s, including their interests in "democracy," and change toward a Western ideal, such as the United States. These were the themes (see below) of the coverage. One problem was finding people who could speak English. A few excerpts from reporters' accounts are offered to demonstrate this perspective.

> I spent one exasperating morning trying to find English-speaking students willing to go on camera . . . Ultimately, they did; in fact, foreshadowing what would prove to be the students' media savvy, one young man made a tortured effort to recite the Declaration of Independence. A Chinese student memorizing Thomas Jefferson was irresistible television. He made air more than once . . .

If the students treated the foreign media with benign indifference during the early weeks of the movement, one man unwittingly changed all that: Mikhail Gorbachev. On May 13 the students began the hunger strike that would become an international cause celebre, and two days later the Soviet leader ensured that the world would take notice when his plane set down at Beijing's airport for the first Sino-Soviet summit in 30 years . . .

Suddenly the students were eager participants in an international media event. In fact, the camera became a beacon. Bringing a camera anywhere, whether to Tiananmen Square or to a back alley, would attract a small throng of boisterous demonstrators, all of whom, it seemed, had something to say . . .

Television crews were not only welcomed, but by unanimous consent they were anointed as heroes . . . It is worth noting some things that made covering the demonstrations with a camera distinct from print reporting. We discovered that the best way to get a coherent sound bite about the movement's goals was to ask, "what do you want?" People inevitably replied: democracy and freedom of the press. Yet of the 30 or so people whom I asked, "What do you mean when you say 'democracy?' " only one replied that he wanted the right to vote. Correspondents' descriptions of this were in vain, overwhelmed by the endless sound bites and picture of people calling for democracy. (Reiss 1989:28–29).

In order for the Chinese student movement to have the epic proportions it did, it had to become a news story, but for it to become a news story, it had to be managed, interpreted, and presented through media formats. What happened in China was informed by Western news criteria and techniques. Indeed, it was the very same techniques that broadcast heart-rendering images of hundreds of thousand of students (and later, workers) challenging their elderly leaders that would also work against these people. This occurred in two ways: One, the Chinese government edited the tapes to show their own population that the students had killed soldiers, and then some segments of the soldiers' "self-protective" retaliation would be shown. The temporal sequence was altered. But it was the second use of network visuals that was most astounding and totally unanticipated. The satellite–video-tools of significant social definition and world-wide notoriety would be turned against the students as government officials began intercepting network satellite transmissions to the United States that contained visual identifications of a number of participants. One journalist told this story:

But not even the government's plague of lies prepared us for its willingness to use American television as an instrument of repression. During the week after the massacre, Chinese television showed tape of a man, accusing of being a rumormonger and urging that citizens turn him in. It was ABC's tape. Correspondent Jim Laurie had conducted the interview, but only a few seconds had appeared on ABC. About 90 seconds appeared on

Chinese TV, suggesting that the Chinese had pirated the image as it was being transmitted via satellite. (Reiss 1989:30).

This interpretation was later supported.

ABC News had not broadcast the footage used by Chinese television and thinks that Beijing's intelligence service must have intercepted the satellite feed as it reached the U.S. Recently, China launched a new wave of arrests and investigations. U.S. officials say it is widely believed in China that the latest detentions are based in part on pilfered American television footage of last summer's demonstrations. (Peterzell 1990:7)

Panama.   The way sources are cultivated and restrained can be illustrated with the coverage of the Panamanian invasion. Briefly, General Noriega was the Panamanian dictator who was put in power by our CIA to do their bidding, but as relationships deteriorated, and his increased greed was surpassed only by a penchant for flaunting his invincibility from the United States, Noriega's days were numbered by a massive airborne invasion. In general, military coverage is carefully controlled, especially when the journalists depend on the military for credentials, transportation, sustenance, and, of course, transmission of news reports. Although we do not have the same quality of information about the Panamanian incursion as we do about the British expedition to the Falkland Islands in 1983 (cf. Morrison and Tumber 1988), Boot (1990) argues that the press pool was directed away from the main fighting by the military escorts.

Instead of being taken to cover combat stories, the pool was led on tours of deposed dictator Manuel Noriega's secret lairs: behold the cocaine, the firearms, the Hitler portrait. Then it was onto the next hideaway: skin magazines to the left of them, voodoo paraphernalia to the right of them (buckets of blood, chicken entrails)—into the valley of shame strode the fourteen . . .

Consequently, the Army in Panama saw to it that there were no independent, close-hand accounts of the assaults, bombings, and strafings that made the Panama victory possible—no televised pictures of dying Panamanian civilians and U.S. soldiers who paid the price for that victory . . .

On the whole, news organs seemed to relish the plight of Noriega—the press needs villains, just as government need enemies, and in the age of Cold War thaw a depraved dictator filled the bill rather well. (Boot 1990:18–20)

Apples.   Two of the most exciting scientific stories to hit the press in 1989 were cold fusion, or the extracting of energy from hydrogen, and apples, or more specifically, the preservative known as Alar. Both involved very questionable claims about the success of scientific experiments generating energy, on the one hand, with the carcinogenic impact of eating apples treated with Alar, on the other hand. Like most public issues, they had a media component, but they are unique in what they portend about the explicit use of media outlets to bypass conventional scientific publications and review. Advocates of both went directly to press releases, and in the case of Alar, the Natural Resources Defense Council (NRDC), an environmental advocacy group, hired a public relations firm to publicize its findings. Indeed, NRDC officials granted CBS' "60 Minutes" "exclusive coverage of the report, which would be issued at a news conference the day after the CBS broadcast" (Haddix 1990:45). Even though some parts of the report were leaked, the impact on some 26 million viewers was enormous. A spokesperson and coordinator of Mothers and Others for Pesticide Limits commented on the tactics used:

> I think those tactics have to be used . . . It's like handicapping yourself if you don't do it. You must use the media to get your message out. Not to use the media is naive. (Haddix 1990:45)

Others who were interested in this issue agreed, and turned to an influential critic of the environmental lobby, Elizabeth Whelan, who has mastered the source role in her campaigns—often supported by chemical companies—to react to campaigns, like the Alar crusade (Kurtz 1990). In addition to financing a documentary narrated by Walter Cronkite (the most trusted man in America when he worked for CBS earned $25,000) on the exaggerated claims of "environmentalists," Whelan does quite well in media-speak:

> Television producers like Whelan because she's colorful and succinct, skewering her adversaries with such phrases as "toxic terrorists" and "self-appointed environmentalists," and referring to their research as "voodoo statistics." Newspaper reporters often dial her number because she is an easily accessible spokesperson for the "other" side of many controversies. (Haddix 1990:44)

These examples are intended to illustrate how media logic has joined the practical use of sources, visuals, and newsworkers' use of themes and angles. Since most sources are shared by various media, the long-term consequences for format development and event emphasis become intertwined. In this sense news, as currently practiced, is an institutionalized process and, not surprisingly, there are similarities between newspapers and television operations. The work of Ericson et al. (1989) makes it clear that there are also important differences. These include format, criteria of performance, and news content.

The hardest part of improving newswork is to recognize mistakes (Altheide 1980). Moreover, before this can occur, there must be a willingness to acknowledge that mistakes are possible and a realization that the news process itself can lead to systematic distortion, thereby depriving the public of a more adequate understanding. The works of Friendly (1967) and Schorr (1977) provide numerous samples of the distoring impact of organizational and practical concerns of newswork. The mistakes we are interested in are not simply those involving misquotes or incorrect facts; these are readily observable, and simply corrected. *We are referring to the emphasis and interpretations given an event or a series of events that are based on assumptions incompatible with the reality and complexity of those events.* These usually surface after the fact—for example, after a politician has been drummed out of office. Moreover, often they are pointed out by both scholars and prominent journalists. For examples, the events of Watergate were distorted by conceptually joining discrete events and calling them all "Watergate" (Altheide 1976:155–172); this interrelation essentially has been confirmed by Nicholas Von Hoffman's (1977) assertion that the media were "out to get Nixon." However, major mistakes can be made without deliberate intent.

Conclusion

We began this chapter with the statement that journalism is dead, and we have attempted to trace some of its undoing. In general, the successes of journalism led to its own undoing, within the context of media formats. We do not mean to imply that there are not talented men and women who are committed to covering events; we only contend that the organization and formats of media—especially television—dominate and essentially define all other journalistic practices. The parameters of journalism are set by formats and not professional standards of reporting, fact gathering, careful analysis, etc. Phase 4 of media analysis underscores the importance of technique and media logic reproducing itself. Anyone who doubts this claim need only check the curriculum of almost any journalism school. See if the curriculum significantly transcends formats of technique.

We argued in our initial look at media processes in 1979 that the logic of media work in general and photo work in particular is different from that of everyday life. For this reason, we are vulnerable as readers and viewers if we are not aware of the workings of media logic. Our statements are now borne out by changes in technology, production, and ethics.

TV news changed significantly during the 1980s in a number of ways. These changes have been so great, as we have argued, that journalism is now effectively dead. The news coverage we have is of a different order. Technological innovations that permitted more "live coverage" of events, plus the ability to obtain information directly from satellite relays permitted TV stations to rely less on their parent networks for world and national news. Moreover, additional networks, e.g., Cable News Network (CNN), offered alternatives and competitors for affiliate and independent TV stations. It is the changing financial relationship between the parent news organizations and the hundreds of affiliate stations that makes up the "network" that is most important in the changing news brew.

> On the corner that once had three newsstands, there are now 25 . . . Add to all this the competition from syndicated "tabloid talk" shows, all-news radio and home video and you have the makings of a fatal erosion of the networks' franchise. Since 1980 the evening newscasts of ABC, CBS, and NBC have lost almost a quarter of their combined audience . . . network news itself may eventually cease to exist. (*Newsweek* October 17, 1988:94)

More and more "local" affiliate TV stations are either sending their own crews or contracting to "freelancers" to cover "world" and "international" events. However, since the crews seek to give the "world event" a local twist or angle (see below) to which their audience can identify, the major world issues will in all likelihood be covered from a "narrowcasting" perspective, very similar to radio! (*Newsweek* October 17, 1988:95). The prospects for covering certain events through only "local" angles are a bit unsettling. As former CBS News President queried, "Can you imagine how the civil-rights movement would have been affected if only local stations handled it?" (*Newsweek* October 17, 1988:97).

Technological innovations have also entered news formats through the actual altering of visual representations. A blend of editorial comment, "making it more real," and aesthetic preference has led newspapers, magazines, and TV advertisers to "touch up" their visuals to convey a message (Lasica 1989). Our claim is that this ability leads to changes in ethical standards, just as the Chinese officials who doctored the videotaped sequence of events to make their statement. The main point of such efforts is to reduce ambiguity and to transform the message into an image that is compatible with the definition of the situation being presented—and clearly constructed.

These materials illustrate the consequences of applying the news perspective to events that may then be connected in order to tell a complete story. Although this practical approach certainly has its merits for covering many events and for saving time, it lacks the substantive sensitivity that news readers, listeners, and viewers have a right to expect. To further examine how journalists' notions of "good work" are used to distinguish between various reports, Altheide (1978a) examined the criteria used in selecting winners for the prestigious Radio Television News Director's Association (RTNDA) awards. The aim was to further clarify the cognitive and evaluative criteria brought to bear on the selection process of quality journalism. In general, materials obtained from observations of the judging process, as well as a questionnaire survey, indicated that the main criteria elicited as relevant for journalistic performance were technique and technical skill. Virtually nothing was said about substantive errors, misinterpretations, and like. The reason for the preoccupation with technique is the judges' knowledge and competence; they were more skilled at handling equipment, sophisticated editing, and general presentational strategies than they were at many of the substantive issues dealt with in the various reports. In these matters they had what may be termed a "lay awareness" of the complexities, circumstances, and other interpretations. This does not mean that they were incapable of evaluating the reports; simply that they could be far more critical and self-assured in their comments about technical aspects of these entries. In one instance an entry was faulted for approaching a community effort to assimilate a minority group as "too academic" rather than in terms of the feelings of the people involved. Comments like "the film looks green," "lousy cut," "the cameraman has a problem," and "every time we see something by K _____ that is pretty good, but hurt by production" dominated the judges' assessments.

Thus the technological and organizational contexts of "news events" must provide newsworkers with a framework for routinely suiting these events to both visual and temporal parameters. This is what is meant by the news perspective. And this is what has contributed to the death of journalism and the rise of information mechanics.

In our age, news is not merely content; it is form and authority based on that form. News is also a "civic duty," associated with rules of competence for citizenship. To not know what is "on the news" is to be "out of it." But to be a competent news watcher, and increasingly a news critique, one must be informed about news formats, and how to use and interpret them.

We would again emphasize that as currently practiced, news production is directed more by organization and commercialism than it is by an adequate epistemology, including a more updated and sophisticated version of objectivity (Altheide 1976; Tuchman 1978; Phillips 1977). Basic to all these statements is the realization that news is an organizational product used to promote organizational concerns rather than a fuller understanding of complex issues (Altheide 1985c; Ericson et al. 1989).

Journalism is dead. The way things now stand, with profits and the programming perspective dominating newswork, the best that can be achieved in the short run is to attempt to enlighten enough viewers about the way news is being manufactured so that they can engage in a kind of *defensive viewing:* a skeptical attitude toward all but the most basic news reports. We doubt that the total effects of this kind of audience perspective will be completely productive and beneficial for public information in our society, but the alternative of blindly accepting events transformed by the news perspective is hardly tolerable.

A related point that should be considered involves the importance of attempting to understand how the production process itself contributes to what we create and find. Such an awareness is especially important with the producers of knowledge in our society—they are, in many cases, helping shape the criteria that people will employ in their own lives. For example, TV news, and especially the ABC evening news program, "Nightline," celebrated the taking of Americans as hostages by Iranian students in 1978. "Nightline," hosted by Ted Koppel, originated as a program entitled "America Held Hostage." For 444 days, the hostage drama was played out on television, often stressing hostage family members' grief, and consistently associating through personalized media format that the "Iranian people" supported this undertaking, and years later, the involvement by their leaders in other hostage enterprises and terrorist activities (cf. Altheide 1985c; Said 1981). Iranian citizens were consistently joined with the representatives of their government. In June 1990, the Iranian countryside was devastated by a massive earthquake that left an estimated 70,000 people dead and thousands of others homeless and injured. Very little aid was forthcoming from agencies in the United States. Ted Koppel, one of our foremost journalists, asked several guests on a "Nightline" show late in June, "why." Why, he queried, could not Americans overcome some of their hatred of Iran, when so many "innocent people" have suffered? Mr. Koppel never indicated that he understood in the least how his own work and those of hundreds of other colleagues throughout the United States had contributed to this definition of Iran in general, and the symbolic joining of a few leaders with the remainder of the people in general. He had produced the very effect he was trying to understand. All of this set the stage for massive troop build-ups in the Persian gulf two months later, of course Koppel reported it live on "Nightline."

For this reason, we must understand the process of creating the first-order criteria. Although we all start with certain preconceptions and assumptions, only through our efforts to state the impact of these on any resultant "knowledge," "beliefs," and "practices" can we hope to remain free from domineering forms of information that, ironically, can retard rather than enhance human potential. Apart from the impact of media logic and practice on a number of institutions in our society (several of which will be examined in later chapters) there is the awesome effect on mass communications throughout the world. Like it or not, American mass media and standards have traversed our globe and have made no small contribution to the establishment of media organizations, criteria of excellence, and formats for knowledge production and dissemination. Still—at least in American life—we have a basic understanding of the transformation of American politics through media formats. We now turn to this development.

Notes

1. At another level, the very structure of the newscast promotes an order and presentation of reports that has a reality of its own, albeit distinct from that of the audience's. Burns (1977:203) offers a cogent appraisal of this procedure:

   This "de-contextualising" of the news, the brevity of each item, and the varying visual impact make the continuity provided by a news presenter and the editor a human necessity. And it is the continuity, the "re-contextualising," which drives the broadcaster to resort to the imputation to the audience of the corporate idea of its stockpile of common assumptions and beliefs.

2. These remarks are grounded in the theory and research in phenomenological and existential orientations (Schutz 1967; Douglas and Johnson 1977), as well as that of symbolic interactionism (Blumer 1969), ethnomethodology (Garfinkel 1967; Cicourel 1968; Speier 1973), and, perhaps most directly, dramaturgy (Goffman 1959, 1967; Lyman and Scott 1970; Lyman 1978).

4

Media Politics I:
The Politicians

"Yet the scary implication remains that some day in the not-too-distant future, the image may be everything."

(Christopher Lehman-Haupt, 1988)

Even though we predicted in 1979 that media logic would continue to pervade big-time politics, we did not fully anticipate the extent to which this would occur. The media and politics sustained each other, but as the role of mass media became more powerful than mere politicians, the latter adapted to the former, and they both changed (Cook 1989). Political media, as much as any single source, contributed to the death of organized journalism.

Power at any point in history travels along communication formats, which were in turn shaped and influenced through previous acts of power (Couch 1990). As Simmel (1950) taught us, cultural patterns and forms that are constructed for one purpose can take on a life of their own. Just as bureaucratic forms are relied on today to "communicate" rational control, coordination, and efficiency, so too are mass communication forms and processes (cf. Nimmo and Combs 1983). And just as virtually all modern leaders of corporations or nation-states have failed to transcend the temporal and administrative control of the bureaucracy forms in trying to exert their own influence, so too have politicians and other power wielders been unable to totally dominate the mass communication process. Rather, the story of the modern age can be told in terms of how leaders and power wielders have had to adjust to both bureaucratic and media logic.

Media logic and accompanying images are most prevalent in political affairs during campaigns, but they are also significant as politicians portray their positions on issues and crises. In the context of politics, media logic and the dominance of certain formats, especially television, are ap-

81

parent in the selection, organization, presentation, and emphasis of political behavior (cf. Becchelloni 1980). The major point of this chapter is that political behavior today is intertwined with media formats to such an extent that politics is *media politics*. Consider a few examples: President Reagan (and every U.S. leader since President Carter) organizes statements around "photo opportunities." In 1990, a Republican candidate for governor in Arizona, Fyfe Symington, distributed *video casettes* containing an eight and a half minute videotaped message to undecided Republican voters! (Arizona *Republic* July 3, 1990). Such activities cannot be easily explained by older perspectives on media effects, which we termed Phases 1–3 in our Preface.

Media Politics in Phase 4

Although there is much agreement among scholars that the mass media play an important role in political behavior, there remain important differences of opinion about its role. Recall that earlier approaches to mass communication (Phases 1–3) stressed the messages, or content of what was communicated (Entman 1989) Those approaches, especially Phase 3, noted how messages were infused with ideological symbols and assumptions. Of course, we readily acknowledge how all cultural products, such as mass media messages, are reflexive of the language, mythology, and taken-for-granted notions that contribute to an "ideology," but our focus—and that of researchers in Phase 4 of media studies—is on how these messages are products of communication forms. It is these forms and logics that are transforming our social worlds into media worlds, and for this reason we need to be very clear about how the media processes influence messages.

A major distinction of researchers working in the latest phase of media analysis is that messages do not exist by themselves. Indeed, a message does not exist as a message for a human being until it is interpreted through a symbolic process (Maines and Couch 1988). This insight, which has been widely documented through research on parasocial interaction, or how audience members interpret, use, and interact with mass media, has not been integrated within a broader conceptual framework for understanding media effects in general, and political information in particular (cf. Horton and Wohl 1956; Lang and Lang 1968; Levy 1979; Lull 1982).

Researchers in Phase 4 of media analysis are able to incorporate many of the earlier findings, insights, and understandings about media effects into a broader and more encompassing theoretical perspective that includes media processes, media logic, and formats. From this perspective,

Lehman-Haupt, in the above quote, is partly correct: The image is increasingly important, but it is the media logic that pervades how an audience member recognizes something as a "message," interprets it, and then plays with it, invoking it in certain situations. Images do not have a clear meaning until audience members interpret it through a process of symbolic interaction. It is for this reason that focusing only on the message or "manipulating images" is an incomplete approach to understanding media effects. Indeed, it is the expectations and experiences of the viewers, the context within which a message is cast—during a Presidential campaign or some other time—the nature of the medium, and the viewing situation, that determine the nature of the message and its effect on audience members. As we stressed in the last chapter, TV viewers throughout our society, and especially young people, are very good media critics, and are aware that images are constructed in order to manipulate them, but they may still choose to situationally integrate those messages into certain activities and identities. Thus many young viewers of TV ads "play" with the messages, may repeat them with friends, but are not directly manipulated or "duped" by them.

When the "presidential look" that is associated with TV debates between candidates comes to be viewed as "essential" for a candidate to be viable, this is media logic. It is media logic because the criteria, its look, form, and overall mode originated from the media technology and perspectives of workers (journalists) themselves. Yet, viewers in general, and inquiring journalists in particular, expect politicians to fulfill these espectations, especially in presidential "debates."

To reiterate our basic point: power and politics are enacted when they are manifested and made visible through a communication process (cf. Combs 1984). Analysis of specific political contexts suggests that the process of constructing order can be discerned by deconstructing the codes of enactment and presentation (cf. Clift 1987). Movers-and-shakers, lobbyists, and vested interests continue to work "behind the scenes" and strive to play the audience in order to enhance their own interests; however, this is now being done through the formats and discourse of the mass media, and especially TV. Our intent, then, is to emphasize once again that media logic and formats do not dispense with conventional power and manipulative zeal, but rather are a mode of discourse through which *all public pronouncements are shaped and marketed.*

Political institutions have been the most affected by media practices and formats because politicians, their advisors, and even their critics now routinely rely on the grammar and timing of mass communication. Indeed, it is partly because of the way in which media logic essentially has redefined political action and rhetoric that we confront the problem of the political spectacle again. When we addressed the political issue in our 1979 volume, others had noted that politics were being transformed by electronic media. We extended that argument, delineating how the criteria of media impact and success were gradually merging with the production of political ads, and the timing of appearances. In those days, however, it was not uncommon for major national politicians and their staffs to deny that they were consciously pursuing and using media logic. That has now changed; "current" politicians, most noteworthy Ronald Reagan and his excellent "image staff" of "spin doctors," explicitly noted how they incorporated the TV timing and logic into their day-to-day operations. The account that unfolds is somewhat complicated, but can be easily summarized: Since the mid-1970s media logic has dominated politics in several respects: (1) big time presidential campaigns, (2) the style and themes of political messages contained in news reports, and (3) the substance and focus of political events and issues, which are selected, organized, and presented according to media logic and formats.

The impact of media logic on social institutions and related activities will vary according to the nature and extent of the media's involvements. Since politics has been most closely aligned with the rise and evolution of media forms (with the exception of the "entertainment business"), it is not surprising that political life today bears the clearest mark of the media's influence (Tracey 1977). For this reason we devote three chapters to the relationship between politics and the media; the present focus will be on the format of public politics, and Chapter 5 will look in more depth at the process of media politics by examining in detail the Bert Lance case of 1976. For suggestive comparisons, a more cursory examination will be made of President Carter's problems with the media in 1980, former Vice President Mondale's uphill contest to unseat President Reagan in 1984, and the Bush–Dukakis contest in 1988. Not all aspects of these campaigns can be adequately dealt with in this brief overview, but the continual, yet changing role of the media can be set forth in a conceptual way suggesting the power of a new approach to understanding the significance of media logic for our age.

Power is communicated. Politics has always blended well with the dominant media of the day, although all politicians have not, e.g., Richard Nixon; indeed, politics quite often controlled and helped shape these media. But it is in more recent times that the phenomenal growth and power of the mass media have come to reciprocally, if not directly, influence the nature and form of political life (Minow et al. 1973; Blanchard 1974; Gilbert 1972). Most recently, the Reagan administration became quite skilled at "learning" about the media procedures and "codes" and then giving the media what it wanted, that is, they provided the media with the results dictated by media logic. Although many in the press would refer to this as manipulation—and it obviously was—one could also make a case for "learning": Politicians had been taught the media logic for several decades, they learned it, and then gave it back to the camera. And they talked about it. Very openly.

Roger Ailes (1988) was one of the best at this. A former executive producer of the Mike Douglas show, Ailes' expertise in coaching chief executive officers (CEO) and politicians was requested by President Reagan's staff just after the first debate in 1984 with democratic challenger, Walter Mondale. In that debate, aides had feared that Reagan did not fare well and seemed to fumble around. Ailes subsequent involvement in and direction of a large portion of Reagan's public appearances were informed by his knowledge of television formats and journalistic perspectives. Although it would remain for people like Michael Deaver, Richard Darman, and communications director David Gergen to tailor journalistic and media opportunities that would benefit the intended image and emphasis of candidate-President Reagan, it was Ailes who stressed the lack of content and details in Reagan's appearances. His words about how TV changed things—from politics to public speaking, to informal "cocktail" conversation—are tough to top. About all audiences, he wrote (Ailes 1988:14, 12):

> In the video age we're all broadcasters. We transmit our own programs. We receive ratings from our audiences.

And

> When someone speaks to them, they want to relax and listen just as they do when a TV professional entertains them in the living room . . . Subconsciously, the style that's acceptable on a television show, informal, crisp, and entertaining—becomes the modern standard for an effective communicator.

The issue is not merely the extent of media contributions to the decision-making process, but the way this process has been transformed through an underlying media logic. We do not attempt to define what the "proper role" of the press should be in governmental activities. There is no question that the press has both a constitutional and an actual share of the political process. Indeed, Burns (1977) has argued—at least in the British case—that the original designation of the press as the "fourth estate," a term coined by Edmund Burke in the eighteenth century, was a response to the government's apparent lack of concern with public opinion:

> The very existence of newspapers and the nature of their contents presumed the existence of a public, political, opinion external to the small

enclosed world of parliamentary politics. Further, the role they assumed was that not merely of carrying information but of articulating and expressing public opinion. (Burns, 1977:176)

Our concern is with the broader but more basic political effects of new forms of technology combined with old journalistic ideals, compounded by the rapid growth of commercialism, the entertainment format, and an occupational milieu that bureaucratizes politics as a form of programming. Consider the issue of "charisma," that many scholars and others mistakenly conclude resides within an individual rather than an interaction between an audience a medium (even conversation) and a speaker. For presidential advisor Ailes (1988:91), the issue is clear:

It's tougher today to be viewed as charismatic. In the heyday . . . the press was not nearly as diligent as it is now in finding and exposing weaknesses in public figures.

We do not think that this statement is irrelevant for the shortened political careers discussed in the next chapter, including Bert Lance, Senator Muskie, and Gary Hart. For Ailes (1988:152), the adversary relationship is not only clear, it is absolutely essential to operate with this in mind:

With the media, make no mistake, you are always on defense, but if you do it right, you can occasionally score.

This appears to be the context for the ambiguity described by Burns (1977:174):

The essential ambiguity in the political role of the press, a role broadcast journalism has seemingly tried to adopt, lies in the way it has claimed to serve as the mirror of events and the voice, the "organ," of public opinion, and also to be seen (and occasionally claim to act) as the controller, regulator, or even creator of events and public opinion.

That there is strong support for this view will be illustrated below. However, before exploring the ways that media logic has infused and is now taken for granted as part of our political institutions, we will look briefly at the nature of various media formats in order to further clarify this perspective. This will be done by comparing the ways in which various media covered the Presidential election in 1976, with some additional comments about the campaigns in 1980, 1984, and 1988.

Formats for Presidential Politics

Political messages are constituted through a communication process involving a medium, a technology, rules or "codes" for constituting the intended message, and an audience that *actively* interprets and constructs the meaning. We have been arguing for some time now that communication *formats* join these overlapping moments into a coherent whole; the audience members, for example, recognize the temporal and spatial relationship that makes up a "shape of a message" before obtaining any meaningful content. As these formats change through history, so does the communication process, especially the "content" or interpreted message. Such changes can be seen over a period of several thousand years in which, for example, primarily oral technologies (Couch 1984) have been replaced by the electronics of the nightly newscast (cf. Harris 1974). But the message has also changed as the temporal and spatial underpinnings of electronic imagery have been substituted for an embodied voice.

As noted in the earlier discussion of entertainment and news, formats provide workable solutions to very practical problems, including the nature of content and emphasis, mode and style of presentation, and the relationship of one episode or event to the entire program, or document. In a sense, formats are inevitable when messages are presented in an organized and rationalized manner. Thus the goals and purposes of the medium presenting the messages have no small impact on the order and logic that shapes such messages. It is the character of these messages or "texts" that concerns us.   .

In a cogent discussion of the way in which political "spectacles" are routinely constructed, Murray Edelman (1988:19) stated,

> As soon as "opinion" is recognized as an ambiguous reference to texts, as truly of language that circulates in a culture and present themselves for acceptance or rejection, it becomes evident that opposing texts become bulwarks of one another while isolated texts, unsupported by opposition, are really vulnerable to new language.

It is the grammar and organization of such texts, rich in ideological inferences, that suggest the relevance of format and media logic for any message. Certainly one reason a predictable range of political messages is routinely offered to various audiences is due to the trade-off between dissimilar formats and audience members' expectations and frames of reference during interaction with particular media.

Consider how taken for granted the TV formats were for a key Reagan aide, Michael Deaver, who, in an editorial in *The Washington Post*, "Sound-Bite Campaigning: TV Made Us Do It" (October 30, 1988), spelled out how professional image managers learned from the media how to produce an image. Deaver's pronouncement signals the death of organized journalism because he clearly articulates how the "source"

and "channel" are no longer separate. The world of one has entered
that of the other, and both are transformed. From a politician's perspective, "long live journalism!"

> My own contribution to campaign innovation resulted from observing the
> medium as we prepared for the 1976 presidential race. I noted how the
> people who run television news were reducing a candidate's thought-
> ful and specific speech on an issue, say, an upturn in the economy, to
> a 10-second sound-bite, which was then followed on the screen by an effec-
> tive visual of someone, usually in the Midwest, "whose life remains un-
> touched by the prosperity claimed by President Ford," as the voice-over
> told us.
>
> The point is that rather than inventing the effective visual or the 30-
> second sound bite, we simply adapted an existing TV news technique that
> was already widely used. That's why it always amuses me to watch someone
> like Tom or Peter or Dan sitting in a million-dollar set, their physical ap-
> pearance the envy of every undertaker in the nation, criticizing a politician
> for trying to control his or her image . . .
>
> There's nothing mystical about what I and others in the Reagan White
> House did with television. A good illustration might be a story about an
> increase in home construction starts. In my judgment, this was a major
> story, of importance and interest to the American people.
>
> So, in our morning issues conference, a meeting much like those held
> in the editorial offices of newspapers and television networks and stations
> all over the country, I decided to "lead" with the housing story. But rather
> than have White House Press Secretary Larry Speakes hold up charts
> or issue a press release, and thereby bury the story in the business seg-
> ment, we took the president to a construction site. There, wearing a hard
> hat and standing in front of homes under construction, he announced
> the housing start numbers and what that meant to the American people
> and the national economy. Naturally, the story played big on the evening
> news.
>
> An enduring shibboleth is that a skilled practitioner can make someone
> appear to be other than what he really is.

In short, Deaver made it clear once and for all that it was no longer
newsworthy to claim, as many novitiates of the media have done, that
"The objective was . . . to transform [the press] into an unwitting mouth-
piece of the government" (Hertsgaard 1988:31). This was not accomplished through fear and intimidation, but by using the codes, language,
logic, and formats of the news media.

[Although Deaver's points are quite straightforward, a brief comment
should be made about his usage of 10- and 30-second sound-bytes. In a
previous study we found that one feature of the format for TV news is
the use of visual grammar, in which "complete" news reports lasting
from 30 seconds to more than 5 minutes are really made up of a series
of 10-second "information units" (IUs) in which an actor is shown taking
some action toward an object. Similar to sentences, these IUs make up

newscasts and are oriented to the visual (Altheide 1985. Deaver is correct.)]

A significant part of a medium's choice of format is its presumed target audience and the interest in and use of that medium by the audience. Obviously, no medium can be everything to everybody, so potential target audience members are regarded in piecemeal fashion; what interest of potential viewers, listeners, or readers will be served by a particular publication? Although media do compete for markets, only relatively minor segments of that larger potential market are sought out. The different focuses between radio, television, and magazines reflect the way the respective media agents plan, define, package, and distribute their "products." Moreover, it is important to stress that the various media are not necessarily competing for the same market at the same time; rather, different parts of the market and different uses are the key to understanding advertising, programming, and packaging techniques.

Television

Content.   Materials selected from the ABC nightly newscasts in 1976 will be used to illustrate the logic of formats. We begin by briefly examining the topics presented. Of those topics presented at least three times in ABC news reports, several dominated air time. The first was polls: more than 15 percent of all stories presented more than three times dealt with viewer polls regarding who people would vote for, who was leading, what issues people felt were important, and who people felt would do the best job. Other more frequently appearing topics (that is, 5 percent or more of topics appearing three or more times) were Carter's *Playboy* interview regarding "lust in his heart," campaign activities (crowds, waving to bystanders, motorcades), and the nature and significance of TV debates. Included in the specific issues dealt with most often were taxes, unemployment, abortion, and crime. Inflation, Watergate, welfare, arms, and foreign affairs each comprised about 2 to 3 percent of the topics presented three or more times. By contrast, the topics that comprised less than 2 percent of recurring stories included energy and peace. In analyzing the relative emphasis on topics throughout the campaign, campaign coverage, polls, and the presidential debates received proportionately more coverage, with one exception. This occurred between September 1 and September 20, when taxes and abortion were treated in 13 percent of the stories, followed by unemployment (10 percent, with the campaign activities and polls receiving 8 percent and 5 percent, respectively).

Data obtained from CBS and NBC indicate similar trends in coverage, although these networks—especially CBS—focused more on the politics of Watergate and certain charges that Carter had accepted campaign gifts during his tenure as governor of Georgia. The Ford stories were particularly stressed on September 22, 26, 30, and October 13, 21, 26, and 27. Political polls were featured on one NBC special (October 25). The poll was conducted prior to the first debate and stressed three things: (1) Do the voters know what is important? (2) Has either candidate gotten his ideas across? and (3) What is coming through to the voters? Results were presented to the following six questions:

1. How much difference does it make to you who becomes president?
2. How much difference is there is what kind of president each would be and what he would accomplish?
3. Who would do a better job on foreign affairs?
4. Who would work for a better tax system?
5. Who will do better against inflation?
6. Who will do better at streamlining the federal government?

Finally, all three networks devoted considerable attention to the three political debates. NBC presented an insightful special report on September 23, just before the first debate. The focus was on the background and cosmetics, including inside looks at the respective strengths and weaknesses of both candidates regarding certain combinations of lights, cameras, and the height of the podium. The significance of the debates to television—at least from the perspective of some broadcasters—was suggested in a comment by NBC correspondent John Hart:

> People remember what they've seen better than what they've heard. The cosmetic men have caged all known visible risks, except for what the candidates will do on the air . . . on their own. (NBC News Special Report September 23, 1976)

Scheduling and Organization. To a large extent, the content presented in a TV newscast is inextricably tied to the organization of newswork, including number of personnel, division of labor, technological considerations, and, of course, scheduling of events. In most cases, TV reports are about events that were planned or known about in advance. The logistics and transporting personnel and equipment, obtaining the film, tape, and other materials, and then editing them in time for presentation are basic considerations. This is why presidential and other politically related events are routinely scheduled several days in advance. This is also why candidates for office plan their activities so that any "significant" statements will be made in time for reporters to send their material to New York for telecasting. This is particularly important when the different time zones are considered; a statement made in San Diego at 3:00 P.M. will not arrive in New York in time for the evening news.

These practical considerations lead newsworkers to select events that are compatible with the overriding organizational logic. A related concern is to select portions of events that are easily presented in a short time span and that can be encapsulated as the significant aspect of an event. Events such as press conferences and charges–countercharges are preferred, since brief statements by two parties can be used to illustrate a particular issue or difference of opinion (cf. Porter 1989). By the same token, televised debates, although not yet common, are preferred by TV news crews, since the event itself is oriented to television's organizational concerns and is usually planned in consultation with TV producers. In this sense, the "format" and organization of debates are a direct outgrowth of the organizational and technical logic that constitutes current TV practices. As noted by another media analyst, Michael J. Robinson (1977:10):

> Without doubt, the single most important development during these years was the Kennedy–Nixon debates. And if the "Great Debates" were a boon to John Kennedy, they were an even bigger bonanza for the media professionals who had services to sell. Indeed, because of the debates, the amount expended by Presidential candidates for radio and television increased by nearly 300 percent between 1960 and 1964, a rate of increase never achieved before or since. The Kennedy–Nixon debates signaled the beginning of the audio-visual orgy of the 1960s.

Much the same is true of the national political conventions occurring in halls that have been transformed into massive television studios. Further, conventions, like televised debates, provide journalists with an opportunity to discuss issues with the candidates as well as evaluate their overall performance. But the significant point here is that the criteria used for assessing a candidate's *competence* depends on his TV *performance,* which includes quick and smooth responses to often ambiguous questions about even more complex and rapidly changing issues.

In brief, the organizational imperatives of TV are more compatible with specific events that can be located in a particular space at a particular time. As Epstein (1974) has shown, if this is not possible in fact—if the event to be treated is a concept, a social movement, or something amorphous—TV will simply focus on a particular city and an event within that city and present it as part of a national trend. Television's reluctance to deal with "abstract" topics is illustrated by John Whale's analysis of the "viewability" criterion and its impact on the coverage of Mayor Daley's conduct at the 1968 Democratic National Political Convention.

> Television viewers were never given more than a cursory explanation of why the mayor of a provincial city was able to rule not only on his own region but a national political convention with an iron fist. They could not

have been. The structure of patronage was too complex, too abstract, too private to be set out on television. There was nothing to photograph. (Burns, 1977:207)

The crowning point of any candidate's campaign is the party's National Political Conventions held in the summer before the presidential election. The way in which television coverage has transformed these events has been widely documented and will not be repeated here (cf. Altheide 1976). Although most of the materials to follow examine the coverage of the 1976 campaign, jumping ahead to the 1988 convention coverage illustrates how the conventions themselves have become not only TV studios, but that the "show" of politics actually starts the journalists themselves. Weiss' (1988:29ff) account of the Democratic Party Convention, which was held in Atlanta, is particularly revealing.

> The convention saw the birth of a unified Democratic party, delivered with Reagan-era propaganda skills. Its twin, or its afterbirth, some related trend . . . was the absorption into the journalism community of more and more political operatives with axes of their own to grind. The causes for this are well known. The power of the party and its nominating convention has shrunk, yielding to the primary process, which is largely a creature of television . . . But TV is never sufficient in itself to form public opinion. What matters in the world of spin is how conventional wisdom solidified over the next few hours or days, often in print.

The role of the journalists to fill in the coverage, which is largely scripted, is quite problematic because it is difficult to be enterprising and innovative when others have thought out various angles to cover the candidates' orchestrated moves into photo opportunities. Weiss (1988:29) reaffirms in 1988 what Altheide (1976) learned at the 1972 National Political Conventions: It is a show, with all the attendant problems. As Weiss observed, "Division 6 of the DNC's convention media operations was titled Spin Control Coordination (a handbook advised staff members to 'track location of top Democratic pundits and operatives and work to coordinate their availability to print and broadcast media.' " What is a journalists to do under such circumstances? Ah ha! Cover each other with interviews.

> Just walking around the thriving Village [the *Omni* convention hall] you could feel the press's awareness of its role. *Newsweek* circulated a press release listing nineteen reporters and editors who were available "as broadcast guests" for radio and television interviews . . . and when a delegate came into the Village and tried to take pictures of some news organizations, she was prevented from doing so. No wonder. It was as though the journalists, aware that the delegates had no power, meant to keep them in their place." (Weiss 1988:29) . . . But the most curious incursion by the

political community on view in Atlanta was the ten-month-old *Presidential Campaign Hotline,* a daily computerized report that essentially covers the coverage. . . . One politico spoke of *Hotline* . . . as a means by which the press could be all the more reliably shepherded . . . This was the overwhelming spirit of the convention (and the central discovery of the DNC): the more reporters there are, the easier it is to spread such a line. (p. 30)

However, at this convention, like so many others, the astute journalists were generally aware of the staging, despite its normalization. Altheide (1976) found that many objected in 1972, but apparently journalists had become better socialized workers by 1988 because Weiss (1988), at least, reports relatively little discontent. An exception was ABC's News president Roone Arledge, whose vocal threat to not air the "staged and boring event" itself became a major story! Indeed, the nature of the coverage of this, and other campaigns, became a commonly used news angle. For example, Weiss (1988:33–34) observed a press conference being held outside of CBS staging area to dispel the rumor that Dan Rather and Walter Cronkite were feuding. His account of the other subordinate journalists who were eagerly seeking out a story is priceless:

A dozen reporters stood outside [CBS' area], and as was so often the case at the convention, one began interviewing another. A third commented wryly on the interview: "Reporter interviews reporter about press conference given about press."

Style and Mode of Communication. The scheduling concerns noted above, along with the widely shared view that TV journalism must be entertaining and highly visual, have led TV news crews to trim stories in order to support the all important film and other visual materials. This is done in spite of the official view that film is meant only to illustrate the significant findings or analysis of the reporter. To the contrary, the commitment to certain kinds of images as the crucial mode of communication actually limits what a reporter can do on a particular assignment. One consequence of this framework is to stress action, movement, facial expressions, and visual process—including the use of graphs depicting trends in opinion polls—over the cognitive and analytical approaches that are most obviously manifested through talk and more linear forms, such as detailed tables and charts.

By 1964, it had become clear that what was good footage for the networks could become a national priority overnight—perhaps without respect to the merits of the case. It was not simply a matter of terrorists eventually coming to steal attention on television. It was that the needs of the television news organizations had already begun to define our political agenda for us—as newspapers and radio had done before, but with less force and without the overwhelming commitment to what might be called the "tyranny of film." (Robinson 1977:13).

A related and significant point is that reporters are as much a part of the "report"—if not more so—than the person or circumstances that are reported. This means they also must be visual, "on the scene," which presumably lends credibility and immediacy to their narratives. But, as stressed above, the narrative is often second to the style and imagery. For example, Daniel Schorr (1977), in writing about his experiences covering the Watergate story, was constantly doing "stand ups" in front of the Democratic National Headquarters in the Watergate building complex. Indeed, virtually anything critical about Nixon and his administration came to be visually associated with this setting. In much the same way, the presence of reporters in Washington, D.C., is illustrated by showing the White House or another widely recognized public building in the background—there can be no doubt that they are on the scene and presumably "inside" what is happening. Of course, in most cases these reporters are simply fed highly edited information that could best be regarded as a form of "bureaucratic propaganda" (Altheide and Johnson 1980).

The role of polls and TV spots was also pronounced in the 1988 campaign. When Democratic Presidential candidate Michael Dukakis' staff complained about the wide-ranging analyses being undertaken by TV journalists, ABC correspondent Jeff Greenfield replied, "It is the job of politicians to act, it is the job of reporters to analyze." In reflecting on the "sophisticated" mass mediated image strategies so widely used in this campaign, Jackson advised Dukakis to "begin to have daily press conferences and not depend on the networks to give him 30 second sound bites."

The general impact on political news is to focus on those aspects of a campaign that are compatible with providing visual evidence for a reporter's assessment of a particular situation or strategy. Often, this appraisal is either based on generalizing themes or angles that the reporter establishes or borrows from a colleague even before arriving at a particular scene. Thus style and movement, as well as physical aspects of "confrontation," "anger," "support," and so on, are more compatible with the needs of television and are therefore more "communicative" to the news cast's definition of its target audience. Not surprisingly, the use of TV debates is quite consistent with this logic; like any staged event, it enables the television apparatus and the candidate(s) to use each other in promoting essentially the same purpose: present an image and style.

Debatable Politics.   A brief comparison between presidential debates in 1972 and 1988 suggests that the media appetite has digested political action. According to Gilbert (1972:169), the first televised debate between John Kennedy and Richard Nixon in 1960 was decided on image:

As the two men appeared side by side on television, Kennedy projected the image of a dynamic, intelligent, and articulate leader while Nixon appeared to be in ill-health, nervous, and unsure of himself. Particularly damaging to Nixon were the reaction shots which caught him while Kennedy was speaking and which transmitted his face, pale and haggard, his eyes darkened by a combination of illness, fatigue, and the vagaries of studio lighting and his skin, streaked with perspiration, into millions of homes across the nation. The practical result of the comparative appearance of the two men was that Kennedy was judged to have won the debate by a decisive margin.

The power of television imagery is further suggested by research findings that radio listeners evaluated Nixon's performance more favorably than the television audience (Gilbert 1972:170).

The impact of this debate on future political strategy was most vividly seen 16 years later when incumbent Gerald Ford debated Jimmy Carter. Ron Nessen's (1978:262–264) account of Ford's preparation illustrates the encroachment of media logic on the political process:

No one at the White House worried about Ford's ability to answer factual questions. He knew the material, dealt with it every day in the Oval Office. . . . The president knew *what* to answer; in preparing for the debates, he needed to master *how* to answer, in order to emphasize his strong points and emphasize Carter's weak points, in memorable language. . . .

As for the mechanics, Ford was advised to stand at all times during the debates, assume that a camera was always focused on him, make notes while Carter spoke. . . .

Rehearsals were held in the Family Theater on the ground floor of the White House, where a replica of the stage layout for the debates was constructed. This permitted Ford to familiarize himself with the setting, get the feel of his podium and of the location of Carter's podium, and try out the signal-light system which indicated how much time was left to complete the three-minute answers and two-minute rebuttals. During the rehearsals, aides took turns firing questions at the president for hours while he developed and sharpened his answers. The sessions were videotaped and played back for criticism. . . .

Carter walked on stage first, grinning but looking uncomfortable. Then the president entered, exuding authority and presidential presence, tall, athletic, dressed in an impeccable blue suit, quiet tie and—the impact was immediate—a *vest*, which created the overpowering image of a self-assured executive. TV adviser William Caruthers had also persuaded the president to abandon his resistance to television makeup.

But it is one thing to "appear presidential"; it is another to get the image and other messages across to the audience and particularly the most significant audience—the journalists. Although no definitive study exists to assess the influence of journalistic impressions on audience assessments of debate performance, Gladys and Kurt Lang (1977) have found that a university audience's assessments do change over time. Specifically, these researchers report that respondents who did not indicate a preference for either Ford or Carter prior to the first debate were able to make an assessment of each candidate's chances for winning after the debate. There was, however, one important distinguishing factor: the amount of time between assessments. Those persons who responded immediately tended to give the advantage to Ford, while those who responded four to seven days after the debate tended to think that Carter had the best chance. Although evidence has not been amassed to show that it was "postdebate" discussions that accounted for these differences, individuals involved with the respective candidates act as though this were the case. Again, Ron Nessen's (1978:266) description of the 27-minute technical interruption during the first debate is instructive:

> The Ford staff realized almost immediately that the networks would have to fill the air time. So [other aides] and I rushed to the lobby, where, as we had expected, the network TV correspondents were fairly panting for someone to interview.
> The three of us rotated among ABC, CBS and NBC, explaining why we thought Ford was the big winner, for nearly ten minutes before Jody Powell and other Carterites caught on to what was happening and showed up at the cameras.

And the self-fulfilling nature of media reports for opinion-poll results also was evident:

> The press gave wide circulation to an instant poll of 600 viewers by the Roper organization within minutes after the debate went off the air. It showed Ford was perceived to be the winner, 39 to 30 percent calling it a draw. Later, polls by the AP, CBS and NBC's "Today Show" reached similar conclusions. (Nessen 1978:267)

In this context, polls become another form of television ratings and work with the same kind of programming logic (Wheeler 1976).

The initial efforts to produce a mediated image of Kennedy in 1960 were improved substantially in 1976, and were taken to a new level by the Reagan staff in 1980. By 1988 the same general procedures were widely acknowledged by politicians, journalists, and a growing percentage of the audience. The major theme, as we have stressed, is who is leading and who is trailing. With this message overriding other considerations about issues and clear positions, the news media focus on opinion polls to generate stories about winning and losing. The debates fulfill this role very well.

The pervasive role of media formats can be seen in the initial TV appearance of Bush and Dukakis in 1988, which was advertised as a "debate." First, it must be remembered that years of experience have taught candidates and their staffs that they must speak to temporal and spatial constraints of the news media. There are several implications of this. First, all meaningful political activities should be viewed as media opportunities. Second, and related, any statement or event should be considered for the way in which the news media will use it and edit it for rebroadcast, perhaps at a later time. In this regard, there is no such thing as an "old" item; all exist in the same temporal framework, that of retrievable videotape. Third, statements and events should be done with the media formats, including their visual grammar, in mind. Fourth, candidates use the audience members' stock of knowledge about media images, scenarios, cliches, characters, and advertisements as resources in promoting their own message about a topic. However, often the message is very incomplete, especially when compared to an articulate written paragraph, with a series of logically connected sentences organized around a beginning, middle and end. Fifth, the journalists and the "organizational machinery" that empower these artful "actual accounts" are the most significant audience for all "on the record acts."

These points can be seen in the 1988 campaign in general, and the "debates" in particular. Consider the way in which both candidates artfully drew on TV discourse, including characters, to show their competence and wit even as they complied with the temporal and spatial format requirements of TV. Specifically, this campaign, as suggested above, epitomized the use of 30-second sound bites, or cute, curt statements that were made with future replays in mind (Mickelson 1989). During the "debates," statements were conceived, organized, and presented with the awareness that it was not only simplistic themes that would count—a carry-over from previous elections—but also that they would be "clipped" and edited for rebroadcast later on within the formats of regular evening newscasts. In effect, the summary clips of the debates would stand for the debates themselves, which, as we have already seen, were orchestrated at the outset in order to play to the themes, myth, and images that viewers were presumed to have. If it seems like a huge circle, it is! Consider the role of one liners. Following the debate, one network newscast summary led off with, "The two candidates came prepared to zing." Then Dukakis was shown saying, "if he [Bush] keeps this up he's going to be the Joe Isuzu of politics." (Isuzu is a car advertised by a man who intentionally and blatantly lies about its capabilities.) Bush is then shown saying, in reference to Dukakis' failure to clean up Boston Harbor while Governor of Massachusetts, "that answer was about as clear as Boston Harbor." Both aids and "spin doctors" claimed victory.

When taken together, the three components of the TV news format provide an orientational map for examining the expanded use of television by candidates. For one thing, more astute politicians are either aware of the logic noted above and/or employ media experts, who are often recruited from the advertising ranks. These people are image managers and are well schooled in packaging. For them, the issue is not whether politicians are competent, knowledgeable, or genuinely concerned, but whether they can impress TV viewers that they possess such qualities. Through the efforts of such image managers, politics has been transformed into a television format and the process is becoming rapidly institutionalized. This is perhaps best illustration by Gerald Rafshoon, the full-time media expert on President Carter's White House staff. For Rafshoon, the major issues are appearance, timing, and presentation—the key criteria of the TV format—and all other material, such as foreign policy announcements, governmental appointments and programs, is to be used to promote a favorable impression. In the extreme case, the avowed purpose of government becomes merely the resource to promote the image of government and government officials, and this may be necessary even when one's opponents are busy at work using the same logic of format to attack programs and policies.

Perhaps the best indicator of the role of media logic in current political life is the contrast between the information value of news coverage and political advertisements. In a sense this is a bogus distinction, since few politicians permit access to events by news crews (or anyone else) unless that tactic becomes self-serving. To this extent, most news coverage is carefully orchestrated (or at least the attempt to do so is made) and even the most knowledgeable journalists are aware of this process and comply with it—often not without a few satirical comments. For example, President Carter would routinely appear wearing blue jeans during his campaign for president in 1976. The same was true of a riverboat cruise set by former President Ford to promote over the evening news the message that he cared about the South. But political commercials made by the candidate's organization and explicitly intended to promote a certain image are not blatant and contrived, often using "natural settings" to avoid the "commercial" flavor or using people who appear to be reporters but are actually campaign workers or hired actors. The intertwining of the various forms of blatant manipulation, entertainment, and "objective" information suggests that an overriding media logic joins the alleged differences.

The above points are helpful in understanding how one study found that commercials for candidates in the 1972 election actually contained more useful information regarding a candidate's position on various issues than did the news coverage of those candidates (Patterson and McClure 1976; Patterson 1980). Indeed, these researchers, in their study of viewers' perceptions of news and commercial information, discovered that viewers received more of an awareness of the candidate's views from commercials. One reason for the relative ineffectiveness of newscasts, these authors report, was the disproportionate amount of time (coverage) given to campaign activity (a network average of approximately 130 minutes) compared to the coverage of a candidate's leadership qualifications (an average of about 15 minutes per network), and the candidates' stands on certain issues (an average of about 35 minutes per network).

Formats Across the Media

The logic of media work promotes the use of particular formats, which in turn can help generate formats in other media. Further, the media–format relationship is not a static one, but is subject to considerable interaction. A good example is the way television programming has adopted the "magazine format" in programs such as "60 Minutes" and, more recently, "People." The latter, like the magazine, lumps together personalities already familiar to audiences via television and other media. For example, the opening of the October 16, 1978 program included the following:

> And later on in the show, we have a look at baseball's most controversial character, Reggie Jackson, a superstar who hits like a champion and talks like one too, and in true Reggie form you'll see and hear him shooting his mouth off, and Leif Garrett, the 16-year-old-teenage heartthrob who gave Kristy McNichol her first TV kiss on "Family." It seems everywhere Leif goes he draws hundreds of girls who would give anything to switch places with Kristy, and get ready to laugh at the hottest comic in America, Steve Martin, he's nutty, he's zany, he's Steve Martin, and coming up in a moment, you'll see me go through an exhausting day in a health spa, stretching, flexing, weaving.

As could be expected from our earlier comments about the impact of format on content, the ensuing interviews and film clips with each of these persons emphasized their "private–public" dimensions as a common bond of media personality was established. Such promotion has its merits for the careers of the people involved and it provides the programming departments of the related networks with more media-related material to give their audiences something they already know about and will be comfortable with. But it would be a mistake if the viewing audience felt that what was being portrayed was "really in-depth," "unrehearsed," and a good indication of the "real person." (Of course, in some cases the personalities actually start believing their media image, even to the point of referring to themselves in the third person.) The portrayal is for entertainment, as a way of "involving" the audience in a scenario of "let's pretend this public and contrived inter-view is really spontaneous and revealing." Thus we feel we have a window on the action of the "real people" when, in fact, all we have in a peek at the ordering of media logic.

Image Experts

The use of media machinery and techniques to facilitate better com-munication and information dispersion has rapidly evolved from primarily a *means* to involve more people in the nature of issues, decision-making, and the like, to something far different. The logic, techniques, and machinery of mass media are now widely used to con-vince the potential voters—and at other times all citizens—that certain individuals and programs are preferable to others. Jules Witcover (1977:15) observes:

> Still, for most Americans, watching the campaign's climax on television was merely a continuation of what had gone before. The campaigners often lost sight of this fact, but for the great majority of voters, the presidential campaign was what they saw on television. . . . That had been the case at least since the election of John F. Kennedy in 1960, but it was particularly so in 1976 for one important reason: Carter and Ford were the first to run under the new campaign finance law that channeled the presidential campaign into the television studio and America's living rooms as never before, and off the streets of the nation.

We are not simply referring to campaign strategies, but to widespread image-making that, through the technology and logic of the mass media, can fundamentally alter visual and auditory signals in a highly deceiving manner. Moreover, virtually all candidates, in altering their images, begin to look remarkably like one another. But how they are competing is increasingly geared to media logic; indeed, this logic has fundamen-tally overtaken political life.

A complete history of political image-making has not yet been written, mainly because the sophistication of technology and expertise is still ascending (cf. Hart 1987). But Dan Nimmo's (1976) overview of political packaging illustrates the rise of this new art form. The 1950s marked the introduction of fully orchestrated image-making. Eisenhower, the candidate, was presented on television as "up front" and would respond to an unseen interrogator. The 1960s saw a slight change, as still photos of candidates were used and then discussed by a narrator. Thirty-minute documentaries were shown of the candidate's style and qualities advantageous to him. Also developed during this decade was the staged spontaneous exchange between a candidate and a panel of "average" citizens. Strategies were also used to capture news coverage. The early 1970s saw little change, although the techniques had been perfected, but during the 1972 presidential campaign 60- and 30-second spots showed candidates in work situations with rolled up sleeves, walking the streets talking to people, in committee meetings, and so on. Also used were 5-minute televised interviews with candidates addressing issues or responding to questions from interrogators who were dressed to resemble journalists, as well as film clips that would be sent to the news media mostly of "pseudo-events"—episodes and activities that were staged for publicity purposes (Boorstin 1961). The hype grew even bigger by 1976.

> It could be said, indeed, that by 1976 television had very nearly crowded out the old-style meet-the-people campaigning, or at the very least had intruded itself so completely as to have destroyed its naturalness. Crowds at an airport fence often worked as hard to capture the eye or hand of a well-known television reporter, or to be filmed by his cameraman, as they did to shake hands with or catch a glimpse of the candidate. . . . In this scheme of things, it was not together [sic] inappropriate that Election Night in America should have become in some ways the greatest media event of them all. (Witcover 1977:17)

The work of image makers such as Tony Schwartz, Gerald Rafshoon, David Garth, and Roger Ailes (to name a few of the more prominent people) is not merely good public relations, but packaging images that, according to various formulas, are intended to win elections. According to Tony Schwartz (1974), the basic idea is to create an image that strikes a "responsive chord" in the viewer; you do not want to convey detailed information regarding complex issues, but hit them quick even when they are not aware they are being hit. Good "spots," according to "media experts," may not even be initially recognized as commercials. Through sophisticated production techniques, and the use of opinion polls that define the "safe" and "volatile" issues in certain districts, messages can be put together to associate—indeed embody—the candidate with problems and perspectives already familiar and perhaps important to the voter. In this sense, according to Schwartz, the audience is packaged to make an association between their concerns and beliefs and the person who can speak to them. A current image giant is David Garth, of whom Anson (1978:25) has written:

Win or lose, at the center of Garth's technique are his commercials. The
look of a Garth spot is unmistakable: 30 or 60 seconds of videotape
("Film," explains one of his producers, "is more dramatic, but not sufficiently immediate. We're after reality"); a candidate standing against some
suitable backdrop, talking directly to the camera, or, alternately, a series of
people describing how a candidate helped them; a touch of voice-over; fact
after fact supered in the lower third of the screen; and, at the close, a
complicated tag line. . . . No music, no flash, no bouncing babies or walks
on the beach, just simple, direct, and as Garth would have you believe,
honest.

While Garth's ideas about ads are now "state of the art," and particularly his emphasis on employing Schwartz's notion of the "responsive
chord," what is crucial for our purposes is the format of emotionality.
Roger Ailes (1988) has taken the logic of ads and transformed it into
interpersonal communication, press conferences, and even presidential
debates. His work is one of the most direct statements that shows how
the media logic of TV, and particularly, with ads, has infused spoken
public discourse.

My experience is that you can improve your voice more by working on
emotional expression than on mechanical skills. (p. 37, italics added).

People who are the best communicators communicate with their whole
being. They're animated, expressive, interesting to watch—just as they
should be on television. Once you recognize these changes in communications techniques brought about by television, you can take some of the
basics of video age communication and transfer them to a meeting in your
office, a business negotiation, or a sale to your client. (p. 36)

To reiterate a dominant theme in this work, media logic has transformed discourse from one mode to another. Ads and commercials are
now the most significant formats, especially regarding time, rhythm, and
tempo, of mass media communication. Just as we note above that commercials sought to strike a responsive chord from the audience, presidential advisors also try to use their candidates and "public discussion"
opportunities, such as "presidential debates" to present a commercial-
type of message. They do not want their candidate to go into details;
they are irrelevant for effect. They want their candidate to strike the
"responsive chord," to tell the people what they already know (or think
they know). One of the best at this, Roger Ailes (1988:17–18), explained
how he coached President Reagan just before the second debate of the
1984 campaign:

"Mr. President," I said, "there are five strategies you can choose from. You
can attack, defend, counterattack, sell, or ignore. You've picked defense,
which is the weakest possible position. If you do that you'll lose again . . .
You didn't get elected on details. You got elected on *themes*. Every time a

question is asked, relate it to one of your themes. You know enough facts, and it's too late to learn new ones now, anyway." (italics added)

Although the messages cannot have an overriding effect on changing people's minds about what or who to vote for, and, at least as currently constituted, can do little in a few minutes to inform people—and indeed, change their views—about issues, there is reason to believe that the style of politics has been affected and that distinctions between style and substance increasingly are becoming cloudy, especially at the public level, where the mass media can be found and which is the source of public information (Seymour-Ure 1974; Kern 1989).

As we argue in some detail in the next chapter, politicians are increasingly sensitive to media perceptions of actions, and often take those actions largely on the basis of what they feel it will do for their media images and what effect it may have on opinion polls. Polls are particularly crucial when a president's "popularity" is widely reported to have "dipped" and generally a flurry of media-inspired events are required to "pull it up." Presidents Kennedy, Johnson, Nixon, and Carter (the hostage rescue attempt), and Reagan did this, each with more skill and daring than the predecessor.

During the 1988 campaign between Democrat Michael Dukakis and Republican Vice President George Bush, a number of references were made during the "debates" and press conferences about media managers, image experts, and managers who attempt to scalp the human candidates into persona (including their hair!), caricatures that are imitations of a perfect image. During one discussion on the ABC TV show, "Nightline" late (10/17/88) (which originated with coverage of the Iranian hostage situation) in the 1988 presidential campaign, former Presidential candidates Jesse Jackson and Barry Goldwater agreed on the style being imposed by current news formats. Stated Jackson, "TV has been used in this campaign more as a shield and as a prop than as a medium of communication." And, "Dukakis [should] begin to have daily press conferences and not depend on network news to give him 30 second sound bites." In reflecting on the changing style of political campaigning as contrived anticipation of the audience's action, former Republican Presidential candidate said (on television, of course!): "candidates . . . don't listen to their own instincts," and he advised future politicians to tell "Madison Avenue" to take a hike.

The debates are an opportunity for journalists and audience members who admire or aspire to act like journalists to use these messages for their own purposes. An overriding concern of news organizations, of course, is who won or lost the various debates. As noted in previous work (Altheide 1976), the issues are not important unless they make a "mistake" by stumbling on an issue or some relevant fact; it is performance that counts, including delivery, humor, and how easily the discourse is translated into game-like metaphors.

We will not scream out to the reader that presidential debates do not serve the voters, because we assume that more and more people know this. But what is not so widely known is that the debates serve the news organizations, especially TV. There are several reasons for this. First, the TV format captures the debates; technology, organization, scheduling, and presentation all take place along the lines dictated by TV formats and media logic. This is true of the makeup the candidates wear, it is true of the audience—which is only a prop for the television audience, and it is true of the questioning and flow of dialogue. This becomes even more apparent when the panel members who ask the questions act in such a way as to negate the staging of a contrived event; they do this in order to play their parts effectively as journalists imitating journalists. What journalist—a real, genuine, non-role-playing journalist—would ask a presidential candidate during such a debate if he would be angry and upset if someone raped his wife and killed her? This actually happened during one debate. This bizarre query was justified on the basis that the candidate (Dukakis) was opposed to capital punishment! The point is that the journalists are celebrated on such a forum and they take every opportunity to present a provocative self for their national audiences, as well as their producers and executives who are in charge of their careers.

The debates serve TV news in another way as well. They provide an opportunity for local news organizations to develop a "local angle" by using various ploys to get audience reactions. This would work fine, except that the audience members are also knowledgeable of the TV news formats and particularly reportage styles, and tend to act like reporters. A Republican supporter who was found in a Phoenix bar gave this edited reply to the debate. "It takes that man [Bush] a while to get warmed up, and if you noticed, once he got going, he was in there." A Dukakis supporter (who was also quite active politically) contributed this to the quality of air in Phoenix: "He's sure of himself. He had a lot of convincing facts and his philosophy, I think, came through very well." Great sound bites.

The Nixon administration revealed that the pre? and other significant audiences had become disgruntled and outright resentful of popularity-restoring actions (Oudes 1986). Although the reasons for this are varied and analysts do not agree on all of the factors, it is clear that one contributor to the disenchantment with the Nixon public relations, media-inspired pseudoevents was the use to which they were put, as well as Nixon's refusal to permit the journalists and others to dictate to them how and when he should use the media, including news. Bonafede's (1978:66) analysis also suggests this:

Nixon, of course, corrupted the public relations resources at his command. Nonetheless, in this age of the ubiquitous eye of television, subliminal advertising, human merchandising, sophisticated image-making and scientific public opinion polling, it is understandable that our presidents should view public relations as a theatrical panacea. Hokum and hucksterism have been integrated as a part of the presidential establishment. Consequently, it is difficult to determine where shadow fuses with substance. Perception becomes reality in the hands of political cosmeticians.

A corroborative statement is offered by Nixon's own hand in a memo he sent to H. R. Haldeman on December 1, 1969:

> I think last week illustrated my point that we need a part- or full-time TV man on our staff for the purpose of seeing that my TV appearances are handled on a professional basis. When I think of the millions of dollars that go into one lousy 30-second television spot advertising a deodorant, it seems to me unbelievable that we don't do a better job in seeing that Presidential appearances [on TV] always have the very best professional advice . . .
>
> My point is that [my TV shots] should always be absolutely top-rate in every respect, and I should spend at least five or ten minutes with whoever is the TV producer to get his suggestions as to how I should stand, where the cameras will be, etc. . . . .
>
> As a matter of fact, the advice for the two-minute shot is probably more important than for the 30-minute appearance. Over a period of 30 minutes the audience will forget the technical difficulties if the subject is engrossing enough. In 2 minutes, the impression of the picture is fleeting but indelible." (Oudes 1989, quoted in *CJR* May/June, 1989:46).

But none of the past presidents measures up to the new standards of media-politics that produced and were refined by President Carter, and his successor, President Reagan. First, consider Carter. Former Johnson aide George Reedy observes that although Kennedy is credited with being the first television president to make speeches on TV, Carter did much more:

> Carter communicates over television with symbols. They are complicated—the sweater and the walk down Pennsylvania Avenue. He is a man of the television age, who does it naturally. It is not a stunt—Lyndon Johnson did stunts. Carter has made a reality out of Marshall McLuhan's theory that the medium is the message. He uses symbols which convey substantive messages. (Bonafede 1978:67)

The use of media-inspired—if not media-directed—events does not stop when a president is elected to office, but continues throughout; keeping his position is difficult, especially if his opponents are using their own media ammunition to poke holes in a particular hype. Indeed, they may even call it a hype and a public relations stunt, all the time making it difficult for the accused to counterattack with the charge that the opposition is simply using their own hype! So success constantly must be publicly engineered, which often means proposing bizarre and/or even very risky political moves. Carter's promise to the North Carolina tobacco growers that the tobacco industry and government can work together to make America healthier is an example of the bizarre (Arizona *Republic*, UPI, August 6, 1978):

> As I am deeply interested in the small farmers of this nation, as I am deeply and permanently committed to a fine tobacco-loan program, obviously I am also interested in the health of America. . . . I don't see any incompatibility.

His pursuit of a Mideast settlement on television, using the classical talk-show format featuring Barbara Walters as "host" and Sadat and Begin as "guests," not only fell flat—at least initially—but led some analysts to observe that putting things in the media light, especially in a quasi-talk-show format, can produce unrealistic expectations among the citizens of the respective countries, and each leader's subordinate but still influential respective legislative bodies, as well as among other countries that are likely to be involved. The great potential problem is acting as though things are worked out, when in fact the most significant "details" still loom quite large. If immediate progress does not occur, then the journalists and others will begin speaking of failure, stalemate, and other images of gloom. Could this then lead to more impatience, higher demands, and even charges of bad faith, scheming, or—in the extreme case—the suggestion that it was merely a tactic in a long-term struggle of one-upmanship? Possibly. As one observer writes:

> Many observers felt that the series of spectaculars staged by Sadat and Begin had raised public expectations to a dangerous level, and to a degree, the two leaders themselves appeared to have let their expectations of success get out of hand. . . . While President Carter's remarks Wednesday—in which he tilted markedly toward Begin's insistence on no Palestinian statehood and the continued presence of Israeli troops on the West Bank—did not give a boost to the process of mutual political support begun by Sadat and Begin, it did not kill it either. In fact, the *only genuinely harmful effects of the Carter statement were to tarnish the American image as an impartial arbiter and, regrettably, to push the Middle East issue back on to the media stage, however briefly.* . . . The two sides will carry on their argument quietly and patiently and mostly out of the public limelight until there is real progress to report on the basic issues. (Schanche 1978, italics added)

The prophetic force of this cautionary note was apparent when talks stalled over "major issues," but the lessons about media politics involving real and brutal differences apparently were not well learned, because by October 1978, a meeting between Carter, Sadat, and Begin at Camp

David was concluded with historical handshaking and reaffirmed commitments to achieve a peace settlement within one month of that date. Weeks passed and little progress was made, and by February 1979, both sides were "publicly" (that is, over the respective media) expressing disappointment with the willingness of the other side to make concessions. Finally, it took President Carter's symbolic show of force—a personal trip to the Mideast—to get the parties together. There was never any question that Carter was desperate for a treaty, since the American media had previously played up the scenario enacted at Camp David; Carter would have a treaty because to fail in this endeavor would be defined as a "major failure," something Carter's already badly tarnished media presidency could ill afford. The treaty finally came. In 1979 we wrote,

> Whether "peace" will follow is less certain, since the main "stars" will have to continue to operate on a stage of conflict and historical hatreds not entirely amenable to TV logic.

The significance of that statement for media logic would echo several months later when 52 American hostages were held for 444 days by Iranian students and supporters of the Ayatollah Khomeini (Chapter 6). Elsewhere, Altheide (1985a) has provided extensive documentation to date of the mass media coverage and its significance for Carter's presidency, U.S. foreign policy, and an image of a weakened America, which candidate Reagan promised to restore. The media continued to play a role for Carter's candidacy as media logic infused the hostage deliberations and virtually brought to a stand-still other pressing issues. Indeed, one of Carter's advisors, the late Arnold Raphel, wrote in a subsequent report that an abortive hostage rescue attempt that resulted in the loss of eight American lives could be partially attributed to the press of mass media coverage and formats. The hostages were released on Carter's final day in office, as Reagan won the 1980 and then 1984 elections by overwhelming majorities. Media logic was dominant.

Conclusion

Political life has been recast to fit the demands of major media. The logic of formats that has grown out of the organizational side of media work has greatly informed political styles and, in some cases, issues, and even outcomes. Candidates now orchestrate statements and activities in order to obtain news coverage, and to appear on shows like "Nightline." No longer can these media be said to either mirror or simply transmit messages; and it is not enough to say that the work of media merely "distorts" these messages. Rather, the logic and procedures of media work have been adopted by politicians and other who must "make points" (opinion polls as well as ratings). In this sense, we have witnessed a fundamental change of political content, organization, and style. The criteria of media success are now inextricably joined with success in public life. For good or ill, the last several decades have witnessed the engulfment of one institution by another. They share communication formats.

The media formats powered by their own logic have become increasingly adapted by all parties to the communication process. As noted in the previous chapter on news, the studies of news and social control and especially news sources of Richard Ericson's et al. (1987, 1989) make it quite clear that traditional sources for news organizations, e.g., government agencies and bureaucracies, have adjusted to news formats and now time and frame their messages, intentions, and vocabularies within these guidelines. Politics has also continued to incorporate new themes and formats, including the way journalists now attack political coverage.

5

Media Politics II:
The Bert Lance Case and Beyond

Character and legitimacy are constituted in public life through the news media. The mass media formats construct the criteria, procedures, and discourse for the definition, recognition, organization, and presentation of moral character. It is noteworthy that in our era when virtually every president over the last 50 years has played a leading role in the slaughter of thousands of human beings that the idea of character and personal morality has emerged in political life. What does character and integrity look like? Who will chronicle it, point to its shortcomings, and how will this be played out in the mass mediated theater? We present the first major post-Watergate "morality play," the Bert Lance story, to illustrate how political decision-making has been shaped during the last 20 years, and to suggest where it will take us into the next century. One thing to us is clear: no serious student of American culture and especially the mass media's impact on social life can neglect the impact of the Bert Lance case on emerging news–political–morality–control issues.

Character and legitimacy. Some people have it and some people do not. Thomas Eagleton learned about it in 1972 (Altheide 1976, 1977). Bert Lance, who we will come to know in some detail, learned about it in 1976. Jimmy Carter, who fired Lance, felt it in 1980. The entire Democratic Party bore witness in 1984—when party regulars rejected Lance as Chairman, and 1988 added Gary Hart and Joseph Bidden who were sacrificed to the legitimation of political reporting. Gary Hart's philandering was documented, while Joseph Biden's speeches were found to contain "plagiarized excerpts" from statements made by a member of the British parliament. They all were on the wrong end of news themes, and, in particular, the significance of "character."

Oliver North, on the other hand, had gobs of mass-mediated character. All he did was coordinate the illegal laundering and transport of funds to provide arms and other support for the "contras" who opposed the elected government of Nicaragua. He also traded arms with Iran for

American hostages (not "Carter's hostages," but later ones). He appeared before a congressional committee, candidly admitted that he had lied to Congress, had destroyed official documents and other evidence, and had knowingly conspired to provide firepower that subsequently contributed to the slaying of thousands of people. He explained that he did it for a higher good, to stop communist aggression. He did it because his commander-in-chief, Ronald Reagan, did not like the government of Nicaragua and believed that the "contras" would be better for U.S. interests. But most importantly, for our purposes, he told about it in his Marine uniform, with medals, with his wife beside him, and with stacks of telegrams in camera frame. This is character in a media age. Some people have it and others do not. How is this done?

The roles of the news media as intermediaries between an event and its presentation, as well as the constitutive role of these media in shaping the events themselves have been noted above. Just as presidential politics increasingly reflects the logic of media work and thereby becomes but an extension of media programming, so too does the public treatment of daily governmental affairs. It is useful to conceive of the public political process as a kind of believable soap opera in which the ambiguities of decision-making, inherent conflicts, and the mundane realities of daily political life—as well as the contexts in which all politicians are enmeshed—become obfuscated in favor of making clear-cut distinctions between right and wrong, good and bad, and real and unreal. Stated differently, the logic of political life as presented in the public arena—the arena controlled and defined by the mass media—can be conceived as a literal dramatic presentation where the actors do not need a "director"; instead, they know the essentials of presentation of self and substance. But unlike "real plays," the drama of politics in the age of the mass media, particularly television, has real-life consequences; elections may be lost, policy can be affected, wars can be waged, and individual lives and careers can be ruined. In this sense the fictive and practical organizing principles, techniques, and logic of media work not only have pervaded big-time politics, but actually have transformed the political process and, in so doing, have further obliterated the line between reality and fantasy. The reality of TV has become the practical reality of politics. Those participants in politics as a vocation must be skilled as actors and critics; they also must be apprised of the different perspectives and interests of the various audiences to whom a particular scene is presented. Thus, it is not just the "mass audience" that matters, but also the special audiences, such as a Senate committee, who are likely to regard a particular performance as having consequences for their own activities (Altheide and Johnson 1980). In this sense, then, there are multiple audiences, and within the logic of media culture winning with some—such as the "mass audience—does not necessarily guarantee success with all. Indeed, the largest audience may not be the most powerful; rather, the audience that controls legitimacy and that can cause the most trouble is the one that counts. In the case of elections the mass audience prevails, so certain tactics will be employed. But in other goal-seeking endeavors—for example, surviving politically or getting programs through Congress—the key power wielders may be a handful of men and women.

What the power brokers often consider are not just the "facts," but how the media coverage looks (Dunn 1969). Indeed, some of the masters of controlled imagery worked in the Reagan administration. As chief of staff Michael Deaver explained:

> The majority of the people get their news from television, so you have to pay attention to them. You're aware of how we construct events and craft photos that are designed for 30 seconds to a minute so that it can fit into that "bite" on the evening news. We'd be crazy if we didn't think in those terms. (*Washington Journalism Review* 1984, 6 April, pp. 23–25)

He reiterated this point four years later, but with more detail about scheduling. "The only day I worried about was Friday, because it's a slow news day. That was the day that bothered me most, because if you didn't have anything, they'd go out and find someting" (*Mesa Tribune*, 10/2/88). The charge of Deaver and his colleagues, Richard Darman and David Gergen, was to develop news stories and angles, always anticipating their planning of an event with the query, "what will be headlines be about this?" This is media logic.

It has become common for members of government to communicate with each other through the mass media; the media become a kind of community bulletin board with specialized messages. The increasingly important role of the news media as a significant audience in its own right is best understood by looking at specific case studies to note the relationships between certain events, individuals, institutions, and the media.[1]

The following analysis of the media's impact on political life focuses on the coverage of the Bert Lance case in 1977. We include it in this revision of the book because it illustrates the process, thinking, and perceptions of a congressional committee, that is itself media oriented, it illustrates the impact of mass mediation on challenging character and legitimacy, and it became the working model for mass communication operatives and perspectives to cover future events and issues.

Even though Lance was never found guilty of anything illegal, he became "damaged goods" and would continue to be encapsulated within major media themes as "improper" and "not above reproach" by the media perspectives, which not only cover national politics, but which actually constitute the public awareness of leaders, political processes, and issues. All charges were eventually dropped against Lance, but his media stigma played a role in his future efforts to help the democratic party. (We would have included the entire case study of the Oliver North case, but it continues to unfold at this time.)

Transcripts of the hearings before the Senate Committee on Governmental Affairs (SCGA),[2] along with televised broadcasts of the hearings and conversations with some journalists who covered the story, provided the data on the issues as they were presented and discussed. In addition to viewing newscasts on all three networks during the key period between September 1 and September 22, 1977, transcripts of all TV coverage by CBS of the hearings were obtained, and incomplete transcripts were obtained from ABC. Newspaper reports and news magazine coverage of what came to be known as the "Lance Affair" were also used in the analysis.

Contrasting what was actually said in the hearings with the media coverage and overall treatment provides an opportunity to further examine the logic of media decision-making, technique, and emphasis.

The thousands of pages of news reports and SCGA transcripts about the Lance hearings make this issue a prime candidate with which to investigate and illustrate the logic of newswork and show its impact on modern political life. In setting forth the logic of newswork as a unique way of looking at events in order to treat them within certain practical and organizational parameters, we do not intend to avoid the other spheres of activity that influence the events before they became enmeshed in the news process. Rather, we seek to clarify how newswork is an activity in its own right, with its own rules and standards of competence. Further, business—especially banking activities—as well as highly politicized investigative committees such as the SCGA also have their priorities and practical concerns. However, when an event is taken out of one context and placed into another and viewed from that standpoint, certain distortions may occur. We believe that as newswork increasingly has come to stand on its own as a way of treating events, it has become dissociated from the plethora of realms of activity and contexts of meaning that have their own priorities and rules. Our task, then, is to illustrate the nature and significance of the news perspective as *a major definer of reality* by contrasting coverage of the Bert Lance case with certain details of that case as it related to actual banking procedures and norms, as well as the typical manner in which the SCGA operated and how it was influenced and shaped by the news coverage.

In sum, we aim to (1) clarify the logic of the news perspective and show how it is part of an occupational and organizational orientation,

(2) show how the Bert Lance case was presented, distorted, and influenced by news coverage enmeshed in this logic and its now very powerful context of meaning, and (3) compare briefly this case with some more recent political dramas in order to enrich our expanded understanding of the role of media formats in political outcomes.

The Lance Case

Bert Lance, a Georgia banker and former candidate for governor of the state of Georgia, was appointed to head the Office of Management and the Budget (OMB) by newly elected President Carter in November 1976. His appointment was confirmed by the SCGA during hearings held on January 17 and 18, 1977. During these hearings many facets of Mr. Lance's financial background were discussed, including campaign indebtedness for his 1974 gubernatorial attempt, personal bank overdrafts, and correspondent banking relationships with other banks. Also, as former president of the National Bank of Georgia, Mr. Lance owned stock that he pledged to sell by December 31, 1977. A related pledge was that in his position as head of OMB he would refrain from acting on banking policy matters that could affect the nature of banking practices and especially—or so it was implied—influence the financial gains of his own stock.

Mr. Lance assumed his duties as director of OMB and continued to serve uneventfully until July 11, 1977. At this time President Carter wrote a letter to Senator Ribicoff, chairman of the SCGA, explaining that the pressure on Lance to sell his stock by a certain date had contributed to a bad market situation, which would mean the loss of a significant income for Mr. Lance (estimated at $1.5 million) as well as financial hardship for other stockholders. Carter requested that Lance's obligation to sell the stock by December be lifted and that the future of the stock be left in the hands of a trustee.

The SCGA was to meet in July to discuss extending the deadline for selling the stock. Meanwhile, on June 28, Lance sent Senator Proxmire, chairman of the Banking, Housing, and Urban Affairs Committee, a letter indicating that the Carter administration disapproved the "Community Reinvestment Act of 1977," a measure designed to increase credit in inner-city areas. This measure would have a direct bearing on the banking industry by requiring it, in Lance's words, "to make difficult judgments using vague and subjective criteria" (Hearings 1977:2, 15). Of course, other objections were cited, but the significant point is that Proxmire, who had been the only one to vote against Lance's confirmation via the Senate Banking Committee, interpreted this negative reply as a violation of Lance's pledge to remain uninvolved in banking-related issues. In a letter dated June 30, 1977—just two days after receiving Lance's negative comment—Proxmire urged Senator Ribicoff to direct his committee to "investigate this violation and obtain assurances that it will not happen again." And in another letter to Ribicoff dated July 14, Proxmire wrote, "I hope the Committee will insist not only in his promise but satisfy itself that in the future the procedures will in fact insulate Mr. Lance from banking decisions" (Hearings 1977:2, 16).

This last letter was especially timely, since the second round of hearings was scheduled to start the next day (July 15) and would continue, following an interruption, on July 25. Moreover, the letter, along with several news reports—particularly one in *Newsweek* magazine—about Lance's indebtedness revived some old questions about Lance's finances. Thus the charge by Proxmire that Lance had violated an agreement, the other claims about Lance's indebtedness, and allusions to financial wheeling and dealing provided committee members with ample opportunity to ask further questions about the man who had been running the OMB for six months.

The role of the committee was never really clear, since it could not "unconfirm," yet several members, particularly Senator Ribicoff and Percy, pursued the matter with a vengeance. All the materials studied leave little doubt that their aim was to bring pressure to bear on the Cater administration to have Lance resign in order to, as Percy often put it, "defend himself against these charges." Meanwhile, between July 15 and July 25 numerous press reports regarding apparent irregularities in Lance's financial negotiations were raised, as were questions about the amount of information the SCGA initially possessed when confirming Lance as director of OMB in January.

The role of the press began to take on paramount importance since the committee learned a great deal about Lance, and even though most claims were called "allegations," the committee felt no qualms about checking them all out (something that later events would show the committee staff had done previously). The overall aim throughout these hearings and the meetings that followed in September was to enable committee members to present their competence and sense of justice to the American people. For example, Senator Percy's opening statement on July 15 stressed that

> we have to be extraordinarily careful to have no appearance of conflict of interest, because of your very close relationship with the President, or the appearance that somehow a special case has been made for you and that we are letting standards down. (Hearings 1977:2, 7)

Senator Percy's presentation of the committee as a guardian of public decency is a specific case of congressional use of investigative committees to promote their own competence to the news media and the mass audience. One reason this trend developed was because the "executive" tended to monopolize all the coverage. These points were made 30 years ago by Francis Rourke (1961:128–130):

> The recent upsurge in congressional investigations primarily reflects an attempt on the part of the legislature to restore a balance of power in the area of publicity. No aspect of congressional activity other than investigations is as capable of attracting the attention of the public and of the communications facilities that both direct and reflect public interest. Investigations are a form of entertainment. . . . While acting as auxiliary and *ad hoc* instruments of law enforcement, legislative committees have no power to impose punitive legal sanctions, except for a refusal to answer questions. Nevertheless, their direct power to punish is considerable. The core of this power is the ability of a committee to inflict the penalty of adverse publicity upon those called before it.

This broad context of competition for communication pervaded the Lance affair for reasons that will be dealt with below.

When the hearings continued on July 25, numerous news stories reified and further supported the claims of truth by others who had charged Lance with improprieties. Moreover, the committee relied on the press to direct their questioning and focus. Senator Ribicoff in his opening remarks said:

> I have read in the press and I was given to understand that I was to receive a telegram from Mr. Mitchell in Atlanta concerning the prospective sale of the Lance stock. . . . (Western Union) have no evidence of this telegram . . . although news accounts indicate that there is such a telegram.

> Mr. Lance, we are here to give you an opportunity to respond to allegations reported in the press within the last week concerning your financial activities and those of the National Bank of Georgia. . . . [Following this] I will ask you a series of specific questions based upon the allegations printed in the *New York Times* and the *Washington Post* last week. (Hearings 1977:2, 49)

In addition to using the hearings to promote the image that the committee members were doing their jobs, the hearings also permitted the members to be sensitive to the "public" and to act as though their actions were largely determined by it. As Delmer D. Dunn (1969:167) observed of officials, "They equate press reaction with public reaction . . . and then equate press interest with public interest." Senator Roth's comment on July 15 illustrates a common sentiment that was expressed repeatedly throughout the Lance case:

> Mr. Lance, I am not interested in seeing you suffer a significant loss, or the other investors in the bank, but my concern basically is what this does to public confidence. (Hearings 1977:2, 22)

Later, however, Senator Roth noted that it is often difficult to avoid the "appearance of conflict of interest," given the complexities of some members of the public and especially the press.

> But it does bother me, when we are saying to thousands and thousands of civil servants, due to no action on their part, who are being put in a position that could result in substantial losses to their family, that in today's world, you really cannot get anybody, because we are so interrelated, that there cannot be some appearance of conflict of interest. . . . We are going to get less trust, rather than more, because we are having artificial situations created, and then when you reach the realities, changes have to be made. (Hearings 1977:2, 22)

Senator Nunn also realized the absurdity of expecting anyone involved in managing the budget to remain uninvolved in economic and/or banking policy. "How can we remove a man who is head of the Office of Management and Budget for having economic discussions?" (Hearings 1977:2,29). In responding to Senator Percy's point about avoiding "the appearance of the conflict of interest on his personal financial situation," Senator Nunn commented:

> I do not think it is possible. I do not think it is possible for anybody in the U.S. Senate that votes on economic policy, to not affect his own economic position, no matter what his interest is in. (Hearings 1977:2, 29)

And Senator Glenn concurred that being extremely sensitive to conflicts of interest can be counterproductive:

> I have voted in favor of every bit of ethics legislation we have had. It is concentrated primarily in keeping an openness of background, openness of record. However, I think we have gone completely ethics happy around this place. I think we have gone crazy on it in some respects, because we are driving good people out of government. . . . I have to agree with Senator Nunn, we are beginning to reach a point where cash only is acceptable, and then you will have to keep it at home, you cannot put it in banks, we regulate banks. (Hearings 1977:2, 32)

As these statements indicate, the committee began to focus not just on the two "commitments" Lance had made during his January confirmation, but also on his overall financial situation. We will see below that one reason for this emphasis was the way the news media delved into bits and pieces of it and therefore created further allegations about Lance's banking practices. However, at this point we want to stress that Lance's debt situation was originally a minor issue and only later became a major one, largely due to newswork. Senator Percy's opening statement on July 15 puts Lance's debt situation in the context of big business:

I have heard criticism of your incurring a great deal of debt to buy stock. Well, if you are criticized for that, I should also have been criticized throughout most of my life, because there is no way that a person without means can acquire an interest in a business that he is managing and working in without incurring debt. . . . I had to go through the same thought process you did for 20 years. I was highly in debt. The measure of success was a larger debt every year, not smaller. (Hearings 1977:2, 7)

Nevertheless, a few minutes later, Senator Ribicoff again stressed Lance's debts, an issue that would continue to be raised.

And I think a clear review of all your debt situation, is more important than the bank situation. If that could be cleared up, I do not see why this matter cannot be resolved. (Hearings 1977:2, 32)

But the matter was not resolved, especially since "allegations" about Lance's past financial practices kept appearing in the news media.

A third set of hearings was held in September to further investigate charges against Lance, including how fully he had cooperated with the committee on its initial confirmation hearing in January. Of particular importance was a report filed after the July hearing by the Comptroller of the Currency. This report dealt with unpublished appraisals of Mr. Lance's banking practices.

Senator Percy set the tone of the hearings in his opening remarks on September 8:

This committee is faced with the unquestioned responsibility to examine all allegations confronting Mr. Lance as well as implicated governmental agencies and private institutions. . . . The central issue . . . is whether Mr. Lance was qualified to be nominated to and is qualified to hold the high office of Director of the Office of Management and Budget. The door to nomination and confirmation for high public office swings both ways. Our judgment in that process is based on the expectation that wholly acceptable personal and professional values and practices, consistently evidence in private life, will serve as the touchstone for guiding a person in meeting his public duties. . . . This committee must weigh the available facts which have come to light regarding Mr. Lance in order to determine, on balance, whether the committee should recommend to the President that Mr. Lance be removed as Director of OMB. (Hearings 1977:4, 1–2)

After noting that the report of the Comptroller of the Currency raised serious questions about whether correspondent banking relationships involving Lance had benefited his ability to acquire personal loans, and that his prior banking practices were "unsound," Senator Percy called for his resignation.

In calling for Mr. Lance to step aside or resign, I would like to make it clear from my standpoint that coupled with that statement was the state-

ment that I was not prejudging the case and the presumption was one
of innocence. I was taking into account the defense of his own personal
reputation the time that will take, and for that reason Senator Ribicoff and
I called for action, and I hoped Mr. Lance would have responded. (Hearings 1977:4, 2)

But Bert Lance did not resign, although he was constantly asked if he
would do so—even *told* he should do so—by members of the press. That
is, he did not resign until he, along with President Carter, felt the full
power of the news media in defining an unworkable situation. The third
round of hearings continued until September 19, including three days
of testimony by Bert Lance and questioning by SCGA members. Finally,
he resigned on September 21, 1978.

Our study of the entire series of events suggests that Lance resigned
due to enormous pressure generated from the mass media on President
Carter and his administration, as well as other elected and nonelected
government officials. Indeed, President Carter publicly affirmed his belief that Lance had adequately dealt with the allegations against him, but
still accepted his resignation:

He was given, this past weekend, a chance to answer thousands of questions that have been raised about him, unproven allegations that have been
raised against him, and he did it well. He told the truth. And I think he
proved that our system of government works, because when he was given
a chance to testify on his own behalf, he was able to clear his name. (Carter
Presidential Press Conference September 21, 1977:2)

The following pages will illustrate the role of the news media in the
Lance affair, noting the organizational and practical reasons for a particular orientation and the consequences it had. We will also point out how
the entire political process is now inextricably tied to the logic of media
work and has been transformed by it into an extension of media production. Three general contexts for the part played by the news media in
this case study will be dealt with: (1) the aftermath of Watergate, (2)
expanding ties between the mass media and government, and (3) news
values and the news production process.

The Aftermath of Watergate

Lance was a victim of a complex effort by certain government officials
and the news media to avoid another Watergate (cf. Harris 1974). We
are referring to the fear that many people shared about the impact of
"shady pasts" and withheld information on good, honest government.
Included in this rhetoric was the constant appeal by Carter during his

presidential campaign that a break with the past was necessary and that the old politics had to be put aside, including backroom deals and compromised integrity, and that only the most open administration could restore the American people's trust and faith in government. Carter's campaign, promising a change from the tactics of the Nixon administration, appealed to many people, especially since earlier mass media reports about the nature of the events of Watergate painted the picture that Nixon's was "the most corrupt administration in history" and implied that things were somehow done differently in Nixon's White House years than in those of any previous administration. Despite a good deal of historical evidence that the general approach of the Nixon staff did not fundamentally differ from previous presidential administrations—although certain specific tactics may have differed—the mass media painted a black picture of Nixon (Altheide 1976). This was achieved in several ways: (1) treating the events of Watergate as if they were all part of a "whole" rather than discrete events, (2) the immense coverage given the "cover-up" of Nixon and his aides about their own involvement, (3) the congratulatory conclusion to Watergate—Nixon's resignation—suggesting that bad people would be prevented from holding public office, and the related media coverage about the nature of Nixon's and his aides' lives outside of office, further indicating that they were "egomaniacs," "power hungry," and "nuts," and (4) Carter's campaign based on born-again Christianity, integrity, honesty, and the favorable coverage this received in contrast to Ford's former ties with the Nixon administration—including the infamous Nixon pardon (Nessen 1978).

With Carter's emphasis on being a "nonpolitician" and an alternative to Washington politicians came his promise to run an administration openly and honestly and to be unquestionably ethical and "beyond the appearance of impropriety." This point was finely honed by the news media's attention to detail in covering Lance, and it was constantly referred to by members of SCGA who also wanted to promote themselves as honest politicians and as individuals bent on avoiding another Watergate. For example, during the third Lance hearings on September 8, Senator Roth quoted President Carter:

> Like most Americans, I was taught that just staying narrowly within the law is not enough. Just staying within the law will never be enough for a Carter campaign or a Carter administration. . . . The Watergate tragedy . . . showed that concealment of a mistake or impropriety can be more serious in some instances than the impropriety itself. I think the main thing is a complete openness of any sort of relationship where a conflict of interest might be involved.

These are the words of our President. I agree with them, and so do the American people. I believe the question is whether or not these high standards are met in the case of Mr. Lance. (Hearings 1977:4, 3)

This question of "high standards" came to haunt Lance as the news media continued to hold up Carter's campaign rhetoric to careful scrutiny. News reports even gave committee members important information about Lance that was used during the various hearings. One example occurred on September 16, when Senator Roth questioned Bert Lance about a question that ABC reporter Sam Donaldson had asked President Carter:

Now, I would like to ask you again—on August 14, 1977, in an interview, Mr. Donaldson had this to say about the President in connection with you and your position.

Mr. Donaldson: "But I think you have a higher problem than perhaps past Presidents because you have a higher standard. The question is not illegality. As I understand it most of these investigations are not dealing on the question of illegality, but simply propriety of a man that might be able to do something that is common practice in the banking field and yet personally between, whereas the ordinary citizen, and you ran against people that didn't pay their fair share, wouldn't benefit. Now here is a question. Don't you have to hold Mr. Lance to that higher standard?"

The President: "Yes, I think so, and I believe that Bert would agree that a high standard has to be maintained."

Senator Roth then queried Lance:

Now, I would just like to ask you again, do you agree or disagree as the President has indicated. (Hearings 1977:4, 1014)

As Lance provided answers to these questions—some relating to matters that had occurred four years earlier—he was inevitably attacked as being "legalistic" rather than simply admitting that he had been unethical or perhaps even immoral. For example, on September 17, Senator Javits questioned Lance regarding his responsibility to fully inform the committee about certain financial and banking problems during the original hearing in January. Lance replied that he had told the committee what they wanted to know, emphasizing that the Comptroller of the Currency's report had not found any prosecutable violations regarding Lance's banking practices. Lance then added that although certain specific activities may appear atypical, when considered in the context of the South and small-town banks, plus the difficult economic conditions at the time of the presumed infraction of rules, what his bank did and what it was "held in agreement" to correct were really quite common. He noted that many banks were deficient by Comptroller of the Currency standards regarding classified loans (70 percent of sample banks), violations of law and regulations (55 percent), inadequate routines and controls (44 percent), overdue loans (35 percent), and more (Hearings 1977:4, 1127). He then continued:

> Over half of the frequently cited problems involve the banker's loan quality and credit procedures, and they go on about that, and then the final thing . . . it says:
>
> "Do examiners find the same problems in large and small banks? Problems varied among banks of different sizes. As shown below, problems related to the nature of the banks' business such as classified loans, classified asset and inadequate capital were more often cited for large banks than small. The problems most often cited for small banks were generally related to policies and procedures. (Hearings 1977:4, 1128)

Following Senator Javits' request that the report be placed into the record, and affirming with Mr. Lance that the report was a generalized statement about all banks, Javits again stressed Carter's standard:

> Now, was it your understanding of President Carter's standards for his Cabinet and Cabinet level officials that the standard of ethics would be what everybody is doing, the average, or the standard would be higher than that? Were you, when you sought to qualify before us, seeking to meet a standard of, well everybody does it so I do it too, or were you trying to meet President Carter's standard that my people shall be superior in terms of their ethical standards and their observance of ethics? (Hearings 1977:4, 1134)

The news media also used Carter's "high standards" as a basis for challenging Lance's legitimacy even before he was finished testifying in September. For example, in the first of five Special Reports on the Lance situation (September 15), anchorperson Walter Cronkite suggested that the main question was whether Carter and aides withheld information from the SCGA, which in turn raised the issue of the erosion of public confidence in President Carter:

> The fact is that the Carter administration itself shares the witness stand with its Budget Director. . . . Perhaps the main question is whether his aides—or Mr. Carter himself—in any way participated in withholding information to obtain Senate confirmation of his Budget Director. If that should be proved by these hearings . . . this nation's recovery from the dark days of Watergate would have suffered a severe setback, and cynicism and doubt again could ride triumphant over the President's promises of honesty, decency, integrity. (CBS News Special Report, "The Lance Hearings" September 15, 1977).

And the day before on the CBS Morning News, the context of Watergate and its bearing on the Lance case were made even more explicit by one reporter's comment:

> The original allegations about Bert Lance are becoming less important than the question Senator Howard Baker asked of Richard Nixon, "What did he know, and when did he know it?" Still another question bothers an awful lot of people, "What else don't we know about Bert Lance?" (CBS Morning News, September 14, 1977)

The Lance case was infused with what may be termed the "Watergate syndrome." Although all participants—including SCGA members and the news media—were using the Lance case to further illustrate how the procedures and ethics of government officials and journalists would prevent "another Watergate" from developing, it was also clear too some SCGA members that the Lance situation was being influenced by this focus on corruption and "covering up." Senator Nunn put it this way during the second Lance hearings on July 25th:

> I know that there is a pervading sentiment here in Washington today that we should not cover up anything. Certainly I share that. We seem sometimes to be so obsessed with the coverup syndrome though. Mr. Chairman, not this committee, but it pervades the entire mood in Washington, that we are in danger of covering up the presumption of innocence here in Washington. We are seemingly—and when I say we I include the news media—we have lost the capacity, I think, to presume that a man is innocent, to presume that a man is honest and to presume that a man has integrity. (Hearings 1977:2, 5)

Senator Nunn then cited the example of the impact of such presumptions and press coverage on the life of Bo Callaway, a Republican party official who innocently suffered from Watergate:

> So whether it is a Republican or whether it is a Democrat, whether it is a Bo Callaway or whether it is a Bert Lance, I think we have a presumption of innocence and I hope all of us will keep that in mind both in this committee and in the media. (Hearings 1977:2, 5)

The role of the press in the definition, presentation, and outcome of the Lance case cannot be doubted. Not only did the specter of Watergate loom large, but many journalists felt concerned about treating both Republicans and Democrats the same, since they were sensitive to charges of bias and being "out to get Nixon." Although the latter claim has been supported by one of the strongest Nixon attackers, Nicholas Von Hoffman (1977), the impact of occupational norms and prescriptions for covering events has received less attention. These will be dealt with in some detail below.

The effect of news reports on defining the problem and adding to the series of allegations that the Carter people had "covered up" something was a statement by former Nixon speech writer William Safire, who, while writing for the New York *Times,* insisted that all the truth about Lance was *not* unknown and that shady Carter practices were behind it. He called this "Lancegate." Mr. Safire's most significant contribution was raising the kinds of questions that were raised about Nixon's predicament: What did he do? When was it done? Who knew about it? Shouldn't we know more? Most importantly, Mr. Safire's experience with the role of the news media in the downfall of the Nixon administration made him all too aware of the cumulative effect of asking one probing question after another and the likelihood that other media workers would pick up on it, as would important governmental committee members like the SCGA in order to protect themselves from future news charges of negligence. The effect can fundamentally alter a particular"-fact." One example was a Safire report of August 1, 1977 titled the "Lance Cover-up," which noted:

> 7. Under 18 United States Code 656, and after the 1975 decision in United States versus Brookshire, the United States Attorney in Atlanta began an investigation into misapplication of funds in Lance banking operations. On December 2, 1976—one day before President elect Carter named Mr. Lance to his Cabinet—U.S. Attorney John Stokes ordered the investigation quashed, over the objections of his investigators. Mr. Stokes, a Nixon appointee, was then continued in the U.S. Attorney's office by Mr. Lance's friend, Griffin Bell. Mr Stokes denies a quid pro quo, and quit last week. Did a deal fall apart? (Hearings 1977:4, 258)

On September 2, Mr. Stokes told a team of SCGA staff interviewers that careful examination of the Lance banking situation and his alleged role in an embezzlement scam indicated that no prosecution was warranted in the former, whereas in the latter Mr. Lance had in fact been the person who called the embezzlement to the attention of the FBI. Stokes further testified that he had been told by an Assistant U.S. Attorney that the case had been closed in September 1976. The man in charge of the case, Mr. Bogart, expressed an interest in reopening it after the election and after initial news reports that Lance might be nominated to an important position.

> Stokes: I was told two months ago that it was going to be closed. Now the election is over, there's a man about to be nominated possibly . . . for national, some kind of national office. . . . Now if we're going to prosecute it and it's a good case, we're going to be criticized anyway as taking some

kind of political cheap shot at somebody, trying to do a hatchet job by a lame duck D. A. or administration. If we close it, I'm sure somebody is going to say well yeah, just trying to help out, the case should have been pursued and so forth. I saw that there was no way to make a decision either way that wasn't going to be the possible subject of some kind of criticism. (Hearings 1977:4, 802–803)

Stokes also told staff members that Mr. Bogart became interested in reopening the case because Bogart wanted the publicity that would accompany someone like Bert Lance.

Here it is nine months later, eight months later, and all of a sudden now that Mr. Lance may become a national figure, all, we've got to get all this additional material. . . . I felt that the time had come to take some definite step. I thought it was more entitled to a critical analysis having sat in the office all this time and nobody doing a thing. If it were all that good where was all these requests for materials back in April and May, and in September and in October. *Now suddenly it's front page news and we've got to request all this information.* (Hearings 1977:4, 815; italics added)

A few minutes later Mr. Stokes was asked whether he had now changed his mind regarding the original decision not to prosecute Lance:

Staff: Finally, Mr. Stokes, you are quoted in the newspaper about five or six days ago as saying if you had it to do over again, you would have prosecuted. I believe you said that. Knowing what we know about the newspapers I wondered if you could establish the record on that. Did you, in fact, tell the newspapers that, or what did you say?

Stokes: No, I didn't tell them that. I told some reporter, and I might say I've been called by dozens of them from different parts of the country, that had I known . . . that the Comptroller had in effect ordered some auditor to give the bank a clean bill of health in an audit that fall and I was trying to ask these reporters whether that reported as a fact or conclusion or what. Now I said if that had been known to me at the time we were making our decision, I said I would have been more inclined to keep the case open a while longer and look into it. . . . I said that would cast in question the reliability of the Comptroller's report, which we had. . . . However, I told the reporter, and I would also say that I still don't believe that anything further we could have done, or any further information or records you would have ever gotten would have changed my opinion of the prosecutable ability, the prosecution merit of the case that I closed. (Hearings 1977:4, 826–827)

In short, the case was deemed not prosecutable, but when it was examined within the context of a nonlegalistic perspective, certain incidents did seem less than honest and open. What the SCGA members did not want to contend with, however, were charges that they had not been diligent enough in their efforts to investigate Lance initially in January.

Thus the investigations continued and more charges surfaced, each one receiving a large play in the news media and in turn being investigated by the SCGA. The news media were working hand-in-hand with SCGA and were doing their work for them, as well as fundamentally distorting important facets of the Lance case.

The Government–News Media Connection

Just as Watergate propelled the news media into a dominant position of power in American politics, it also made politicians both envious and wary of the work and role of journalists. Politics in the media, as we have stressed throughout this work, did not begin with Watergate, but was a logical progression from the earliest period when politicians began considering the role of media in planning press conferences, making speeches, selecting campaign styles, and, of course, planning political conventions and overall imagery (Barnouw 1975). Indeed, the time when the news media were "just one factor" has passed into something much greater; media people are now major advisers in total imagery. As media people work with pollsters in assessing which direction the public is leaning—and which way it might be led to lean—substance is increasingly taking a back seat to imagery. Today, image is the important substance. For example, President Carter's media adviser, Gerald Rafshoon, recently decided how many Carter staff members should appear on a morning news and talk show and what topics should be stressed (Phoenix *Gazette* July 26, 1978).

The Bert Lance case served to further establish the significance of media logic and procedures for governmental committees and the issues with which they deal. Many journalists now openly help set agendas or "alleges" and decide what the outcome will be. Not only were dozens of press reports used by the SCGA in their investigation of Lance, but some members of the press felt little hesitation about imposing their perspective on the events. Moreover, their points of view often were not stated as personal opinions but were replaced by such terms as "everybody says," "the public," "all of Washington," and "a lot of people." ABC's Sam Donaldson illustrated this point quite well when, during an ABC special report on August 18, he said:

> The thing that struck me here today, Ann, was that Mr. Lance, the President, and other White House staff, who were not present today but who have talked to reporters, are clearly trying to draw the issue on the question of legality. . . . But a lot of people think that the question of Mr. Lance's activities and his continued usefulness to the President rests on a higher standard. . . . Mr. Lance said that the report [by the Comptroller of the Currency] cleared him of all impropriety, he acknowledged that it did in fact mention the question of the propriety or impropriety.

And later Donaldson commented on Lance's indebtedness:

> Well, of course living beyond one's means is not illegal, and certainly may
> not even be improper, or all of us might, in fact, have to resign our posi-
> tions. But the question becomes, does it not . . . do we want the Director
> of the Budget to have exhibited this type of practice? (Hearings 1977:4,
> 202–203)

One consequence of this kind of reporting, and the mass of charges
published about Lance, was to essentially alter the role of the SCGA.
Specifically, during Lance's first confirmation hearing before the SCGA
in January 1977, the majority of questions asked by committee members
pertained to issues and procedures relating to the Office of Management and the Budget, as well as Lance's general philosophy regarding
government monetary policy, cooperation with the various congressional bodies, and more (Hearings 1977:1). Only about three pages of
the 45-page transcript of this hearing (plus some 60 pages of documentation) referred to his 1974 gubernatorial campaign debts (Hearings
1977:1, 63 and 111), press charges that Lance had somehow influenced
the closing of the investigation of his banking practices by the Justice
Department (1977:1, 64), banking loans to Jimmy Carter before he was
elected president, the speed with which he was disposing of his assets
and possible conflicts of interest (1977:1, 115), and finally, "questions
involving your associations with various banks" (1977:1, 124). In each
case, Lance's brief explanation was accepted. Lance was then confirmed.

But his confirmation became uncomfortable when, as noted above, he
requested an extension on the December 1, 1977 deadline for liquidat-
ing his stock in the National Bank of Georgia and when he signed a
letter disagreeing with Senator Proxmire about an urban banking and
housing matter. This led Proxmire to challenge Lance's commitment to
refrain from involving himself in banking matters. In addition to these
two events, there was the extensive press coverage that grew out of more
detailed investigations of Lance's career as a banker. Thus on the second
day of the second set of Lance hearings—July 25—SCGA Chairman
Ribicoff noted that although he agreed with other senators that not every allegation made about an individual needs a response:

> We felt Friday and I feel today that the nature of the allegations made
> were of such a serious nature that would not just go away without giving
> Mr. Lance an opportunity to come and give us his part of the story. We
> would have been derelict in our duty as a committee if we did not arrange
> this meeting today. (Hearings 1977:2, 49)

On adding that the Comptroller of the Currency's report was not yet
completed and that Senator Proxmire was still expressing an interest in
"how does the Comptroller of the Currency handle problems of banking

regulation," Senator Ribicoff informed Lance that he was being given the opportunity "to respond to allegations reported in the press . . . concerning your financial activities" (Hearings 1977:2, 50). The allegations included (1) Lance's personal relationship with the first National Bank of Chicago and the correspondent relationship between this bank and the National Bank of Georgia, (2) the deposit of Teamsters' funds in the Trust Department of the National Bank of Georgia on a trust account relationship, (3) Lance's relationship with a man involved in an energy exposition scheduled to be held in Knoxville, Tennessee, (4) campaign overdrafts, (5) charges about the correspondent relationship with Manufacturers Hanover Bank of New York, and (6) Lance's request for an extension of his agreement with the President to sell his National Bank of Georgia stock by December 31, 1977. Lance answered the specific allegations and SCGA members' questions on July 15 and 25, but the most important point to be stressed is that by this time the function of the committee had gone beyond merely being concerned with qualifications, competence, and even the nature of Lance's background. It was now wholly involved in an extensive review—and meticulous scrutiny and second-guessing—of Bert Lance's prior life experiences. The sweeping scope of the investigation was now focusing on competence and general background checks, and had shifted to issues of morality, decency, and other highly subjective domains. Most importantly, this was done from an absolutist perspective on morality and business practices in general. As noted above, the context of the various activities, including those noted in the reports by the Comptroller of the Currency, were essentially ignored.

The way in which his past life and experiences that occurred in varying contexts and with different purposes could be used as a measure of future performance puzzled Lance as well as several senators. On September 17, Lance said:

> How do you judge performance in a government position as opposed to performance in a private position that happened some years previously? It is very difficult to judge yesterday's performance by today's rules and regulations. And I think that is what we have seen in this instance. . . . We have talked about overdrafts. We have talked about the other circumstances. It would have been better if that had not happened, but I think I have not made excuses. I have given reasons why that took place. (Hearings 1977:4, 1029)

Senator Danforth agreed that the role of the Senate in these matters was not all that clear.

> Well, somehow we have got ourselves into a position in this country where we have accepted as conventional wisdom the notion that if there is a suggestion of the appearance of the possibility of some impropriety, we must

then conduct extensive investigations and hold endless hearings. And I, myself, question whether that is the appropriate role for the U.S. Senate.

It seems to me that the appropriate role of the senate is to inquire into a person's past life during the confirmation process. Absent fraud in that process that a card laid is a card played, and that our role after that is to oversee the performance of a department and of an office and not to maintain continuing inquiry into somebody's personal life. (Hearings 1977:4, 1029)

But it was not Lance's performance as Director of OMB that was under question but the allegations and ad hoc role of the committee that was largely defined by the press.

The new rules of the committee in their investigation of Lance can be seen further by comparing Senator Percy's above comment about full-scale investigations of both government and private institutions to determine their standards, with a point raised by Senator Jackson on July 15 about the ambiguity of standards:

Mr. Chairman, it seems to me that the heart of our problem in trying to resolve questions such as Senator Nunn and Senator Percy have discussed is that each committee has a different standard. We have allowed appointees to hold stock. The last, I think, was Mr. Duncan, who had about $15 million in Coca-Cola stock. I supported retaining his holdings with the understanding that he would have nothing to do with any sales of Coca-Cola either within the Pentagon or within in the Defense Establishment. (Hearings 1977:2, 30)

Moreover, the tremendous amount of news coverage notwithstanding, even Senator Proxmire, one of Lance's early accusers about defaulting on an original pledge to refrain from being involved in banking matters, told a network correspondent on August 28, 1977, that Lance was being treated rather uniquely.

Reporter: Senator, do you think that what is now the public record about Mr. Lance's past banking activities, the fact that there was a finding of unsafe and unsound banking practices with regard to this Calhoun Bank, the fact that there were questions about the overdrafts at his Calhoun Bank, do you think things like this disqualify him or should have disqualified him, if they were known then, for confirmation as Director of OMB?

Senator Proxmire: Well, Bob, I think that's a very good point, because I think, to be fair to Mr. Lance, we haven't done that to other nominees. All of the criticism of people who've been in office for any length of time has been their conduct of their office, not what they did beforehand. And virtually all of the reports on Mr. Lance have been what he did before he came to office. . . . But he's in office, and I think that we should largely judge Mr. Lance on what he's done since he's been there. And *I think we could probably dig up material on almost anybody in office, if we went back far enough and dug deeply enough, that would be embarrassing to them, especially somebody who's been involved in banking, who's made a lot of money in a short time.* (Hearings 1977:4, 236; italics added)

Senator Proxmire, unlike the journalists who covered the Lance affair, was aware of the role of the SCGA and knew that its jurisdiction of inquiry was limited to certain specific issues of competence. Although Senator Proxmire did not feel that Lance had done all that well during his short tenure as Director of OMB, he nevertheless felt that, in retrospect, things would not have changed much.

Reporter: Do you think the Senate would confirm him today knowing what it does now about his financial dealings?

Senator Proxmire: I think the Senate might very well confirm him, knowing what we know now. I hope not. I would have gotten more votes than any own lone vote which I got when I opposed him. But if he should come up—if that hearing before the Government Operations Committee had been as comprehensive as we—the information we have now, I doubt if I would have gotten more than five or six other people that would vote with me against him. (Hearings 1977:4, 238)

The comments from Senator Proxmire and others suggest that Lance was treated in the original hearings in much the same way most aspiring conferees are treated; they are ritually and courteously led through the confirmation process, barring any obvious instances of criminality, fraud, or immorality. In Lance's case, however, things changed when "new information" was reported about his banking practices and personal finances—especially his overdrafts. But the crucial point to stress is that these factors alone would not have made any significant difference in the disposition of his case as far as the SCGA was concerned. For one thing, they were legal. With one possible exception, all charges leveled at Lance were extralegal in character, although they implied that illegality had occurred. For example, an article by William Safire, "The Skunk at the Garden Party" (New York *Times* September 8), claimed that a loan given to Lance had not been fully collateralized. If so, then the legality of the loan would have been in question. However, what had actually happened was that the collateral value was diluted over time, so that although it was originally fully collateralized, it was not at another point in time. This is legal. When Senator Nunn asked the Comptroller of the Currency, John Heimann, about this allegation, Mr. Heimann contended on his sources of information:

We have diligently attempted to keep a listing of allegations, regardless of the source of the allegations. . . . Of course, they have been reported to us by two forms, members of the committee staffs . . . or allegations made in the press. (Hearings 1977:4, 328)

Among the allegations that were making news was the charge that Lance had engaged in "corresponding relationships," an exchange in which money from one bank is deposited into another, which bank in turn may provide certain loans and other services for the "correspondent bank." Excerpts from Comptroller Heimann's remarks to the SCGA illustrate the routine use of correspondent relationships and the role they play in banking.

> I would like to add one other thought to that, correspondent relationships per se are not bad. They are a very important segment of the banking institution, and provide important services throughout the banking industry, to serve all of the people and the industry of this country. What we are concerned about is possibility of abuse in borrowing and correspondent relations. I have noticed there has been a great deal of discussion about correspondent relationships in the press, and I would like to take this opportunity to say that the correspondent relationship itself should not be looked at as some deep dark, or mysterious system. (Hearings 1977:4, 153)

A few moments later he added some insights regarding this notion of "abuse."

> I am not sure I know of what abuse means, except to note that, number one, from the point of view of the banks making the loans, we do not see sufficient evidence to warrant control. (Hearings 1977:4, 153)

News coverage of the correspondent relations issue is illustrated by a few excerpts from CBS newscasts:

> Then Lance's bank in Calhoun and the two state banks all deposited funds in non-interest-bearing correspondent accounts in the Fulton bank, the bank that was willing to lend Lance and his friends their money. Comptroller Heimann says there is "some evidence that, but for the correspondent accounts, the loans would not have been made." (CBS Evening News September 9, 1977)

> The Comptroller of the Currency has issued another report on Budget Director Bert Lance's financial activities, again finding nothing illegal in them. But the stories of overdrafts and sudden switches from this account to that must sound exotic to the average depositor, who would have the bank breaking down his front door to seize the children as collateral if he tried anything like that. . . . As reports about Lance mount, so do the cause for his resignation. The Washington Post today, also the New York Daily News and the New York Times—The Times says, in part, "For the President to ask for Mr. Lance's resignation is not, finally, to surrender to lynch-mob injustice, but to demonstrate an understanding of the rough-and-tumble of national politics." (CBS Morning News September 8, 1977)

The "national politics" referred to are the issues and strategies preferred by the major news media. The news media, in effect, insisted that their standards of proper conduct and fair play be observed, even if their criteria were far removed from the workings of the day-to-day world. This includes the standards to be used by certain members of the SCGA, who were extremely sensitive to press reports and used them to guide their investigations.

One underlying assumption throughout coverage of the Lance case was that he had clearly violated either the "letter or the spirit" of certain banking and financial regulations. Although there is a large body of banking regulations, how they apply and the limits of their interpretation vary greatly from one situation to the next and are subject to routine negotiation. Moreover, the various banking committees that have a hand in specifying these procedures are aware of this. When asked about Lance borrowing from nine different banks because of his establishment of correspondent relationship with these banks, senator Proxmire commented:

> Well, it should be made illegal, in my view, and I'm going to do my best to see that we make it illegal, or that we change the rules of the game so that instead of having a compensating balance that doesn't draw interest, interest would be paid and the services performed by the big bank would be charged for. Then you'd have the whole thing in the marketplace, and I think it'd be done on a far more objective and fair basis. (Hearings 1977:4, 239)

And a few questions later:

> There's a great deal wrong with regulation. We've known that for a long, long time. . . . You see, what happens is, if you have a permissive regulator who lets the banks they regulate get away with murder, then other banks that are under the supervision of the Federal Reserve, for example, under the supervision of the FDIC will opt out from under that to be under the supervision of Comptroller. . . . And in order to remedy that, I proposed legislation to consolidate bank regulation into one regulator. (Hearings 1977:4, 240)

In addition to the complexities of banking laws, the Comptroller of the Currency lacked systematic data on normal banking practices, including routine violations. When Mr. Heimann was testifying before the SCGA on September 8, he said:

> It is only fair to say that there are no accurate statistics, there is no quantification that would be of sufficient depth as to make a judgment as to normal or not normal, to tell this committee that the three primary regulators are in the process of sending out what we call a special report which will address itself to the following area, overdrafts, in the commercial banking system, family, or insider overdrafts, bank stock loans, correspondent

relationships. . . . We will have I believe between 90 and 100 days the kind of survey which can give a reasonable recommendation as to what is normal, and what is not normal. We, however, not knowing in the true sense of the word what is normal has to be compared to what, have phrased our report in terms of what we deem to be acceptable as a regulator. It is difficult to say what is normal without statistical base upon which to predicate what is normalcy. (Hearings 1977:4, 148)

Mr. Heimann's point was further supported by a study of some 600 banks made by the Comptroller General of the United States on January 31, 1977, which found that there were numerous problems and rule violations and practices differed by the size of the bank (Hearings 1977:4, 1129ff).

Still another sample of the way news reports attempted to define the role of the SCGA in their investigations of Lance concerns his overdrafts. This practice, the study found, also varies greatly from one bank to another and from one part of the country to another. In his testimony to the SCGA on September 13, Donald L. Tarleton, Regional Administrator of National Banks in Atlanta, Georgia, discussed the "overdraft problem" in this area of the country:

It [insider overdrafts] does not exist in the majority of banks, but we are not surprised when we run across it. I might also add that there are varying degrees of this practice, and we do not necessarily automatically enter into an enforcement agreement when we come across it. In fact, we normally get it cured in other ways. (Hearings 1977:4, 537)

And in his testimony before the SCGA on September 15, Lance explained the overdraft situation.

Much criticism has been directed at me by certain members of this committee regarding the large overdrafts in checking accounts maintained at the Calhoun First National Bank by me and my family. It has been said that this practice was an unsound banking practice, that its adoption constituted an abuse of my position at the bank, and that it was engaged in to the detriment of other depositors and stockholders. . . . The overdraft policy of a bank simply involves the decision to extend credit to depositors, and the policy varies from bank to bank. Some banks have special overdraft services which they advertise in an effort to attract customers. Though the record has become confused with respect to this issue, there is nothing illegal about overdrafts. Nothing in the banking laws prohibits their use. The issue as to overdrafts thus becomes a question of degree— a subjective determination. The overdrafts which occurred at the Calhoun Bank are a matter of record. However, I do find it curious that the news stories have grouped all overdrafts incurred by me, by my family, and by relatives and in-laws and imply that I personally had overdrafts of $450,000. This is a gross distortion of the truth. . . . The Calhoun First National Bank for years followed a liberal policy with respect to overdrafts. . . . The liberal overdraft policy of the bank was available to all depositors. (Hearings 1977:4, 901)

Mr. Heimann had earlier confirmed Lance's statement when, on September 9, he responded to Senator Percy's query about overdrafts:

Senator Percy: Yes, I think an understanding, a better understanding of this is useful because there has been a great deal made of this in the press.

Heimann: Now it was the policy of the Calhoun Bank prior to 1974 not to charge interest or service charges on anybody's overdraft. In other words, whether that overdraft came from an officer or director or from just a customer of the bank they did not charge interest. So in that sense it was not preferential. (Hearings 1977:4, 311–312)

The significance of the overdraft issue, when viewed in the context of the news interest in developing a simple standard, is illustrated by one CBS reporter's observation on September 8:

Murky legal and ethical questions concerning Lance's bank dealings remained, but there was no new major damaging allegations, and that, alone, has to be a welcome change for the embattled budget director. Comptroller Heimann will be back before the committee tomorrow. (CBS Evening News September 8, 1977)

Of course, more allegations would be made—Lance's misuse of a company airplane, his involvements with a convicted swindler, as well as charges that he helped engineer a "cover-up" of certain information about his banking past. Nevertheless, the key to many of the charges against Lance, and the one the press focused on, was the personal overdraft issue. Senator Eagleton made this point clear on September 19 during his questioning of a staff member who had compiled information about Lance's financial past but who had not provided these data to the committee during the first confirmation hearing. After taking the staff member to task for not divulging all he knew to the SCGA earlier, Eagleton stated:

The linchpin of this case from day one has been the overdrafts. If there had been no overdrafts, if there had been no attention paid to overdrafts, all of the other matters that have been thrown in here . . . might have been a titillating three-hour, at most, hearing on some balmy and warm afternoon in July. It is overdrafts that made this case what it has become, because it was the overdrafts that when described by the headlines and lead stories on the evening news—those overdrafts hit home to rural and real-life Americans. (Hearings 1977:4, 1381)

But by that time Eagleton's point had become pointless; the outcome had already been decided.

Two days after the close of the hearings, on September 21, 1977, Bert Lance resigned his position, having had the opportunity to answer questions and make important detailed statements about the charges against him. But as we have shown above, most of those answers were not taken seriously by the significant audience of the press and selected senators—they were regarded as evading the truth. The truth was, of course, quite complex, but clearly had to be seen in the context of Lance's banking experience in Georgia as well as the then prevailing standards. But the news reports would not permit this to happen and, strangely enough, journalistic powers of investigations were used only to uncover more "allegations" against Lance rather than put them in the context of banking practices. Roger Mudd, noted journalist for CBS news, illustrated this tendency in the CBS Special Report "Lance Resigns" (September 21, 1977):

> Apparently what made Lance's departure inevitable, according to some senators, was his decision to base his defense on a technical legal innocence. The President praised Lance today as a good and honest man who had broken no laws, but as one member of the Governmental Affairs Committee said, that phrase—breaking no laws—was, at worst, reminiscent of an earlier Administration, and at best, sounded strange in a White House where the President himself said the standards of excellence were extraordinary.

A few minutes later Mudd raised the major question that our entire research has addressed:

> It's pretty screwy logic, it seems to me, for the President of the United States to say that Bert Lance took three days before the Senate committee and exonerated himself, and that proved that the—the U.S. system works, and therefore, I'm accepting his resignation. I mean, I can't get from A to C; there's something illogical about this. (CBS Special Report, September 21, 1977:9)

Point "B" was the news media, especially the logic of media work that led to the growing alliance between journalism and government in the Lance case, and also the procedures and routines that directed the focus and emphasis on certain events and themes rather than others. In the next section we turn to the logic underlying the presentation of the Lance story and the media's tendency to overlook some of the most important practical considerations that would have led journalists and, therefore, committee members, to see the matter differently.

News Values and News Process

The handling of the Bert Lance case by the news media and the SCGA is obviously related. We have argued that the SCGA was by and large an extension of the news media's interest and perspective, and that its function in dealing with the Lance situation was more a result of news presentations and resulting pressures on SCGA members to appear competent and reputable than the actions of Bert Lance. Although the domination and virtual control of the confirmation process by a post-Watergate news media is but a logical extension of the growth of media logic throughout our culture (especially national politics), the specific focus brought to bear on the Lance case was more a feature of the production and practical aspects of newswork.

Scheduling and Timeliness. Our discussion of news (Chapter 3) stressed how practical concerns influence what is selected for news presentation (cf. Altheide 1985a; Bennett 1983). Among the most important of these concerns is the number of events generated and publicized for news purposes. Since a large amount of the material for Network TV centers around Washington, D.C., the real heart of national news, any factor influencing the amount and quality of material coming from various agencies and institutions in the capital will have a direct bearing on the amount and the kind of news coverage that will follow (Epstein 1974). And since the work of these agencies and institutions varies by the time of day, day of the week, and month of the year, it comes as no surprise that the amount of news presented also varies accordingly. In terms of the Bert Lance case, the third hearing received a tremendous amount of network and major newspaper coverage, at least partly because it occurred during the summer, the slowest period for news during the year. There are few competing events for news workers to work on, and this was important since news channels and other outlets did not cut back their newspaper space or their air time allotted to news coverage just because it was the slow summer period. To the contrary, news workers act as though there is always news happening, although any experienced journalist is keenly aware of this practical limitation imposed on them.

Despite the significance of slow news for the journalistic interest in the Lance case, little was mentioned about it throughout the Lance coverage. An exception occurred on CBS coverage of Lance on September 22, 1977, one day after he resigned. Bruce Morton, a CBS correspondent who had provided many "comments" about the Lance case, raised the question of "How good or bad a job did the news media do?"

First, coverage was timely. In January, before Lance's original token confirmation hearings, stories appeared outlining what would become the major charges against him. At the time they were competing with a lot of other news. In August, an extremely slow news month, coverage was massive, but it was a major story involving an important official. (CBS Evening News, September 22, 1977)

This view was then supported with a filmed statement by Charles Seib, ombudsman for the Washington *Post:*

> In this business we don't seem to have a way to play a major story except rather stridently. We don't have a way to say, "Well, look this is a pretty good story." We either say this is a great story or it's no story, and so, to that extent, it perhaps was overplayed slightly, but I would say marginally. (CBS Evening News, September 22, 1977)

Another example of the impact of an event occurring during the summer months for its resulting coverage was the Eagleton case in 1972. Thomas Eagleton, selected as the Democratic vice-presidential candidate in 1972, was dropped within 10 days after he told a press conference that he had been hospitalized and treated for mental illness some years before. This happened in July. A network anchorperson explained the impact of "slow news" during an interview:

> There is a problem in journalism which is that journalism is keyed, it's build up to cover the crises, to cover the war, to cover the disasters. Therefore, when you get a relatively placid period, when you get a dramatic development, I think we probably over-react, we over-react objectively, it's just a matter of a bunch of people trying to get a story. (Altheide 1976:142)

When a "bunch of people" try to get a story during a "slow news" time, this often means a bunch of people focusing on the "big story" in order to show their bosses, the competition, readers, and viewers that they are doing a good job. One effect we have seen in the Lance case is for journalist to rehash old material while looking for new material, usually in the form of some kind of "evidence." The repetitiveness, however, is a constant of "big stories" during slow news periods. As Eagleton said of the coverage about himself:

> It was sort of my personal belief that the Eagleton issue would fade away through this month of August, around the first day of August. . . . I thought that [CBS reporter] would get tired of asking me in every city of the country about my health, and that it would run its course. (CBS August 1, 1972)

The constant repetition of this relatively small issue took its toll on George McGovern's ability to obtain more issue-oriented media coverage during 1972. This contributed to his decision to drop Eagleton as his running mate. McGovern explained why he did so:

> [I] was of the opinion that this issue would continue to plague the campaign . . . look at the press, at the news, at the magazines. This has been

the issue that has blotted out the war, blotted out the economy, blotted out all the central questions before the nation. (CBS, August 1, 1972)

This background experience undoubtedly led Eagleton to be critical of the press coverage of the Lance case, and as a member of the SCGA, he knew the impact press reports were having:

> I would like, Mr. Chairman, to comment a bit on the atmosphere of these hearings. . . . Back in the late 1940's and early 1950's the technique and mode of the time was guilt by association. Senator Joseph McCarthy made it a fine art to practice guilt by association. Here in 1977, we have a newer technique, guilt to accumulation. It seems that every day someone will hurl a charge at Mr. Lance and regardless of whether it is true or false, it accumulates. A little bit more mud gets on the character and reputation of Mr. Lance. (Hearings 1977:4, 1019)

Eagleton then gave specific examples of the way Senator Percy promoted the impression that Lance was involved in the embezzlement situation at the Calhoun Bank and that Lance had backdated checks for income tax benefits. Eagleton then continued:

> Yesterday, Senator Percy apologized to Mr. Lance, and in his apology used this curious language, he said "I apologize for any anguish I caused you over the weekend"—marvelous. Anguish I caused you over the weekend. We are playing with a man's character, and his decency and his reputation. . . . Some people, I do not know how many . . . will believe forever that Bert Lance was a tax cheater. I say, gentlemen, that we cannot play so fast and loose with the reputation of any person. All we take to our graves is our reputation. . . . In some measure, Mr. Lance has been irrevocably tarnished. There is no way to undo the wrong. (Hearings 1977:4, 1020)

As more journalists became involved and as reports filled the news columns and the air waves, the complexities involved became very simple, as everyone concerned—including the politicians—wanted it to end through a kind of symbolic execution. William Sexton, Associate Editor of *Newsday*, one of the earliest periodicals calling for Lance's resignation, told PBS's Robert MacNeil that the media may have "buffaloed" Lance because:

> Having developed this momentum . . . there is a rush to judgment on the part of the newspaper editorial writers, on the part of the White House press corps. ("MacNeil/Lehrer Report" September 15, 1977)

One way this momentum develops is the practical wisdom of journalism that not only should one be attuned to the "big stories," but also that journalists can rely on their colleagues to steer them in the right direction. This tendency to simply accept what has been already publicized and then attach one's own block to the expanding pile of news can be referred to simply as "the doctrine of truth in numbers." Thus the more news organs present certain reports and attach significance to them, the more they can be relied on as valid definers of the particular event(s) and the more trustworthy they become. The practical application of this is that these earlier reports can be used in one's own newscast or newspaper articles or even, as we have already seen, as "allegations" for a Senate committee to consider in performing and validating its work.

In the case of Bert Lance, the major networks relied heavily on newspaper reports. A few examples from CBS newscasts illustrate the use of other news reports as a source of information as well as actual material to be used on the air.

> September 3: The saga of Bert Lance went to another installment today. The Los Angeles *Times* says that a preliminary draft of a report by federal investigators concludes that political motivation was behind the clean bill of health given Lance's Georgia bank by the Comptroller of the Currency. (CBS Evening News September 3, 1977)

> September 4: As the Carter's were preparing Friday to helicopter off to Camp David for the Labor Day holiday, someone asked Mrs. Carter if she was looking forward to a quiet weekend. "Yes," she said. "The quiet before the storm next week." Well, if by some chance the President didn't believe that then, he had only to pick up his adopted hometown's morning newspaper today. Greeting him on page one was still another story on embattled Budget Director Bert Lance; this one quoting powerful Senate majority leader Robert Byrd, who says he has counseled Mr. Carter that Lance's effectiveness is being very seriously eroded. Page three contained a reminder that next week will be a hectic time when the Presidents and Prime Ministers of 19 Latin American countries will be here for the Panama Canal treaty signing; plus a reminder that the latest polls show the country is still divided on the Canal issue, with 45 percent of those questioned still against it. Turning to page four, Mr. Carter was reminded that the first of three Congressional probes into Bert Lance's affairs get underway next week—hearings that may take up most of September. On page six, still more from Senator Byrd on Lance. And moving on to page eleven, still another reminder than Mr. Carter's energy plan is facing some serious problems in the Senate. . . . Well, if reading the Washington *Post* was no fun for Mr. Carter, he could always switch to the other paper here—the Washington *Star*. But then again, maybe that was no fun either—what with Pat Oliphant working the weekend shift. (CBS Sunday Night News September 4, 1977)

> September 5: *Time* magazine says this week that embattled Budget Director Bert Lance has twice offered to resign, but White House Press Secretary Jody Powell says he checked that report with the President and Mr. Carter flatly denied. *Time* also quoted another source as saying Domestic Affairs aide Stuart Eizenstat had said Lance would have to resign, but Eizenstat says that's a lie. (CBS Morning News September 5, 1977)

September 8: The Comptroller of the Currency has issued another report on Budget Director Bert Lance's financial activities, again finding nothing illegal in them. . . . As the reports about Lance mount, so does the cause for his resignation. The Washington *Post* today, so also the New York *Daily News* and the New York *Times*—the *Times* says in part, "For the President to ask for Mr. Lance's resignation is not, finally, to surrender to lynch-mob injustice, but to demonstrate an understanding of the rough-and-tumble of national politics." (CBS Morning News September 8, 1977)

The use of media reports further illustrates the working logic of journalists in regard to "objectivity" and remaining "current." To repeat what someone—or some other publication—has stated demonstrates journalistic competence even as it adds significance to the original report. This practice in turn promotes the use of the same report by other news channels and network affiliates. And as the word spreads, journalistic commitment to it increases, as does the interest in pursuing other aspects of the story. In part then, the "momentum of news" as well as the "guilt by accumulation" referred to by Senator Eagleton are involved in the process of newswork at a cognitive and practical level.

That the work and competence of journalists involve essentially passing on and even embellishing what other colleagues say rather than attempting to validate those claims was also apparent in the Lance case (cf. Altheide 1978b). The often-repeated allegations that Lance was implicated with a bank swindler provide a good example. On September 5, Labor Day, the Atlanta *Journal and Constitution* carried a front page story with the headline "Swindler Implicates Lance." The substance of the story was that three investigators from the SCGA talked with Billy Lee Campbell and obtained an affidavit from him in which he claimed that Lance was involved. On the investigators' return to Washington, they met with members of the SCGA—including Percy and Ribicoff—who in turn met with Carter on the same day and asked for Lance's resignation, claiming that they had received "allegations of illegality." On subsequent days this report appeared in the New York *Times* and other major news media, including CBS newscasts. Lance's assessment that

the net result of the developments of Labor Day, 1977, was to inform the American people that Lance, who was already under attack, was now involved in some serious "illegality" that had something to do with "embezzlement" that was of such sinister proportions that the two Senators felt compelled to ask that Lance be fired. (Hearings 1977:4, 894)

Excerpts from CBS newscasts over the course of several days illustrate this point.

September 5: Senator Ribicoff: Certain material came to our attention in which there were alleged illegalities in the conduct of Mr. Lance, and, as United States Senators, we felt it was our duty to bring these alleged illegalities to the attention of the President. I think that it would be wiser for Bert Lance to resign. (CBS Evening News September 5, 1977)

September 6: Chairman Abraham Ribicoff and ranking Republican Charles Percy . . . have told President Carter that Budget Director Bert Lance should resign, because they have learned of new allegations unproven, that Lance has broken the law. . . . Ribicoff and Percy wouldn't say yesterday what these new allegations involve. They are supposed to tell other members of the committee about them this afternoon. It is known that committee investigators have talked to Billy Lee Campbell, a man who is serving time for embezzling from the Calhoun First National Bank, which Lance used to head. Some reports say Campbell told committee investigators that Lance was involved in that embezzlement. But as Percy noted, "He is in jail, and obviously wants to get out. We would be irresponsible if we simply repeated what he said without verification and we have no verification."

A lawyer for that convicted embezzler, Billy Lee Campbell, says Campbell will reveal—quote—"a ton of things" publicly, unless he is called to testify at those Senate hearings on Lance. Campbell is supposed to have told Senate committee investigators Lance was somehow involved in his embezzlement. And officials at the Calhoun bank say that's impossible, and that Campbell never hinted at anything like that during his trial.

The Senate Committee on Governmental Affairs met this afternoon to hear in detail the new allegations that Bert Lance may have committed crimes as a banker. . . . Although senators have not disclosed the new allegations, this much is known. One allegation of illegality concerns Lance's involvement with Billy Lee Campbell, a former employee of Lance at the Calhoun National Bank, now serving an eight-year prison term for embezzling $900,000 from the bank. (CBS Evening News September 6, 1977)

Although this "new allegation" added to the seemingly endless flow of charges of wrongdoing against Lance, its significance for the present analysis is even more striking since the charge was untrue and easily could have been checked out by any journalist seriously committed to accurate reporting. Lance explained to the committee on September 15 how this charge could have been checked out:

If someone were searching for the facts instead of a "smear," the obvious first step would be to go to the assistant U.S. Attorney who prosecuted Billy Lee Campbell. His name is Jeffrey B. Bogart. He would have been easy to find for he was still the assistant U.S. Attorney at that time. If they had talked with Mr. Bogart, they would have learned from him that Campbell at no time attempted to implicate Lance or anyone else. . . . If, by chance, any possible skepticism remained, the investigator could have called upon the lawyer who defended Campbell in the embezzlement case. He would have learned from him that in the many months he represented Campbell, and in innumerable conferences, Campbell never in any way implicated Lance in embezzlement. The transcripts in Federal court show that the judge questioned Campbell in great detail, but again Campbell did not involve Lance in any embezzlement. Apparently, no steps of this kind were taken by the investigators. They talked to Campbell—they received an unsupported accusation—they brought it to the committee—two of whose members promptly took it to the White House and then, at a press conference, informed the American people that they have reported the Campbell charge to the President.

A curious epilogue should be mentioned. Although the Atlanta paper reported that the committee investigators obtained an "affidavit" from Campbell, this proved to be untrue. Not only would Campbell not give an affidavit, he would not even permit his conversation to be taped. . . . And the entire tragic and irresponsible incident could have been prevented by one simple telephone call. If I had been called, I could have, in five minutes, told them who should be seen to get the true story. (Hearings 1977:4, 894–895)

Although it is obvious that the newsworkers fumbled their responsibility in not attempting to verify the truthfulness of what was published, it is less apparent how this series of journalistic indelicacies could have happened during this period of government–press tensions. Why should the press simply accept what a government committee told them? Hadn't they learned the lessons of this during the Watergate period, and hadn't many eloquent voices and triumphant typewriters heralded the end of simply accepting government lines? Hadn't the much-lauded legwork of Woodward and Bernstein of Watergate-exposé fame convinced journalists that there is no substitute for thorough investigation? Why, then, did this embezzlement charge against Lance skyrocket and never die? Indeed, why did the journalists not acknowledge that this was even a mistake?

Answers to such fundamental questions are basic to unraveling the complex but highly crucial components of the news perspective. The first point to be stressed is that the story about Lance's embezzlement involvement was accepted largely because it was consistent with accepted rules of journalistic competence involving evidence, objectivity, and follow-up. Thus we must understand what these journalists felt the broader truth was about Lance to clarify why they thought the Campbell story fit the situation.

One Theme, Many Angles. Several studies have shown how time constraints, limited expertise, and the demand to make newscasts entertaining (if not downright simple) have led journalists to rely on simplifying themes and angle (Weaver 1972; Epstein 1975; Altheide 1976; Tuchman 1978; Braestrup 1978). Themes are general statements or images that may be used to connect one report to another to provide unity to the topics being presented. In elections, for example, the general theme of a "horserace" may be used to add a time-related sense of start-to-finish, along with implicit categories to deal with tactics and strategies as well as gains and losses. Weaver (1972) has convincingly argued that the formats of TV newscasts that structure reports about events in limited time frames benefit from the use of themes. He points out how short and narrated stories can be presented as merely an example of the theme. But the significant point for our focus is that the selection and development of a particular theme provide an important interpretive context for both the reporter and the audience.

Angles are like themes, except they are used to illustrate certain themes that may or may not be made explicit. An explicit theme would be claiming that Candidate X is a "front-runner," and angles that may be used to illustrate this point are the candidate's confidence, sound financial backing, party support, and so on. However, the more a theme is accepted as legitimate by the journalist and the audience, the more likely it is that angles will be used to illustrate—if not prove—the theme, even though the theme itself may be explicitly referred to during each report. Moreover, although any angle or theme may be used on a given story, our research suggests that the dominant theme restricts the choice of angles. Further, there is evidence to indicate that themes have a career: certain themes that may develop out of a particular event can take on symbolic lives of their own and even be used as a kind of explanatory technique for other events. Although more research clearly needs to be done on this issue, there is little doubt that themes last beyond the specific events to which they originally referred, and are likely to be episodically employed by journalists and other who want to connect the drama and excitement of one event to another. Just as entertainment programmers routinely "go with what is working," and attempt to further develop the kind of programs, situations, and even characters that are obtaining high ratings, so too do the news media. We think the Lance case illustrates this process.

As noted above, perhaps the most crucial predictor of what would happen to Lance, as well as a significant influence on how the news media treated him, was Watergate. As shown elsewhere (Altheide 1976:155–172), the word "Watergate" came to symbolize in the press a wide array of events and personalities that were essentially unconnected. Nevertheless, that term came not only to encapsulate all these events and people, but to symbolize political corruption. It was no accident that after Nixon resigned as President of the United States dozens—if not hundreds—of allegations and investigations at the national, state, and local levels of government came to be treated as some kind of "gate": Koreagate, Milkgate, and, of course, Lancegate, a term developed by

Nixon's former speech writer, William Safire, a writer for the New York *Times*.

The concern with corruption and the tendency to greatly simplify the nature of right and wrong, ethics, and a host of potential improprieties were part of the context that led to the suspicion of, and subsequent heavy journalistic attacks on, Bert Lance. Lance emerged within this climate of political experience, of heightened public interest in the role of journalism in our political process, and of the practical cognitive orientation of journalists to "get on a good story" and adopt an interesting theme.

The central theme that was primarily adopted without careful scrutiny of the facts and the various contexts of banking in Southern and rural Georgia *was that Bert Lance was morally, ethically, and even mentally unfit for his office, should have never been appointed, and should—and would—resign.* Summary reports of CBS newcasts—including special reports—between September 1 and September 22, 1977 illustrate this point.

> September 1: After noting that Representative Giaimo stated that Lance should resign and that the charges against him are being proved correct, Lance is shown denying that he will resign and commenting on the role of the press in his case. Others, such as Moore and Church, call for his resignation, and a reporter questions whether Lance's effectiveness as the administration's "point man" has not been lost.

> September 2: White House News Secretary Jody Powell confirms reports that Lance has been borrowing money from one bank to pay loans in another bank, but adds that there is nothing improper about this.

> September 3: LA *Times* report claims that the Comptroller of the Currency's report about Lance's financial difficulties was cleared through political influence.

> September 4: Secretary of Labor Ray Marshall is asked on "Face the Nation" whether Lance can effectively carry out his job as Director of OMB in the face of all these accusations. Marshall replies, "Yes." On the evening news, the White House denies that Lance will resign, but Senator Byrd is reported to say that Lance's effectiveness "is being seriously eroded." The reporter reads critical headlines from stories in the Washington *Post* about Lance and Carter.

> September 5: It is noted that stories about Lance are still in the press. *Time* Magazine reports that Lance will resign; Percy and Ribicoff on the SCGA call for his resignation. Percy says this is desirable so Lance can "defend himself against allegations."

> September 6: Percy and Ribicoff call for Lance's resignation, and Percy charges that "new allegations" regarding Lance's involvement have come to light. Reporter summarizes other allegations including misuse of bank airplane, SEC investigation, correspondent relations, and implications that the original Comptroller of the Currency's report about the Calhoun Na-

tional Bank was influenced by political pressure. On the evening news the reporter says, "CBS news has been told there are at least three serious allegations of illegality against Lance." Another reporter wonders if this isn't hurting Carter's image, and it is suggested that Lance could better defend himself if he resigned. Fernand St. Germain, Chairman, House Banking Subcommittee says, "While I do not want to rejudge, the evidence I've seen to date leads me to believe that Mr. Lance, his family and friends regarded the Calhoun First National Bank as their playpen to be used as they pleased."

September 7: Charges against Lance are repeated, and the growth of the SCGA into a full-scale investigation of Lance is reported. The Comptroller of the Currency, John Heimann, says that the evidence against Lance "does not warrant prosecution." Ribicoff retracts an earlier statement that Lance was being smeared by the press. The effect of Lance on banks is suggested. Lance's personal financial problems are dealt with, and a reporter in a "comment" states that Lance should be able to defend himself and not just resign, but "the climate in Washington dictates fate, they [Lance's defenders] don't."

September 8: After noting that the Comptroller of the currency's report found nothing illegal about Lance, the reporter states "as the reports about Lance mount so do the causes for his resignation." Editorials from the Washington *Post*, New York *Daily News,* and New York *Times* calling for his resignation are cited. Reporter also states that following the hearing, "universal assumption in this city is that Mr. Carter then will ask Mr. Lance to resign." Ribicoff says he was misled at the earlier hearing.

September 9: A reporter states that Agriculture Secretary Bergland says, "Lance's effectiveness has become badly impaired, and hinted Lance may have to resign." A spokesperson for the American Bankers Association denies that Lance's practices are typical; concern is expressed about how the public may perceive bankers. The effect of great press coverage on Lance's capacity to carry out duties is noted. Opinion poll shows Carter's rating is down.

September 11: "Face The Nation." Senator Jackson says that "decency requires that he [Lance] be heard," and adds that Carter has been "temporarily hurt." Reporter refers to "All the President's Men," and Jackson says that it doesn't really matter if Lance violated the law, what about his "background record of performance."

September 12: Powell is reported to have known about Lance's overdrafts, and the Comptroller's Office says that overdrafts are common in rural Georgia, but Carter's support of Lance is reported to have shifted. Bloom, Department Comptroller, is reporter to have said that his report about Lance was influenced by concern for his career. St. Germain says the Lance situation is an opportunity to reform banking, even though the President of the ABA says overdrafts are not common.

September 13: Cabinet appointees discuss Lance, including Andrus (Secretary of Interior), who says, "you [media] people are finding him guilty." A reporter asks if this is Lance's last cabinet meeting. Bloom is reported to be upset with Tarleton's lifting of restrictions on Lance's banking, and Lance denies that he will resign.

September 14: Powell plants an invalid charge in the press that Percy misused a private plane; Percy refutes this. Charge about pressure put on bank examiner involved in the Lance case is repeated, and the concern with how much was known about Lance before his nomination is made, along with the charge that perhaps a "cover-up" has been going on, in much the same way as in the Nixon administration. Lance's financial situation is noted, and Eric Severeid states that things look bad for Lance.

September 15: Overview of questions likely to be put to Lance when he appears before the SCGA. CBS news presents a case involving lending of money to bank controlled by Lance from another which received a contract from Lance's bank. In a "comment," reporter says a "whiff of blood is in the autumn air," and equates Lance's situation to a play, "The Chamberlain's Trial." Support for Lance in Calhoun, Georgia, is shown. Evening news opens with "The big story: Bert Lance's day in court . . . a hot seat or a seat of redemption. . . ." Lance deals with several charges, including overdraft policy and his use of collateral. Jackson voices concern about public confidence in Lance to head OMB. Cronkite asks reporters how Lance did.

Special Report: Lance challenges Percy's allegations and the publication of them regarding his involvement with an embezzler, as well as the charge that Lance had backdated checks. Lance attempts to explain overdraft policy of bank. Ribicoff is presented wondering why Lance did not stop the practice, and Jackson refers to the impact of all this on "the average man in the street . . . in the minds of the public." Even though Lance questions the truth of alleging that a "cover-up" has taken place, Cronkite—after asking reporters "how he did" and referring to the charge of "sloppy banking practices"—concludes with "while it is high drama . . . perhaps the main question is whether his aides—or Mr. Carter himself—if any participated in withholding information to obtain senate confirmation."

September 16: Lance returns before the SCGA "picturing himself as a man whose human and Constitutional rights have been violated." Reporter contends that the committee, the press, and Congress were ready for "a public execution . . . but the victim refused to die." The hearing is treated as a "theatrical event," and reporter says Lance did well from a soap opera fan's point of view. Another reporter says "Lance is the kind of person who can defend almost any cause," and "he's a very persuasive witness in his own defense." Question is raised whether Lance's overdrafts violate the "spirit of federal banking laws." Lance denies this. Eagleton charges Percy with publishing highly damaging reports about Lance, all of which were untrue. This is reported as an example of the internal strife within the committee, and Lance is reported to be exploiting "the political cross-fire."

September 16, Special Report: The SCGA is reported to have "tried to gain the offensive." Senator Roth uses a news report (ABC's) to question Lance's standard of ethics. The Percy–Eagleton exchange is reported regarding the allegations and aid in publishing them by Percy. Notes that Eagleton "went through the same kind of public wringer." The game metaphor is big; e.g., reporter notes that the "committee got to him on a few point"; queries are raised if the White House is helping organize the defense; and finally, Cronkite asks the reporters, "who's ahead—Lance or the committee?" Following a commerical, Cronkite apologizes, saying, "This isn't an athletic contest," adding that, "We, the public, might be excused for losing track of the real meaning and purpose of this inquiry when the committee itself seems to have so much trouble with that matter." He repeats the "principal point: was the committee misled, deliberately or otherwise."

September 17: Javits says, during this third day of questioning, "What we're judging is your ethics and your competence." Senator Nunn says the charges would not hold up in a court of law. Three big questions are now said to define the case: (1) the kind of banker Lance was; (2) whether he improperly obtained bank loans; and (3) whether he tried to hide or cover up any of this from the SCGA. Reporter notes that "regulators and investigators had found again and again that he had not violated the law." Carter is quoted as saying that even a series of incorrect allegations could so damage a man that he would have to go. Reporter wonders who " everybody" is that is always being talked about, and concludes it is really "nobody."

Special Report: The use of a bank-owned airplane is referred to and Percy refers to a double standard which people like Lance adopt, unlike the "man on the street." Lance presents documentation from a study by the Comptroller of the Currency about banking showing how widespread are certain practices and rule violations. Javits says this is not good enough for Carter's standards, and wonders if Lance is "bewildered by financial troubles." Reporter notes that Lance's financial affairs are a "maze." Percy wonders if the "ongoing criminal investigation" would deter Lance from doing his job. Reporter concludes that others are investigating Lance.

September 18: SCGA staff members are reported to have denied that Lance told them about the agreement between Calhoun Bank and Comptroller's office; Ribicoff and Percy again say he should resign. Although Eagleton attempts to put Lance's situation in the context of rural Georgia, Serafin says "Lance's future remains uncertain."

September 19: The impact of Lance on the President is noted, but Carter feels his testimony has helped Lance. Public opinion, reflected in calls and letters, is "heavily for Lance." SCGA staff members say they don't remember asking Lance about certain liabilities in earlier hearings. Justice Department sets up panel to check out Lance.

September 20: Poll shows people to be divided on Lance question. Justice Department will be looking into banking and securities and tax questions regarding Lance's use of bank-owned airplane. A viewer's poem, entitled "Bankers are Just like Anybody Else, Only Richer," is read to help explain "what's involved in the Lance case." O'Neill says that Carter will have to decide what is to be done to Lance. St. Germain asks Justice Department to check if a Lance witness committed perjury.

September 21: Morning news reporters that SEC is preparing a civil suit against Lance; Senator Byrd tells Lance he should resign, but reporter states that firing Lance when he hasn't done anything illegal goes against the "public sense of fair play." It is also noted that the definition of ethical banking does vary from city to city and from region to region. A report about Carter's upcoming news conference, states that the "White House is now stone-walling all questions about Lance's future." Percy meets with

Carter. In the evening news it is reported that Lance resigned. After saying that some of the coverage was unfair, Carter states, "In general I think the media have been fair." Questions are raised about Carter's credibility among the news media, although Senator Nunn reiterates Senator Eagleton's charge that Lance was a victim of "guilt by accumulation"; "The media plays a very important role in national life . . . the news media can do a little self-examination." Mudd suggests that Lance's phrases, like "I did nothing illegal." were too reminiscent of another administration. Coverage of Lance's wife and hometown are given.

Special Report: Carter's press conference. After Carter reaffirms his belief in Lance and the regrets he has about seeing him leave his job, Donaldson asks him if he felt Lance was still above the "appearance of impropriety."

Special Report: "Lance Resigns." Suggests that all the public scrutiny was too much for Lance. Lance's claim of "technical legal innocence" is referred to and it is noted that Carter's standards of conduct led to Lance's downfall. Mudd says "I think he just got overtaken by events" and later can't figure out why Carter would say Lance was vindicated and yet still accept his resignation.

September 22: Carter's standards of conduct are blamed for Lance's demise, and the three persons selected to serve on the Justice Department panel to further investigate Lance are discussed. His debts are mentioned, along with reports by various agencies which continue to investigate him. Hometown reaction is given, generally supportive of Lance, who is reported to have flown there in a private plane, but the trip was paid for. An aide is reported to have said that Carter can't hold a press conference without the Lance issue being raised, a point followed by a claim that the effectiveness in Washington depends on the "public." Percy says the charges prevented Lance from doing his job; Javits says the public must have confidence in government; and Nunn says that Lance was hounded from office by the mass media. Morton discusses effect of slow news month on Lance, and the ombudsman for the Washington *Post* says the coverage "perhaps was overplayed slightly, but I would say marginally." Morton concludes that with the press, "fewer and fewer holds are barred. The belief is that more and more the public official's private or past life is the public's business, and officials unaware of that new mood can be hurt."

These summaries show that on nearly every day between September 1 and September 22, the topic of resignation was raised and Lance's morality, ethics, and judgment were implicitly referred to—but usually explicitly stated—almost every day as well. Moreover, these points, especially the resignation question, were raised as often by journalists as by politicians and officials who were interviewed and/or quoted. One of the more extreme comments was made by a reporter for another network on September 6, 1977:

This is Sam Donaldson. Many people in Washington now seem convinced that Bert Lance must soon resign. But this morning as he left home for work, Lance continued to express optimism about his future.

Lance: I've been assured that I'm going to have a chance to appear before the Senate committee and answer any and all charges and that's exactly what I'm going to do.

Reporter: Do you think you could better defend yourself against these charges if you were to resign?

Lance: I just said that I've been assured that I'm going to have the opportunity to appear before the Senate committee and tell my story. (ABC Evening News September 6, 1977)

Although all the major networks carried similar reports, the recurring theme pervaded virtually all the news media, including the nation's major newspapers. The Washington *Post* and the New York *Times* called for his resignation on September 8, a week before Lance appeared before the SCGA to testify and explain the various charges and allegations against him. Such points of view were transformed into obdurate reality as they were reiterated and passed from one news organ to another. For example, after a CBS reporter cited all the major newspapers calling for Lance's resignation on September 8, he added:

The universal assumption in this city is that Mr. Carter [following the hearings] then will ask Mr. Lance to resign. (CBS Morning News September 8, 1977)

That the verdict was set in the minds of some people long before all the "facts" were gathered is further illustrated by the following excerpts:

Ferdinand St. Germain, Chairman, House Banking Subcommittee: While I do not want to prejudge, the evidence I've seen to date leads me to believe that Mr. Lance, his family and friends regarded the Calhoun First National Bank as their playpen to be used as they pleased. (CBS Evening News September 6, 1977)

Senator Jackson, a member of the SCGA, provided the following backhanded support for due process in response to a reporter's question:

Herman: Senator Jackson, you say something will happen when Budget Director Bert Lance appears before the committee this week. Can you realistically say, at this point, that there is any way that Mr. Lance can pull it off and stay on the job that he has now—now damaged beyond all repair, as some others have said?

Senator Jackson: Well, I'm sitting, personally, in judgment as a judge in this matter, and I want to hear Mr. Lance. The allegations are very serious. If he can, of course, give clear-cut answers that will satisfy the committee, then that's something else, but as of now, even on matters that are, indeed, in agreement—that is, allegations that have been made that are deemed serious, and his responses, places him in a very difficult position. I'm not asking him to resign at this point. I've not heard Mr. Lance, and I think decency requires that he be heard . (CBS, "Face the Nation" September 11, 1977)

But one of the earliest calls for his resignation came from Representative Robert Giaimo, Chairman of the House Budget Committee. In addition to noting that Lance was becoming a political liability and that he was "in serious jeopardy," he added that "most of the allegations against him are proving to be true" (CBS Evening News September 1, 1977).

The context of this prevailing definition of Lance and the "inevitable" outcome of the allegations against him had two consequences. First, it made more likely the possibility that charges would continue to be made, especially as journalists began digging into Lance's past and details of various transactions. Second, this theme of corruption—and its inevitable result—made the various charges worthy of publishing and checking out and, ultimately, more plausible and believable.

The dominant theme was supported and illustrated with a host of both specific and vague issues and charges. These became angles on which to hang more evidence about the unquestionable background and general undesirability of Bert Lance. These charges included

1. withholding information from the SCGA during initial confirmation hearings;
2. lack of qualifications for the job of Director of OMB;
3. unethical conduct and questionable business practices that involved, over the course of the hearings, at least six charges:
    a. campaign, personal, and family overdrafts;
    b. establishing correspondent relations with other banks and using these to increase Lance's ability to borrow money;
    c. use of stocks for collateral on two different loans;
    d. influencing the closing of a Comptroller of the Currency report regarding his banking practices;
    e. collaborating with an embezzler; and
    f. inappropriate use of a bank-owned airplane.
4. Lance's inability to do his job at OMB while defending himself;
5. his liability to Carter as a "front man" and as a threat to Carter's image;
6. Lance's personal financial difficulties; and, finally,
7. his "technical innocence."

By themselves, any one—or even a combination—of the various charges would have been vacuous and, as Senator Eagleton said, would have required only a few hours of the SCGA members' time. But once the dominant theme was established and accepted by the news media, more specific charges followed, as well as highly abstract charges such as "sloppy banking."

Although the more specific charges could be dealt with through records, transcripts of past hearings, and expert testimony, the more vague but more damaging claims against Lance could not be as easily discounted. For example, the charge of "withholding information" really involved not only what Lance had told the committee, but also what he had been asked during previous hearings, what the committee's staff intended by a particular line of questioning, their emphasis, and other factors. Moreover, materials describing most of the charges against Lance were available to the committee during the initial hearings, but were largely treated as a few specific points here and there, since the dominant theme of his compromised ethical conduct had not been established. Only later were both the charges and his initial statements reinterpreted. The possibility of points, facts, and connections not standing on their own but being highly dependent on synthesizing an array of events and interpretations was seldom considered by the news presentations. Rather, news media presentations were more consistent with the demands of making a simple and concise presentation of each day's new charges and then explaining how these were but part of a larger picture that was somehow becoming less clouded, primarily due to the combative questioning of the journalism–SCGA team.

One example of the material made available to the SCGA was the information about Lance's overdrafts. On September 15, 1977, Lance told members of the SCGA:

> At our meeting on January 13, I discussed with the committee investigators my previous relationship with the National Bank of Georgia and the Calhoun First National Bank. We discussed my financial assets and liabilities, including loans I had obtained from various banks. We discussed in detail the entire matter concerning the Calhoun First National Bank's involvement in my 1974 gubernatorial race, including overdrafts incurred by my campaign committee, the investigation by the Comptroller's Office and the subsequent referral of this case to the Department of Justice.

> I advised them of my personal overdrafts. We discussed previous financial problems of the Calhoun First National Bank and their current status. Specifically, I disclosed and we discussed the agreement between the Office of the Comptroller of the Currency and the Calhoun First National Bank. We further discussed the fact that the agreement had been removed in November 1976, by the Regional Administrator of the Comptroller's Office.

> Statements taken in the recent IRS investigation of the Comptroller's Office confirm my present testimony. Mr. Childers, who was present at the January 13 meeting, was interviewed during the IRS investigation. His

statement, which was released last Friday, reveals that Mr. Childers and Mr. Schaefer of the committee had telephone conversations on January 17 and 18 with Mr. Robert Bloom, then Acting Comptroller of the Currency, during which the committee investigators asked Mr. Bloom "about the campaign and personal overdrafts of Mr. Lance and his family." Mr. Bloom indicated to them that overdrafts of $100,000 to $200,000 would be "in the ball park." In those conversations Mr. Bloom also advised the Senate investigators that "the campaign overdrafts were referred to the Department of Justice and Justice declined prosecution." Finally, Mr. Bloom told the Senate investigators "that personal overdrafts of the Lance, David, and Chance families had been handled internally and administratively, and had been paid with interest." (Hearings 1977:4, 896–897)

After adding that the problem of overdrafts was one of the first things about which he was asked during the initial confirmation hearings, Lance added:

Those who claim that I was withholding information from this committee at my confirmation hearings have, under the most charitable interpretation, ignored the information that was readily available.

Admittedly, discussions I had in mid-January with the Senate investigators regarding the matters which have now taken on such importance did not include a microscopic review of my affairs. The failure to review additional financial data was not due to any hesitation on my part to disclose anything of interest to the committee. I appraised this committee in some detail of my past financial and personal background and answered fully and accurately all questions that any Senator or staff member asked. (Hearings 1977:4, 897)

Before moving on to further illustrate how Lance's version was essentially confirmed by other staff members' testimony, it is important to note what CBS stressed in its evening news and the Special Report presented the same evening. First, the detailed and complex explanation of the overdraft issue that assumed such importance and took more than seven pages of testimony in Lance's original statement was reduced to a small part of the news report about Lance's first day of testifying before the SCGA. Specifically, of the evening portions of Lance's entire testimony for the day edited to news, only 17 lines of transcript—about a minute and a half of air time—were used. Anchorman Walter Cronkite and other reporters were given approximately 126 lines of transcript—nearly ten and a half minutes—to interpret, introduce, and comment on select portions of Lance's testimony. The various Senators' comments in the questioning of Lance were edited to less than two minutes of air time (about 19 lines of transcript). Time allotments for the CBS Special Report, "The Lance Hearings," were split in a similar way. Lance was provided about nine minutes of air time, Cronkite and the other reporters were given about eleven minutes, and the various Senators' comment accounted for about seven minutes. That the relative proportion of air time is the same in both the evening news and the special report is consistent with the *format* of the newscast, which puts a question and an answer together along with a side comment. All this occurs within the context of an overriding "story line" or theme. The respective introductions to the evening news and the special report by Walter Cronkite illustrate the agenda-setting function (cf. Shaw and McCombs 1977) of the format:

> Here in Washington, the big story: Bert Lance's day in court. . . . It was standing room only by the time they entered the hearing, but a seat was reserved for Lance—a hot seat or a seat of redemption only the days ahead would tell. In his opening statement to the committee, Lance gave an aggressive point-by-point rebuttal to virtually every question that had been raised about his financial activities before becoming budget director. (CBS Evening News September 15, 1977)

> Good evening. Bert Lance today got what he had asked for: his day in court, a hearing by the Senate Governmental Affairs Committee. After a summer of battering by charge after charge concerning his earlier financial activities, the beleaguered Carter Administration Budget Director came on as a man injured and angered—and on the offensive." (CBS News Special Report, "The Lance Hearings" September 15, 1977)

After establishing the proceedings as a combative affair, the remainder of the materials simply squared a briefly stated question or issue off against an opponent, who would also be briefly presented. This procedure, which precludes in-depth discussion of complex issues in favor of simplified story-lines, is illustrated with the evening news reports about Lance's explanation of the charge that he withheld information from the committee. A reporter stated:

> Among other things, Lance cited statements contradicting the report that he might have been involved in a bank embezzlement scheme, said he had fully informed the committee and its staff of his past banking practices. (CBS Evening News September 15, 1977)

The remainder of the newscast's report on Lance focused on Senator Percy's disbelief of several of Lance's statements, Senator Nunn's request to have the Justice Department investigate the leaks that have come out of the Comptroller's office during the investigation, Senator Jackson's point that the extent of bank overdrafts can undermine the public confidence in Lance as head of OMB, a reporter's assessment that the pace of the hearings has thus far "been sluggish," another reporter's rundown of the charges involving double use of collateral, supportive statements from President and Mrs. Carter and supporters in Calhoun,

Georgia, and a reporter's summary comment that "all in all, Lance was able to spend more time smiling than squirming today."

Despite the significance of the charge of "covering-up" or "withholding information" from the SCGA for Lance's future as Director of OMB (as well as the scenario that he was a deceptive wheeler-dealer who was up to all sorts of shenanigans), surprisingly little detail about Lance's awareness of what he had told the committee was set forth. The oft-repeated claim among journalists that such a report would not have been allowed within the severe time restrictions does not hold up, since the details of this issue were also systematically avoided in the special report on the same evening. The main reason for this important omission is the interest in promoting an exciting and fast-paced interchange of questions and responses within a dominant story-line. This means that events are depicted and portrayed for their news value in terms of perceived audience interest and capacity to be entertainingly and smoothly presented, rather than in terms of achieving a fuller understanding.

Lance's explanation of the charge that he withheld information about his overdrafts and other matters was given 40 lines of transcript, or about three minutes of air time. And still the main point about what the committee had previously known was not stressed:

Cronkite: Through the weeks of disclosures about Lance's activities, a recurring question was: Why didn't all this come out at his confirmation hearing? Well, Lance addressed that question today. He testified that a week before the hearing, he told members of the committee staff about the various financial matters that are the focus of the current hearing.

Lance: Perhaps the most fundamental charge to be discussed at this hearing is the allegation that I failed to disclose all pertinent facts to this committee at the time of my confirmation hearing. This oft-repeated accusation by certain members of this committee was readily seized upon by the press, who sought to denigrate me—and, indeed, the Carter administration—with suggestions of a "cover-up." Members of this committee have been quoted in the national press as having said the committee had been "misled" prior to my confirmation.

Senator Javits: On January 18th, 1977, you appeared before us for confirmation and, at that time, I questioned you upon these very matters. And these were your answers, and I'd like to read you the whole thing because, though I only have 15 minutes now, I'll take as many 15 minutes as it takes to find out one thing: Did you tell us all you should have told us as a nominee for one of the highest offices in the land?

[Javits then reads excerpts from the transcript of January 17].

Did you know at the time that you had not paid interest—from 1972 to June 1974?

Lance: Senator, the response to the question was yes, that they had been repaid with interest, and that is a correct statement as, I think, was responsive to your question. Now the policy of the bank prior to 1974, as I said in my statement this morning, and I say again, was that interest or service charges were not levied on overdrafts by the bank. From the time that interest was charged—at the rate of one and a half percent over prime—those interest charges were paid, in full. (CBS News Special Report, "The Lance Hearings" September 15, 1977)

Despite Lance's statement about the information he had provided to the committee, the coverage given it in the newscast as well as in this special report—and others that followed—was relatively small. This seems paradoxical in view of the concluding comment made by anchorman Walter Cronkite to this first special report on Lance:

Whatever face the White House chooses to put on the Lance hearings, the fact is that the Carter Administration itself shares the witness stand with its Budget Director. . . . While it is high drama—a man fighting before the world to save his reputation—that, of course, is not the only significance of the Lance hearing. Perhaps the main question is whether his aides—or Mr. Carter himself—in any way participated in withholding information to obtain senate confirmation of his Budget Director. If that should be proved by these hearings—it certainly was not today—this nation's recovery from the dark days of Watergate would have suffered a severe setback. (CBS New Special report, "The Lance Hearings" September 15, 1977)

Thus the central question—according to Cronkite—of another "cover-up" was at least partially dealt with in Lance's opening statement and subsequent questioning, but this was primarily ignored in favor of simply establishing the scenario on the basis of selected events in Lance's past and then providing an overriding interpretation of them. Of course, as we noted earlier, the events of Watergate and the role of the news media in those events had no small bearing on providing an apt choice of scenarios to encapsulate a plethora of Lance-related incidents. Nevertheless, it seems clear that the question of a cover-up was standing on its own, independent of careful scrutiny of the events and charges that had given rise to it. Scrutinizing the testimony and events would have helped settle that question before it was raised and inserted as yet another piece of the "maze of charges against Lance." In short, the presupposition that Lance was culpable of something led to the way this report was newsworthy; and the way it was inserted and presented within the news context was contingent on the news format, image of audience interest, and employment of simplifying angles of represent pregiven—and largely unquestioned—general story lines or themes. And from this Lance could not escape. But the news net was drawn even tighter through the use of "game" and "play" metaphors by network correspondents in presenting a view of the committee hearings that was compatible with the entertainment format.

Politics, Games, and Plays. The Lance case was presented as a game, a play, and as theatre. As a game, the "big" question was who was the winner, who was losing, and what strategy was being used. A few examples follow.

A reporter asked Lance if he had sensed a "possible wavering in White House support for you," to which Lance replied:

> Oh, I haven't sensed that at all. I think that strength and support is very obvious. I don't know how else it—it could be shown any more. I expect that you always hear a lot of comments about wavering and who's winning and who's losing. That seems to be something that you all seem to have a great interest in, especially about who's winning and who's losing. But the strength and support of the White House has been very obvious, I would say. (CBS Morning News September 1, 1977)

> Cronkite: Good evening. Bert Lance underwent a second day of detailed questioning by the Senate Governmental Affairs Committee. . . . President Carter . . . reportedly thinks his old friend . . . has gained ground. (CBS Evening News September 16, 1977)

The game metaphor was evident during the CBS Special Report on the Lance hearings.

> Cronkite: Good evening. The second day of Bert Lance's testimony into his financial affairs took a turn toward the tough side today, as Senate committee members tried to regain the offensive.

> Reporter: He held his own again today, but I think perhaps the committee got to him on a few points, and didn't yesterday. . . . It's the first time that, I think, we've seen him squirm a little. . . .

> Reporter: Lance made a very good appearance, I think everybody agrees, at the start. Also you have to remember that—that these people haven't had a whole lot to cheer about or laugh about lately, so it was just kind of a change for them to see their guy sort of—sort of taking the lead. . . .

> Cronkite: Today it seemed to me, watching the proceedings, that—that there was definitely a defense posture on the Democratic side of the committee, as opposed to the prosecution side, on the Republican side. Is there any indication from either of you . . . that the White House is organizing the defense up there on this committee?

> Cronkite: Let's take a quick poll. Who's ahead—Lance or the committee? Schakne?

> Schakne: No question, Lance is ahead.

> Cronkite: Serafin?

> Serafin: Lance, but there are still a lot of questions to come.

> Cronkite: And Schieffer?

> Schieffer: Lance, but he has, by no means, won.

> Cronkite: I remain uncommitted. Thank you gentlemen.

The last brief exchange was followed by Cronkite's apology for so blatantly comparing the hearings to "an athletic contest."

> Cronkite: The answers were all right, but that really wasn't a very good question of mine a moment ago. It may be the way we all are inclined to think of this Senate hearing: Who is ahead? But this isn't an athletic contest and there is no scoreboard at either end of the committee room. We, the public, might be excused for losing track of the real meaning and purpose of this inquiry when the committee itself seems to have so much trouble with that matter. (CBS News Special Report, "The Lance Hearings" September 16, 1977)

Cronkite's apology can be readily dismissed as rhetoric, since the working logic and assumptions of transforming events into simple encapsulated summary statements for purposes of entertainment rely on the routine employment of standard metaphors and images. The "win—lose" distinction is again apparent in Roger Mudd's analysis of the committee's performance:

> Bert Lance has succeeded in making the committee's record of performance almost as big an issue as his own. He has run rings around it with such ease that the committee now plans to take open testimony on Monday about why it did not know in January what it seems to know now. . . . The result has been that the senators have been publicly embarrassed and, in the words of one, "made to look silly." In recent days, the investigative staff has been beefed up by borrowing from various subcommittees, but it may be too late. *Bert Lance still has this committee on the defensive,* and he may pull off the impossible, making not only the senators look silly, but also their staff. (CBS Evening News September 16, 1977, italics added)

What Mudd did not mention, of course, was that the news media, within their own context of work and meaning, could avoid having to deal with problems of "fact" and "countercharges" of "sloppy work," and could never be made "to look silly." Indeed, the context of their work was significant insofar as the impact of President Carter's final decision about Lance was concerned. This is why the metaphor of game is so important; it is a framework that can be applied to the events in the world in order to make them interesting, intelligible, and presentable within the context of media formats and logic.

Before giving some examples of the play and theatre metaphors, it should be noted that the game metaphor was reinforced by deriving "points" from opinion polls.

> Reporter: There's no question that—that Lance's appearance has been going over fairly well as far as the—as far as the public is concerned. Phone calls and mail at the White House were running four, four and a half to

one against him before his appearance. Since then, the calls—the White House has just been besieged with phone calls, and those calls are running three and four to one in his favor now. (CBS News Special Report, "The Lance Hearings" September 16, 1977)

Reporter: The Lance affair may be affecting President Carter's own popularity. A Harris poll out today shows the President's overall rating is down; 52 percent give him a positive job rating, 44 percent negative, down from 59 to 37 in July, and 69 to 27 in April. And the Harris poll shows that on the way he has handled the Lance affair, Mr. Carter gets a 40 to 33 negative rating, with 27 percent still undecided. (CBS Morning News September 9, 1977)

Reporter: The mail and the phone calls here continue to run heavily in Lance's favor again today, but spokesman Powell says public opinion will play no part in the decision on whether Lance stays. (CBS Evening News September 19, 1977)

Cronkite: An Associated Press poll taken nationwide after Bert Lance's testimony finds that 38 percent think he should resign as Budget Director; 35 percent think he should stay; and 27 percent have no opinion. The poll also finds that 53 percent say the Lance affair has not affected their opinion of President Carter's commitment to high ethical standards; 26 percent say their confidence has decreased; and 8 percent say their confidence has increased. Fifteen hundred forty-eight persons were polled with results subject to a sampling error of plus or minus two-and-a-half percent. (CBS Evening News September 20, 1977)

The use of polls as a form of evidence was carried over to an association of bankers that provided the data for Senator Percy to strengthen his claim that Lance must resign.

Reporter: Percy said he had sampled public opinion and passed the results on to Lance.

Percy: I told him that the strongest critics he has are his own peers among county bankers; that they have been incensed. And I called the President and told him that as well, I wanted Mr. Lance to know the kind of judgments that were being made, not just by the media but by his own peers; by people all over the country; by businessmen, by labor leaders; and I've been all over the state of Illinois. In fairness to him he recounted that this was not the way his mail was running; this was not the way he heard it; and this is not the way the people of Georgia felt. But I told him I could only speak on behalf of the people of Illinois. (CBS Morning News September 6, 1977)

Another metaphor that supported the use of a dominant story line, and which was then supported with various angles, was the play or theatre image. Like the game metaphor, the presentation of the Lance case as a dramatic series of events taking place in a theaterlike setting permitted newsworkers to fit the events of banking and Senatorial hearings into the news context. A reporter drew the analogy out to its fullest extent in the following comment:

> Washington's gulping down its breakfast in unseeming haste this morning so it can get to Capital Hill where a whiff of blood is in the autumn air. All sorts of legal, political and ethical matters are wrapped up in the investigation of Bert Lance by Senator Abraham Ribicoff's Governmental Affairs Committee. But let's not kid ourselves, *this is also theater, with all the human strife and poignancy that theater affords.* The title of the play is *The Chamberlain's Trial.* Consider the cast: Jimmy Carter plays the philosopher king, who came to power with moral instruction for his people. His once glittering and confident court is now soiled by the suspicion that truth, which is the very cement of morals, may not have been fully told when the Lance nomination was sent to the Senate. Jody Powell, White House Press Secretary, is the court's wise jester. His epigrammatic wit once lightened the king's moral earnestness and made it pleasurable. Suddenly though Powell appears as something less than wise or witty. He apparently tried to impugn the reputation of Senator Charles Percy, the ranking minority member of the Ribicoff committee. Ribicoff himself, the unwilling discoverer of wrong. Several weeks ago he accused the press of smearing Bert Lance; then came more revelations. Ribicoff publicly said that he had misspoken. He is the reluctant chief judge in the play. And finally, Bert Lance. He is the chamberlain on trial; a dogged and cheerful loyalist, who placed himself at the King's service long before the king came to his throne. Now facts about Lance's life, other than that early loyalty, may rob him of loyalty's reward, which is power in the king's service. So, it is theater. The audience is gathering, and this morning the curtain goes up. (CBS Morning News September 15, 1977, italics added)

Another reporter skillfully combined the game and theatre metaphors the next day.

> A funny thing happened yesterday on the way to the hanging. The Senate Governmental Affairs Committee had prepared for a public execution; the press was ready; so was the rest of the Congress. But the victim refused to die. Instead, Bert Lance came out swinging, on the attack in a statement which at various times quoted the Bible, the Constitution, and Abraham Lincoln. . . . Hearings like this are several different things all at once. They are, though they don't always look it, searches for truth, and on that level some of Lance's problems remain unresolved. He says he told committee staffers about criticisms of his banking early, before his confirmation hearing. We don't know yet what the staffers will say. Other discrepancies remain. But a *hearing is also a theatrical event, and on that level Mr. Lance was a solid first day winner.* All the thunder was his. And a hearing is a political event. And the more this one turns into party line wrangling, as it seemed to be doing at times yesterday, the better Mr. Lance will look. So, on the first day a visitor could leave the hearing humming a new version of an old labor song—"I dreamt I saw Bert Lance last night, alive as you and me. Why Bert, I said, you're ten years dead—I never died, said he." (CBS Morning News September 16, 1977, italics added)

The Power of News

Lance's fate was sealed when massive journalistic investigations began delving into his past. In the contexts of Watergate and the growing power of journalism, even the President of the United States could not save him from mass-mediated allegations hurled by journalists, journalists-through-politicians, and politicians-through-journalists. In this day of public image and massive public-relations frontwork, simply being charged via mass media connections is enough to taint and delegitimize; this is understood by journalists and especially politicians who depend on media cooperation to maintain appearances of legitimacy and competence, as well as do their own work. In brief, *it is axiomatic that what is presented via the mass media matters and has consequence.* Of course, media impact varies with situations and issues, but the overall thrust is quite consistent.

A related point to be stressed is that the context of media work and the news perspective that it has propagated now take precedence over virtually all other contexts of meaning and logic in the realm of public presentations. This means that any individual, activity, organization, or institution that is treated or covered by the mass media will be affected by them in predictable ways.

Although more research is needed on such effects over an extended period of time—since media influence will change—several general statements now can be made. First, public presentations increasingly demand knowledge of media and especially *news* media, logic, and techniques. Second, the media perspective will be considered—and usually played to—in pursuing any public statements or action. Third, "experts" skilled in the knowledge, techniques, and ways to manipulate activities and events to fit media procedures will become more important and influential in their respective organizations. Fourth, skilled public performances are increasingly demanded from all individuals and organizations who depend on mass audiences for legitimacy and approval. Fifth, any performance that is not approved of by the mass media is not only doomed to failure, but the "actors" in that performance are themselves likely to become objects of publication, allegation, and attack. Sixth, the truth or accuracy of a report has virtually no bearing on the consequences for the individual, activity, organization, or institution involved—only the presentation matters. Seventh, the growing significance of news power in our society will make any criticism of its role either futile or a target for counterattack. Eighth, more public presentations and related tasks will adopt the media perspective, and, in the process, public life will be less a reflection of private life. Ninth, more bureaucratic, organizational, and governmental actions and decisions will (1) take place behind "closed doors," and/or (2) be sufficiently benign to avoid the wrath and potentially destructive application of the news perspective. Finally, any attempt to delineate the nature and significance of the mass media and particularly the news perspective for social life, public acts, and official information will be denounced with moral vigor and will be treated as a major threat to our society's heritage, freedom, and future.

Each of these points summarizes an important dimension of the Lance case: (1) the selection of angles, themes, and appropriate metaphors to set the scene for action and thereby allow the angles and themes to aid in the news process, (2) the overwhelming interest in simplifying the complex process and context of banking in a rural southern community, (3) joining the government in its work and actually doing "politics" even as the SCGA members were engaged in a kind of self-serving amateur investigative journalism, complete with allegations presented through a predefined theme, (4) the symbolic denunciation of Lance by veteran politicians even before the major part of the hearings were under way in September, and (5) the widespread denial by journalists and victims of the contribution of journalistic work to Lance's resignation.

But even the victims can openly confront the role of the news media in national politics, especially if they depend on it for legitimacy. Indeed, during the entire hearings, only Senators Eagleton and Nunn made disparaging remarks about the role of the media in Lance's fate, and Eagleton addressed most of his remarks to the way Senator Percy had provided the reporters with unsubstantiated charges, the publication of which, according to Eagleton, produced a sense of "guilt by accumulation."

> Senator Nunn: Senator Eagleton said the other day it's almost guilt by accumulation. I think all of us can learn a lesson from this. I think the media plays a very important role in our national life, and I would do nothing whatsoever to abridge that and the first amendment rights that we have, and I don't think government should, but I believe the news media can do a little self-examination regarding their own role in this overall matter. (CBS Evening News September 21, 1977)

Note that in criticizing the news handling of the Lance case Nunn is almost apologetic. He must be, since he has a political future to look forward to. The now taken-for-granted supplication to the news media was even more evident in President Carter's remarks after Lance resigned. In response to a question about his feelings if Lance "was unfairly drummed out of the government," Carter replied:

> That's a difficult question for me to answer. I have had personal knowledge of so many of the statements and happenings that have been widely

publicized. Some of them were greatly exaggerated; some of them were actually untrue. On some occasions, the report of an incident was not unbiased, but unfair. In general, I think the media have been fair. There are some exceptions. In general, I think that the Senate committee has been fair. (Carter Presidential News Conference September 21, 1977)

Although the President made some soft criticisms of the news media in the above remarks, he was still condescending; he did not come right out and say the journalists were correct, and he did not completely validate their perspective and logic throughout the Lance ordeal. This led another reporter to ask a few moments later if the President "still feel(s) that Mr. Lance has avoided the appearance of impropriety or whether a new standard is now in operation?" Carter responded:

There's not been one allegation that he violated his responsibility or his oath when he was sworn in, that he'd done anything improper at all, that he's violated any law. And even those allegations that were made about his life several years ago, in my opinion, have been proven false and without foundation. (Carter Presidential News Conference September 21, 1977)

When another reporter insisted that Lance's "overdraft loans of more than $5,000 violated the banking law," and continued with, "but how do you justify this with your statement that he never broke any law?" the President replied:

Well, my assessment is that you are trying to succeed where the Senate committee failed. There was no judgment made that Bert Lance did anything illegal. The only Comptroller's report that I saw specifically said that he had done nothing illegal. (Carter Presidential News Conference September 21, 1977)

But whether Lance had done anything illegal or not was beside the point when viewed from the absolutist perspective of the newswork that would produce simplistic and dramatic reports. Indeed, numerous documents were presented during his hearings about the relative merits and rules of banking practices and even "standards of ethics" in various parts of the country. This was even true with the allegation of "overdrafts," which were construed as personal loans to Lance and his relatives. Lance insisted—and provided documentation—that the Calhoun National Bank afforded a "liberal overdraft policy" to many of the bank's customers. But this was the point that Lance was challenged on by the SCGA members as well as many journalists, which further implied that his financial affairs were a "maze," that he was dealing with a "double standard," and that he regarded the bank as his "personal playpen." This point was raised during an interview with William Sexton,

Associate Editor of *Newsday*, a magazine that called for Lance's resignation early in September. Even though his magazine had pursued the overdraft issue and raised all the ethical cautions in permitting Lance to maintain in office, Mr. Sexton rather sheepishly noted that overdrafts may not be all that bad, and perhaps not that uncommon:

> I not only have an overdraft myself even as we speak, but my checking account is with a fairly good-sized bank in the New York metropolitan area which sends me letters every once in a while encouraging me to make the overdraft larger. ("MacNeil/Lehrer Report" September 15, 1977)

Statements such as this were not widely circulated and could not diffuse the enthusiasm and pressure brought to bear on selected federal agencies to pursue the Lance case even after he resigned. This was done largely to further document the media's charges against him. It worked. In April 1978, the Securities and Exchange Commission and the Comptroller of the Currency charged Lance with civil fraud and asked that his banking activities be restricted. The charges involved Lance's overdrafts, which, the SEC made clear, were not illegal, but that appropriate procedures for recording the transactions and reporting them to stockholders had not been followed. The SEC also charged that it should have been notified by Lance and others who attempted to take over a bank holding company (Los Angeles *Times* April 26, 1978; Phoenix *Gazette* April 27, 1978). Although these civil laws do not carry prison or money fines, the leveling of these charges against Lance was a great symbolic victory for the media that contributed to his leaving office.[3] And perhaps most significantly, it validated the logic and procedures used in the news process that substantially contributed to the definition and solution of the Lance affair, and increased the likelihood that this perspective and procedure would be employed with other individuals, activities, organizations, or institutions in the future. We think the consequences are predictable.

Conclusion

When viewed from the perspective of news values, formats, and organizational routines for making newscasts entertaining, simple, and consistent, the Lance case was an ideal opportunity for journalists to do "good work." The work consisted of transforming the specifics of the Lance case and the SCGA hearings into material compatible with the logic and constraints of the news perspective, which is but a special aspect of the media perspective we have addressed throughout this book. As illustrated above, this meant that certain events would be focused on, treated, and given meaning in order to promote a particular kind of presentation and understanding that was compatible with, for example, scheduling and time considerations, entertainment values, and images of the audience. Although there can certainly be no objection to making a complex proceeding intelligible and putting it in a broader social and political framework, this was neither the intent nor the result of the news presentations about the Lance case. The prevailing logic and guiding considerations for treating this complex topic were not, for example, the day-to-day context of banking, nor were they aimed at illuminating the committee confirmation process—all this was secondary to, or even more remote from, the prevailing logic used in constructing the events of the Lance case to suit the guidelines, assumptions, and rules of competent TV newswork. Our findings indicate that the myriad of details pertinent to the Lance case were regarded in a very occupational and practical way; they were used primarily as a *resource* to aid in the news coverage of the case, rather than being treated as a *topic* or *substance* that demanded careful and detailed scrutiny in order to accurately unravel, understand, and then present the various facts and situations that were the actual foundation for the circumstances surrounding Lances' activities, confirmation, and eventual resignation. But for this type of work to occur the newsworkers would have to, first, be aware of the logic their perspective and workday routines necessarily impose on events and, second, they would then have to be willing to curtail or check these distorting influences. It would therefore mean viewing newswork as a significant context of meaning that transforms experience and substance into workable news forms, rather than assuming that the news process is inconsequential for how events occur, are defined, selected, transformed, and then presented. The work of news, then, is not an organizational mirror for the world, but is in itself a major organization form for interpreting the world of experience. And as we have seen, this work can have grave consequences.

The Bert Lance case is significant beyond its impact on the life of one man and the Carter administration. This case may be regarded as the culmination of a series of events from the era of John F. Kennedy through Watergate, and right on through the Reagan and Bush presidencies. The political order is constituted through communication channels, logics, and formats, which engage the interaction, discourse, and rhetoric of cultural myth makers, players, and audiences. This means that the work of politics is reflexively woven into the work of mass communication and the interpretation and framing of these messages. To say it was "good television" does not make it any more or less "real" than the eruption of Mt. St. Helens; it is the meaning of these events and the procedures become folded into our histories, myths, and collective memories, which sets us all up for the focus of our future scrutiny, hopes, and fears, and interpretive frameworks. Politics is one of our media worlds.

Notes

1. Although this has been done with foreign affairs news (Batscha 1975), the "cold war" (Aronson 1955), a hot war such as Vietnam (Epstein 1974; Braestrup 1978), crime and drug use (Cohen and Young 1973), environmental pollution (Molotch and Lester 1974, 1975), the Eagleton story (Altheide 1976), Watergate (Altheide 1976), and, more recently, the women's movement (Tuchman et al. 1978) and professional sports (Altheide and Snow 1978), the explicit connections to the media occupational culture and the logic that infuses it have not been precisely examined.
2. The Senate Committee on Governmental Affairs documents referred to in the text are listed by volume number in the reference section.
3. Following an even more extensive investigation of nearly two years, Lance was indicated by a grand jury in May 1979. All charges were dropped on June 7, 1980.

6

A Political Kaleidoscope

"Highway to the Danger Zone"

Kenny Loggins

Lessons from Lance

The TV content of political intrigue and accompanying dethronings is enticing. We saw with Watergate, then "Lancegate," how investigative reporting could serve as a "watchdog" of people in high places, and help keep them honest; if not, they would be exposed, tarnished, and removed, especially incumbents. This, according to some informed views, is about all that can be expected of the journalism–political connection. We saw that Jimmy Carter used the media criteria of righteousness to put down all politicians associated with Watergate.

> Ever since Jimmy Carter took them by surprise, journalists have tried to counter campaign media strategies by stepping up their scrutiny of anyone who seems likely to break out of the pack. (Lichter et al. 1988:114)

It would be no exaggeration to suggest that some observers had even prayed for such scrutiny. But Oscar Wilde also had an idea about our hopes and wishes. He wrote, "When the Gods wish to punish us, they answer our prayers." In Part I of this chapter, we provide some materials to illustrate how some recent political scenarios were punctuated with media logic, and in Part II we suggest an alternative theoretical perspective for understanding voting behavior.

Part I

Carter and the Iranian hostages

The Lance affair happened early in the Carter administration but it was not the most important political fallout from the media; the Iranian

165

hostages story holds that distinction. Fifty-two Americans were taken captive from the U.S. Embassy in Iran by Iranian revolutionary guards in November 1979 and were held for 444 days (cf. Altheide 1985c) until President Reagan was inaugurated on January 20, 1981. Their captivity was the most extensively reported continuing TV news story of the past 20 years, and perhaps in U.S. history. For example, Altheide's (1981, 1985c) study of this coverage examined some 925 reports, totaling nearly 26 hours, over a sampling period of 112 days, or about one-quarter of the time period! Each network newscast included a statement similar to those of CBS' Walter Cronkite: "and that's the way it is, June 9, 1980, the 219th day of captivity." One new evening news program, ABC's "Nightline," emerged on March 24, 1980, from its temporary predecessor, America Held Hostage."

An exhaustive study of this unprecedented coverage is presented elsewhere (cf. Altheide 1985c), with additional observations by others (cf. Said 1981) and will not be repeated here. The general findings were that (1) the coverage was dramatic, stressing visuals of hostages, but more commonly, hostage families and their sadness and suffering; (2) government spokespersons from the U.S. dominated the coverage; (3) following the rules of format for access to visuals, the topics and themes differed systematically with the origin of reports, e.g., Washington/New York, other cities in the United States (4) we learned very little about the context of the problem, or the issues surrounding the reasons and events for taking the hostages captive; and (5) Iran, Iranians, and the Moslem faith were stereotyped as crazy, mad, insane, lunatics, and irrational. With the aid of additional documentation and statement from many of the main characters, the role of the media can now be summarized. In addition to a plethora of news reports and scholarly analyses, our sources include statements from President Carter, his press secretary, Jody Powell, a report authored by the late Arnold Raphel, who was a key member of the hostage-negotiating team, and the account by Gary Sick (1985), who was President Carter's principal White House aide for Iran on the National Security Council staff.

The mass media, and especially TV news, influenced the hostage situation because it became tied to Carter's presidency, which in turn was oriented, often unwillingly, to the single major concern of getting the hostages released. Then Republican candidate for president, Ronald Reagan, chided Carter and the Democrats throughout his campaign as being weak, letting a third-rate power (Iran) "bring America to its knees," and vowed that if elected, America's strength would be renewed, resolve would be shown, and pride in America would return. Carter could not reverse the hostage stigma, and was soundly defeated by

Reagan. The hostages were officially released five minutes after Carter's term in office ended (Sick 1985:341).

Several important points need to be noted before proceeding with this analysis of the Iranian hostage scenario. First, many of the statements we draw on for this analysis were made for the "record," and the TV record at that. Although the formats and the contexts did differ somewhat, we should not be surprised if the same media logic that informed the original ordeal, including the "State Department briefings," did not also bear on these comments. And relatedly, when someone, like a former President (Carter), comments on past accomplishments and problems, we should not be surprised if these statements are also made with a future orientation, that is, in anticipation of how how their past performance will be evaluated in the future. Like the journalists who select and edit statements to illustrate a theme, we must choose some segments of comments made by some of the main players in this media drama that came to be known by various names, including "America Held Hostage," "The Iranian Hostage Crisis," and "America's Shame." Despite devoting several years of our lives to studying and understanding these case studies, we do not propose to insult the reader with the authoritative claim that the "final answer" is in, that there are no additional materials or interpretations that may be useful in clarifying the role of the mass media on this issue. Just as our thinking on media logic has continued to evolve over the past decade, our thoughts about events such as the Iranian hostage situation are continually refocused as new information becomes available, often in the form of extensive interviews such as some of the materials presented below. Our general view of the role of media logic has not changed, but we invite the reader to read, reflect, and then seek out additional information about various views on this event, and some of the others ones to follow, in order to clarify the nature, relevance and impact of media logic and formats on big-time politics (cf. Schandler 1977). Here are a few reflections by some of the players in the Iranian hostage drama.

Except for a number of research reports produced by academics (cf. Altheide 1978, 1985b,c), Arnold Raphel (1980–81), a member of Carter's hostage negotiating team, provided the most analytic statement about the impact of the news media coverage on the Iranian hostage situation. In a report to the Foreign Service Institute, this consummate diplomat, who would be killed in a Pakistani air crash in August 1988, wrote:

> The capture of the embassy and the hostages was a ready-made media
> event, assisted by the initial eagerness of the Iranians to have access to the

American media. In such a situation, it would have been very difficult if
not impossible for the Administration to downplay the issue. (p. 20)

Another Carter aid, Gary Sick (1985:220), noted:

> The crisis was the longest-running human interest story in the history of
> television, in living color from the other side of the world. Commercially
> it was a stunning success. Never had a news story so thoroughly captured
> the imagination of the U.S. Public. Never had the nation sat so totally
> transfixed before its television sets awaiting the latest predictable chants
> of "Death to America" alternating with the day's interview of a brave rela-
> tive of one of the hostages . . . Perhaps it was the true genius of America
> to transform a political disaster into a commercial bonanza.
>
> There are several possible explanations for this phenomenon. In the
> first place, it must be remembered, not very much happened. The hos-
> tages were taken, held for fourteen and a half months and then released.
> There was a good deal of political rhetoric all around, punctuated by a
> few moments of genuine drama and tragedy, but for the most part it was
> political shadowboxing, more form than substance.

Eight years after the crisis, Lloyd Cutler, Carter's White House Coun-
sel, stated "It wasn't that the press covered it, it was how they covered
it." For example, ABC's anchor, Frank Reynolds, stated, "This was the
305th day of captivity for the American hostages in Iran." "It became a
running news story. Indeed, Ted Koppel built a new ABC Program,
which is now called *Nightline* but was then called *America Held Hostage*
. . . The result of that was that it was impossible to take the hostage problem off the center of U.S. government activity even though there was a
good case for cooling it" (PBS, "Power Game" January 4, 1989). Koppel
saw it differently:

> The state department, rather than just giving 1 briefing a day, was giving
> 2, sometimes 3 briefings a day. The White House would give a couple of
> briefings a day . . . [Carter] had an agenda; he thought that by focusing
> on this foreign policy issue he could keep Teddy Kennedy at bay in the
> Democratic primaries. It reared up and bit him where it hurt most. But
> he couldn't have known that at the time he initiated that agenda. So both
> Carter and the Ayatollah Khomeini . . . each believing that the press would
> serve his agenda, both were wrong. (PBS, "Power Game" January 4, 1989)

When an interviewer suggested to Koppel that Carter wanted to let it
cool down, but the press (including Koppel) would not, Koppel replied:

> by that time the public was in an uproar, the public could not get enough
> of it. You simply had to listen to radio call-in shows, you simply had to
> look at the front pages of every newspaper in the country. There was a
> public appetite for it that simply could not be satiated.

But, an interviewer might query, isn't this a bit circular, saying that the public demands what the mass media are providing? Koppel stated:

> We are subject to a daily plebiscite . . . and if not enough people watch *Nightline,* the American people by its vote will have determined that it's time to kick Ted Koppel out of office.

Hodding Carter, President Carter's press secretary during the Iranian crisis, discussed the Iranian situation at various times.

> The thing that the Carter administration wanted was a lot of focus on our running around to prove that we cared about those hostages. And for months we encouraged that kind of coverage. (PBS August 27, 1989)

And,

> If the administration had not been a willing participant in this elevation of a terrible story into a national obsession, the media could not have stood with it. (ABC November 3, 1989)

However, Gary Sick (1985:222–223), Carter's aid to the National Security Council for Iran, argued that the President did not attempt to use the hostage crisis and resulting coverage, although he did benefit from it at first:

> The argument can be overdone. Given the overwhelmingly emotional response of the U.S. people and the daily diet of emotionally charged television coverage from Tehran, there were limits on the ability of any administration to move the issue lower on the national agenda. There is no convincing evidence whatsoever that such a strategy would have resulted in the hostages being released even one day earlier. On the contrary, the purpose of such a strategy would realistically have to be seen as political damage-limitation. By downplaying the importance of the crisis, Carter might have hoped to minimize domestic political reaction against himself and his administration in a situation where the United States had very limited means to affect the course of events.

And

> Those who suggested that Carter artificially "hyped" the hostages crisis for his own political benefit got it exactly backwards. President Carter initially benefited from the hostage crisis, as presidents almost always gain public support in a national crisis, and he was quite prepared to make the most of it. However, a more cautious politician, realizing the dangers of failure, would rather quickly have attempted to dissociate himself from the consequences and would have been more inclined to adopt the kind of damage-limiting strategy that later had such appeal to pundits and academic observers. To the best of my knowledge, President Carter never seriously

considered such a strategy, and that, again, was characteristic of the man. (p. 223)

A reporter for ABC, Jeff Greenfield, apparently drew on the research of the news coverage of the Iranian hostage coverage, which showed that very little of a historical or cultural context was presented, when he followed Hodding Carter's comment (above) with,

> It [TV coverage] also showed one of television's endemic weaknesses: the tendency to throw such images at us wrenched out of historical or political contexts

Gary Sick (1985:220) agreed with reporter Greenfield and academic studies by Altheide (1985), Said (1981), and others that the intensive coverage did not seem to produce much understanding by the public:

> In this contest of hate, Jimmy Carter and most Americans were at a distinct disadvantage. Americans did not hate Iran, at least not until the crisis started. In fact, Americans knew little about the country, cared less, and—despite the massive television exposure and the spilling of millions of gallons of printer's ink—managed to emerge from the ordeal with their basic ignorance surprisingly intact. For Iran, the taking of the embassy was revolutionary theater of the highest order; and in the United States, where there was genuine concern for the fate of its fellow citizens, Iran found the perfect audience.

Then, in one of the few statements that President Carter has made about the impact on the TV coverage on the hostage situation, he stated,

> I was relieved, on occasion, when the Ayatollah would exclude the Western media from the streets of Iran because then the threats against the hostages would die down, the public demonstrations would die down. Absent television cameras, Iran became much more moderate in its attitude toward the crisis itself. (ABC November 3, 1989)

In light of this additional material, it is useful to integrate our extensive investigation of the Iranian coverage and other international "crises" in order to further clarify the relevance of media logic and formats for political action.

What we want to stress is how the logic of television became incorporated into the reasoning, options, decisions, and assessments of the event. During a program aired on PBS in 1988 about the "Prime Time President," Former President Carter discussed the impact of TV discourse and formats on political awareness and the sense of significance:

> You even have the feeling that something has not happened unless it is recorded by the television camera and later rebroadcast. It is almost like

you're living in a vacuum if you do something that is significant and then it is not publicized by television. (PBS October 3, 1988)

The Media Script, the Reagan Act

It is not our intent to join in the ongoing debate about whether Reagan won the presidency in 1980 (and 1984) or whether the Democrats and Walter Mondale lost it. Nor will we argue that TV was the only important factor in the outcome. As our work should make clear to the reader by this point, we find conventional political analyses quite flawed in seeking to discover the "underlying issues" that "led people to the polls." Such accounts place far too much emphasis on the individual talent of a political actor, rather than on the communicative and cultural context that informs voters' meaningful interpretations about the nature of life, its problems, plausible solutions, and that can be expected of political leaders. In a mass media age, when all actors invoke media logic in making sense of their lives, it is the scenario that is far more significant than the individual candidate, who, after all, must be able to enact the appropriate characterological expectations of the audience.

What we do argue is that the mass media in general, and TV coverage with its thematic emphases in particular, produced a *cascading of mass-mediated scenarios, events, issues, and discourse* that was consequential for "what won," regardless of "who won." Reagan, the professional actor, we contend, was better typecast for the scenario than Carter and the other cast of Democratic losers. The same was true of Bush's ascendancy in 1988.

All political action is bounded by the communicative contexts and criteria underlying the claims of political actors who seek to define situations. The politics of the last quarter of the twentieth century and those that will take us well into the twenty-first century are reflections of our communication culture. It is the social construction of political worlds that surrounds candidates. The clear trouncings of challengers by Reagan and Bush do give an identity to the world they help legitimate, but they do not control that world; they can participate only within the symbolic mass communication parameters of the postmodern world. We offer a glance at the media stage for the form and content of politics that now confronts us.

What did this world look like? What has been different during this time is that for the first time in American history—and perhaps all history—a single communication format dominates and essentially directs the actions, interpretations, and consequences of political behavior. This is media logic, in which the actors, audiences, and commentators reproduce technological discourse of TV visuals, replays, projections (polls), dialogue, and images. In the first place, audiences—who are also the voters—are evaluating candidates, policies, and priorities on the basis of media logic of believability, namely, does it look and sound right and familiar with other experience, which itself is increasingly mediated. In the second instance, politicians who are coached by advertising experts seek to package their visual presentations in brief, punchy, and thematic ways in order to present the image of leadership, trust, and confidence called for by market researchers unsullied by comparisons with delivering pizzas or publics. In the third instance, the media moguls who have helped destroy conventional political party organizations in favor of prime-time primary elections (cf. Robinson 1977) evaluate the candidates' performances in the discourse of media logic through themes and angles already familiar to the audiences weaned on media criteria. Such themes, as we noted in a previous chapter, may be borrowed from sports ("horse race") mythology ("David and Goliath"), and often the news transformation of spectacular political events such as "Watergate," "Lancegate," "Milkgate," Koreagate," and "Contragate."

Corruption and individual culpability were stressed in entertainment and news programming, but there were also accounts of social problems. There just seemed to be so many, one right after another, so many thrown at voters, and so little systematic integration of common denominators, that they hit very few citizens like a full deck, but more like cards blowing about in the media whirlwind. Civil rights was a thing of the past, the 1960s. Former presidential press secretary, Hodding Carter, who became a journalist, commented on the information onslaught and how it was produced through the skilled application of media logic by various news sources:

> We don't have an independent sense of judgment about the news. [We march to the same beat.] That number is the number that the people who make the news now have. Mike Deaver [Reagan's Deputy Chief of Staff] just said it and it's correct. . . . They know that if they present a story in a certain way, we will go to that story. (ABC August 27, 1989)

And

> Pretty soon, either all issues are seen as being simply transitory and therefore matters of sensation and not reality, or they're seen as equally important and therefore incapable of solution because it's obviously baffling for anybody to deal with that many. (ABC August 27, 1989)

A lot of the "story" and "issues" involved crime and drugs. In the early 1970s, Nixon's crew pushed the "heroin angle" and called network executives to the White House, where they were encouraged to produce law and order stories about heroin on shows such as "Baretta," "Starsky and Hutch," and others (cf. Epstein, 1977, *Agency of Fear*). In the era of the 1980s, the story became cocaine, especially "crack cocaine." Related to both were themes of street crime, fear, out of control cities—and now suburbs—all demanding more and stronger law enforcement at all levels, including a massive shift toward undercover police work and surveillance, e.g., entrapments, "string" operations, which sometimes resulted in officers shooting other undercover officers (cf. Marx 1988).

America was a good society in danger, in need of confidence, moral uplifting values, and someone with whom everyone could identify with and feel good about. Almost everything else, e.g., health care for the elderly, housing and urban problems, could not penetrate the ubiquitous and least common denominator issue that continued its volcanic reemergence during the Nixon years—crime and drugs. Many segments of our knowledge system followed the media leaders, who were often pressured by national politicians to renounce crime. These co-conspirators in advocating targets and programmatic efforts to promote fear, dread, and reliance on big-time protectors were funded by an expanding mine of federal treasure. They included criminal justice agencies, state and local governments, national funding agencies, and, of course, university faculty members. The acronyms of LEAA (Law Enforcement Assistance Administration), NIDA (National Institute of Drug Abuse), NIJ (National Institute of Justice), NSF (National Science Foundation), NIMH (National Institute of Mental Health), SSRC (Social Science Research Council), and numerous others helped initiate the legitimation of fear associated with crime and drugs. Their activities produced more competition between themselves for legitimacy, funding, and growth. They also developed public relations hacks, became skilled as news sources, and thus reproduced the media logic to a new and younger generation of journalists, some of whom had actually "learned" media logic in schools of journalism! More cooperation emerged between reporters and sources who were speaking the same language, using the same logic based on many of the same assumptions. Others have chronicled the impact on social control (cf. Ericson et al., 1987, 1989).

The logic and formats for transforming civic time and importance into the space and temporal dimensions of a TV screen joined journalism, commercials, and entertainment programming until it got to the point where the production rules were quite similar! This coupling was negotiated through a more sophisticated but more narrowly circumscribed "state of the art" technology, including visual and aural synthesizers, computer graphics, reorganization within news and production departments, and transfer of personnel. An example was the movement of ABC's sports coverage whiz, Roone Arledge, to head of the news division! If you could master one, you could master the other since both drew on format and media logic. Animation found its way from the Saturday morning cartoons to the evening newscast's simulation of U.S. war planes bombing Libya, and naval ships shooting down an Iranian passenger airliner!

Audiences were becoming more accustomed to the logic as they experienced it in "commercials," "entertainment," and "news." For example, one poll found that half of those surveyed believed that the dramatic audience vigilante show, "America's Most Wanted," was a news program, with 64% of younger people (under age 30) more willing to accept simulations in newscasts than the older viewers (TDN September 26, 1989:B6).

To sum, important changes in American political life were ushered in and out during this mediatization of political life. First, political parties were essentially destroyed or relegated to third position behind individuals and their own sponsorship (i.e., interests). Second, class and larger aggregate issues such as poverty, race relations, and environmental problems were most easily treated as "documentaries," and deplorable, but narrow constituent problems, which were not easily incorporated into mass mediated platforms. Third, the elected officials went underground, more skillfully posturing "front stage" media behavior to conceal "backstage" activities.

As we predicted in *Media Logic* (Altheide and Snow 1979), media inspired criteria of legitimacy prevailed, as visual caricatures of "competence," "leadership," and "national strength" were drawn from networks' file film to illustrate and reconstitute the major themes of the campaign, and the decade of the 1980s. Recall that the major thematic context for the Reagan ascendancy through the 1980s, carried forth by Bush into the 1990s, was post-Watergate. As we have argued, the flagrant abuses of power by the Nixon team that resulted in the publication of criminal and shoddy political episodes permitted Nixon's enemies to call foul, and successfully label his regime as the "most corrupt in American history." It was "politics" that was held to account for this, at least according to the post-Watergate rhetoric. What was needed, Jimmy Carter urged, was someone who could be trusted to be honest, deliberate, and indeed, this political veteran of the southern wars in Georgia politics, heralded the claim, "I'm not a politician." One man who worked closely with Carter, stated:

> There was not an ideological bone in his body. He was candid and open, almost to a fault—the very antithesis of the classic image of the wily practitioner of power politics. These attributes, together with his quick mind, appealed to a U.S. electorate emerging from the dark experiences of Vietnam and Watergate and gained him the presidency. (Sick 1985:219)

Jimmy Carter did not win the election; Gerald Ford lost.

President Carter was doomed to failure because he chose to act as an independent and rational leader, pursuing issues and policies that he believed in, and even though he lacked the tried-and-true political networks to complete many of his programs, he was not a good role player; he wanted to write his own script, so to speak, and was largely unsuccessful. There was the Bert Lance problem, tied, as we have argued, to the legacy of avoiding the delegitimating practices of Watergate; there was the Iranian hostage crisis, which was played out and thematically telecast night after night as a failure of American leadership, will, and military might; there was the energy crisis and Carter's willingness to ask Americans to conserve, turn off the lights, and face our difficulties. Nobody wanted to hear that because it did not make sense in light of the major media scenarios and logic of the previous decade.

> However, he did not seem to display the same concern for *form* as he did for substance. He seemed unwilling to devote the same degree of care and attention to the atmospherics and public relations aspects of public presentation as he did to the decision itself. Fundamentally, he seemed to believe that if a decision was correct it would sell itself, and his disregard for the potentially dangerous political consequences of his programs at times appeared to to border on recklessness. (Sick 1985:223)

This approach contributed to his political demise. Corporate heads plan and follow "decision-packages," but *TV leaders are heroic and take action.*

A major exception was the Middle East issue, where his Camp David Accords between Israel and Egypt were consummated in a televised handshake between the Egyptian and Israeli heads of state. It is also significant that the man who was often cited as the most trusted person in the United States, Walter Cronkite, had also worked on the air to promote the visitations of Anwar Sadat and Menachem Begin. The international scenario, in other words, had been cast over the years as a televised war, with appropriate dramatic and tragic moments, with leaders routinely presented in "frame" as mourners, advisors, and prominent players. Carter took on the task (cf. Sick 1985:222ff).

> Three presidents had backed away from the political quicksand of a Panama Canal Treaty, but Carter pushed it through and accepted the political consequences. The Camp David negotiations were a political high-wire act undertaken against the advice of virtually all of his political advisers. In the days immediately before Camp David, the veteran Washington correspondent Richard Rovere wrote a scathing and somewhat premature political obituary of Carter in which he commented that Carter had "made some decisions that men with a greater flair for gauging the public temper might have hesitated to make. In summoning President Sadat and Prime Minister Begin to man-to-man talks at Camp David, he is courting a failure

that could be even more costly for him than for them. They risk almost nothing . . . But Carter is involving his own and American prestige in what could be the last unarmed Middle East confrontation."

There was still the Iranian hostage situation, the failed rescue attempt that left eight Americans dead and the military command in disarray, and contrasting images of confidence and leadership. Carter was out of time.

Then there was Ronald Reagan. It was less of a challenge between the man Reagan and the man Carter than the identity of the former with a different world from the latter's crises. The hostages were still held captive, and Reagan's advisors knew that the actor could fill the role. He was good on camera, but more importantly was his ability to resonate positive emotions and talk about the good news of a stronger, brighter, economically free America, with citizens solving many problem by volunteering, with safer streets, and, of course, with stronger military might, more respect in the world, and no guff from terrorists! Moreover, this would all be done with a balanced budget, no new taxes, and, as it turned out, very few cuts in anything except for social services.

During the campaign debates, Reagan looked old, but chuckled his way through allegations of lack of experience. One of the memorable events for Carter was citing his daughter, Amy, as an authority on the future of nuclear weapons. Reagan said that we should be stronger. This message was consistent with the mediated experience of numerous voters and middle class American citizens.

Reagan won (51% to 41% for Carter) in a world made for traditional American values. He gave them his personal signature through a series of fortuitous events, including the following. The hostages were freed on completion of his inaugural address. The United States was strong. Family-based situation comedies continued to be audience favorites. Nancy Reagan devoted her efforts to the "Say no to drugs" program, and TV commercials encouraged children to "just say no." Then Reagan was shot by John Hinckley who was found "not guilty" due to temporary insanity. Robert Snow's (1984) comparative analysis of the news coverage and commentary by several newspapers and the major TV networks showed that the latter clearly played up the "public outrage" theme. Those "liberal" courts! Hinckley testified that he was trying to impress actress Jodie Foster who had starred in a movie he repeatedly watched, *Taxi Driver*. The "missing children" issue (Fritz and Altheide 1987) was constructed through the efforts of moral entrepreneur, John Walsh, the father of abducted and murdered Adam Walsh, who later became a prime mover for a TV show, "America's Most Wanted." Some 5,000 American per week call in tips about how the wanted fugitives who are graphically cast in reenactments of pornographic violence resemble their friends, neighbors, co-workers, and shopping mall patrons. Gonzo justice was emerging (Altheide 1990). There was more on the kaleidoscope. The United States invaded the small island of Grenada in 1983. And won. Bernard Goetz's brutal shooting of three not-so-nice youths in a New York subway led to his being dubbed "the subway vigilante," a moniker that led movie producers to cast Charles Bronson (again) in the movie *Death Wish III*. And the winner of the Boston marathon told Reagan to "stay the course."

Mondale Is Next

Walter Mondale had to challenge this evocative world in 1983 (cf. Bronk 1987; Mayer and Mc Manus 1988). The political campaign was not much of a contest. Walter Mondale tried to discuss certain issues, and hinted at tax increases. Not as practiced in front of the camera as Reagan, Mondale's attempts to deal with ideas in an evocative format of TV coverage did not work. The presidential debate between Mondale and Reagan was classic. Reagan, the experienced actor, was tempted to try to deal with issues at a cognitive level, during the debate. His media advisor, Roger Ailes (1988:17–18), talked with Reagan before the second debate:

> You didn't get elected on details, you got elected on themes. Every time a question is asked, relate it to one of your themes.

He did it, and very well. Reagan won the election by one of the biggest margins in history, 59% to 40%. Four more years.

The "teflon President," as the journalists referred to Reagan, continued his reign with very few problems or detractors. There was little systematic coverage by the news media about the host of potentially significant issues of the period, but at the same time it is important to stress that they were not overly supportive of Reagan. There were numerous critical pieces of the Reagan style, of his lack of involvement and knowledge about the most important issues, and about his "protection" from contrary views by henchmen who fed him one and two liners at a time. It was not that Reagan was stupid—he was not, nor that he was incompetent—he may have been. The thing that careful journalists, including a number of points by his biographer, Lou Cannon, stressed, was his unassuming way of doing things, seldom working hard or long hours, and, in general, seeing his role more as a representative of a style, moral position, and world view. (To be quite honest, these are also our characterizations, but that is not so important!) What is important, however, is the media arena he was to play in, and partially change.

Reagan was good at press conferences because journalists liked him, and also because his "boys" protected him from impromptu questions. He had a tendency to talk during photo opportunities, which his staff was masterful at arranging, but their guidance and control avoided most embarrassing moments. Of course, some slipped through and would become an unguided missile. In one case he acted largely on his own, with the aid of a few highly ambitious advisors, to push his own ill-conceived "star wars" program, which horrified his own science and military advisors (PBS January 4, 1989).

Reagan was presented as having character. In our media age, this means that his "persona," including his style and demeanor, could be interpreted by sympathetic viewers as looking and sounding and feeling like "leadership," "sensitivity," "confidence," and "decisiveness." It cannot be emphasized too much that from our perspective, Reagan "looked like" the kind of leader one would want whose world was essentially in tact, except for a few troublesome problems, such as street crime, inflation, anti-American views abroad—and at home—and terrorists. There it was. Reagan helped people "feel good about America," so that if they were doing allright, things would be allright. The idea was to maintain the believable and anticipated status quo of his constituents, as reported by his skilled pollster Richard Werthlin. Poor people, people of color, and people in countries who were not our friends were of little concern. They were the bad news, and any news reports about their plight could be interpreted accordingly.

Resolve, decisiveness, and sympathy were packaged. When the Marine base in Lebanon was bombed by "terrorists," resulting in 283? deaths, our flawed intelligence agencies reported that the sabre-rattling Muammar Qaddafi was behind it. So Reagan ordered our war ships to level his compound and several additional city blocks, killing dozens of people, including Qaddafi's child. News reports carried numerous accounts of the bombing, complete with animation showing our F-14s in operation. Indeed, ABC creatively led off its report with tape and audio from the hit movie, *Top Gun*. Reagan's popularity soared, even when later information suggested that Libya was not involved in the bombing of the marine barracks.

Contragate

There was trouble ahead as Reagan's second term was winding down. Central America, and especially Nicaragua, was any "cold warrior's" nightmare because it did not fit easily with the old formulas about "American interests" and "national security," while also defying simple leave-it-alone logic that it would someday go away. Whether called "communists," "leftists," "revolutionaries," or "patriots," there was a problem in Central American countries that had either "tilted" away from the U.S. position, or were in danger of doing so. Thus, the United States found itself in the position of opposing a democratically elected government in Nicaragua, which was opposed by a small but troublesome force called the "Contras." With the help of our military, CIA, and a lot of political rhetoric, this Central American country was elevated for dramatic purposes by the Reagan administration. From the perspective of our work, Nicaragua became a symbolic toy to promote U.S. resolve and commitment to "combating communism" and "fighting for democracy," while not having to spend a lot of resources or energy on the problem. Partly because of the penchant of news organizations, and especially TV networks, for visuals and dramatic footage, the slightest fire fight and combat scenarios in Central America provided a great news scene, even though millions of viewers were seldom given enough repeated systematic information to distinguish meaningfully between our "official" position in Costa Rica, El Salvador, Nicaragua, or Honduras. (cf. O'Connor, 1987) Consider the complexity: In El Salvador, we supported the government and opposed the rebels, while in Nicaragua, we supported the rebels (the Contras) and opposed the government. About the only country where the images seemed less problematic was Panama, where the canal was, where we had a military base, and where our man, Manuel Noriega, was in charge. (They were firm allies, at least late in Reagan's administration; that would change early in Bush's term of office when U.S. forces invaded, bombed, and extradited Noriega to the U.S. to face drug charges!) Once again, there had been the experience with Watergate that had prompted a series of legislative moves and laws to attempt to restrict the arbitrary powers of the president and the CIA. There was the appearance of an accountability structure that had to be taken into consideration by the Reagan people.

This was the setting, then, for the conflict that developed between Congress and the Reagan administration about military aid to Central America. Congress essentially prohibited the United States government from providing arms to the Contras. Yet, Reagan, ideological cronies, and his staff were committed to "fighting communism" and "saving democracy," especially the "freedom fighters in Nicaragua." How this conflict came to be resolved is the fascinating story of what came to be known as "Iran-Contra," or "Contragate." Simply stated, it involved a series of secret deals between the United States and representatives of the governments of Iran, Nicaragua, Israel, Costa Rica, Honduras, and others. Of course, secrecy is nothing new to governments, especially the way the U.S. CIA or the Soviet KGB play their games of espionage, sabotage, and assassination. But this one was different because it in-

volved (1) money from private individuals (and foundations) within the
United States, (2) working through CIA, the National Security Council,
and other government operatives, (3) to sell arms to Iran in order to
gain favor in the treatment of some American hostages as well as to
obtain funds, (4) to be used to purchase arms for the Contras in Nicaragua. Recalling Reagan's campaign promise against Carter to never "negotiate with terrorists," helps set the stage for what was to follow.

Oliver North was one of our operatives in these incredible transactions. Numerous administration officials were involved in the illegal and
secret arms deals with terrorists, as well as the Contras. These included
William Casey, the Director of the CIA, and John Poindexter, the head
of the National Security Council. Oliver North, who had served in Vietnam and had been appointed to Lieutenant Colonel, became the fall
guy. He was the messenger, the bag man, and sometimes the negotiator
for several of the transactions. He was also the one who left a paper trail,
even though he enlisted the aid of a secretary to shred many of the
documents, for which he was convicted in 1989.

He became a media star during the Congressional hearings on Iran-
Contra. As numerous fingers pointed his way, North took the stand over
a period of several weeks. North was the perfect media figure, with a
shoulderful of decorations on his marine uniform, which he seldom
wore before entering the hearing room. Handsome, articulate, emotionally convincing, and combative, North faced several tiers of congressional accusers, and proclaimed his guilt! He admitted that he had lied
to Congress on previous hearings, had destroyed evidence, and had
taken numerous evasive actions to throw off investigators. The reason
he did it, he stated, was to serve his commander-in-chief—Reagan, and
to fight communism at all costs in Nicaragua and throughout Central
America.

North became an instant American folk hero. He fit the logic and
formats we have discussed. For one thing, he represented the archtype
of our Western mythology, a modern version of David vs. Goliath, the
rugged moral individual. Tom Wolfe described this type of "individual
warrior" in his brilliant characterization of the first seven American as-
tronauts (*The Right Stuff*). They were lone warriors representing us; they
were willing to die to save us. The "us," of course, meant the United
States. North was doing what was right even though Congress said it was
wrong; Reagan said it was right and he had openly supported the fund
raising efforts of General Secord and others to solicit funds from private
sources to sustain the Contras, which numerous military authorities acknowledged could not have continued without U.S. training, arms, and
other support. They were, in effect, our rebel forces.

North was a major media production. North had character. He was able to present himself as genuine, real, committed. No mere role player or someone who was looking out for their own cushy career path, North was packaged as authentic. There had been nothing quite like it since General Douglas MacArthur's farewell address to Congress when he was relieved of his command during the Korean War. He was our warrior, one above the politicians who sought to limit his actions to invade China!

North was in great demand for public appearances. He became the symbolic hero that is so lacking in public life. John Wayne was dead, but North was alive. Moreover, he fit the format of what a hero should look like and how he should act. The visual juxtaposition of North in uniform "against" the congressmen in suits was powerful. They spoke in turns, with time limits on their questioning; they often read questions and summaries provided by their staffs; he replied and spoke on numerous occasions. They wore suits. He wore his uniform. Our uniform.

He could couch his actions in his love for his country, patriotism, desire to protect his family, and, by implications, all of our families. At one point during the hearings, Senator Daniel Inouye, a Japanese-American who had lost an arm during WW II stated that he too was a patriot, and that he had received medals, but that was not the issue. Still, the audience saw North. He was taking the fall for the President and others above him, who, viewers understood, often had to rely on brave individuals to do their bidding. And after all, what did legality really have to do with anything when one dealt with the international scenario, spy vs. spy, right vs. might, sort of like the James Bond movies and the "I Spy" and "Missions Impossible" (starring Bill Cosby!) TV series about cold warriors who took extraordinary measures for the proper outcomes. It was media politics at its best. Images were registered and the format was enlivened. Regardless of the ultimate outcome, there would be other heroic presentations, but next time they would look like North! Before continuing with the epic story of the engulfment of big time politics by media logic, it is important to stress how Reagan's persona glowed on the tube. The reader can check our assessment with more specific analyses by Kern (1989), Denton (1988), and other works that will be available. Largely because of a communication process that we explicate further below, Reagan represented the first radical shift in American politics from content to a mixture of content and form to pure form: Reagan had essentially no substance beyond the evocative images through which he danced. We do not question his intelligence or even his capacity to "really be a leader," if he so chose; rather, his terms in office were both facilitated and constituted by media logic. *It was unnecessary for him to actually act other than his media presence.*

The most damning evidence we can muster are his own words. During the period immediately following his term of office—especially early 1990—Reagan dropped some political bombs on the citizens via the news media about his "style" of leadership, on the one hand, and his lack of knowledge of the most basic elements of accountability, on the other hand. As part of the Iran-contra trial of John Poindexter (Reagan's head of the National Security Council) his attorneys called Reagan to testify about what he, as President, knew and directed Poindexter to do. His videotaped testimony (a 293 page transcript) released on February 22, 1990 revealed a man who was considerably confused. Not only did he not recall the details of the Iran-contra dealings, but he could not recall the identities of John Vessey, whom Reagan had appointed as head of the Joint Chiefs of Staff. More alarmingly, he testified that he was unaware that his former national security advisor, Robert McFarlane, had pleaded guilty to making false statements to Congress several years prior! He also claimed that "This is the first time that I have ever seen a reference that actually specified there was a diversion" (of funds from the sale of arms to Iran to purchase weapons for the Contras). This "reference," the so-called "Tower Commission Report" on the Iran-Contra, affair, was published and widely broadcast in 1987! (Azizona *Republic* February 23, 1990; *Newsweek* March 5, 1990:16–17). Reagan had been a shell, but a good one. No single individual had been in charge of the United States for nearly 8 years!

The Democrats Try Again, or The Trials of the Trail

The demise of meaningful political parties in the United States further contributed to the impetus of "primary elections" for a range of candidates to throw their hats into the ring, "test the waters," and see how they may fare. This made television even more important as candidates realized that gaining the initial momentum in a key state could lead to more coverage. A number of Democratic challengers entered the primary circus as early as 1986, seeking to become defined by the national media as the "front runner." The cast of characters we attend to includes Jesse Jackson, Bruce Babbitt, Gary Hart, the front runner, who was overcome by a "sex scandal," and Michael Dukakis, the nominee and big-time loser. We have already referred to the Bush–Dukakis debates in 1988, and noted how TV formats defined political discourse.

The complex mass media scenarios and impact in this campaign are hinted at by the self-casting of Bruce Babbitt. Although a minor player in the early Democratic primaries, Bruce Babbitt is relevant for our consideration because of the role he played in a TV movie about the political campaign, called *Tanner for President.* Just as Gerald Ford played himself in an episode of "Saturday Night Live" in 1975, Bruce Babbitt played a challenger to Jack Tanner. The problem of discerning what is real and what is false is suggested by Babbitt's comment:

> What happens to Bruce Babbitt? Am I reality or fiction? Am I politician or entertainer? What I decided . . . is it works very well as long as I am Bruce Babbitt both in Jack Tanner and in the real world. As long as I'm consistent in what I portray. (PBS, Bill Moyers, "Prime-Time President")

The "character" issue was especially important during and before the Iowa primary election. Despite having some of the most favorable press coverage, Jesse Jackson was not a big factor in this campaign. Some of the reasons for this will be suggested below. One exhaustive study of TV news coverage of the 1988 campaign examined some 1,300 network reports (Lichter et al. 1988). We will refer to this work more a bit later, but for now it must be stressed that although this research confirmed prior findings about the "horse race" theme dominating the political coverage, these researchers also came up with some rather surprising results about the way in which TV formats help transform a "neutral" trait like "character" into something negative and reactive. Generally, when "character" was a theme for a report, it referred to something negative or critical. Lichter et al. (1988) found that more than half of the 153 character stories in the campaign coverage were about Gary Hart! (Bush had 18). This suggests that responding to media challenges and definitions is likely to be counterproductive and has a negative impact. The researchers expand this general thesis to interpret how the Democratic challengers played to the TV formats to destroy each other during the primary period:

> Since television conveys conflict better than explanation, the candidates quickly learned to deliver the kind of pithy put-downs more likely to generate replays the following evening. It was a classic case of each individual acting in his own interest to the detriment of all, as TV debate coverage began to resemble a Don Rickles routine. (Lichter et al. 1988:78)

The complex relationship between media coverage of politics, audience involvement and interpretation, and voting preferences will be examined below. We can continue with a quick comparison of media coverage to voter preferences. In the 1988 presidential election, Lichter et al. (1988:108ff) found that the overall ratio of good to bad press for the Democrats was 56% and 54% for the Republicans. This slight Democratic edge notwithstanding, George Bush defeated the Democratic challenger, Michael Dukakis, in 1988, by the margin of 54% to 45%. He apparently overcame the media tag that he was a "wimp," that is, indecisive and incapable of making tough decisions. This was not as large a trouncing for the Democrats as the previous two outings, but it was still considerable by presidential election standards. But it is how he did it that is fascinating, and further demonstrates how media logic dominates politics.

If the reader perceives that the last several years have seen the Democrats lose decisively, that is largely correct. The Democrats were out of touch with media logic, not only in terms of their own campaigns, but also the images of problems and life that resonate this logic. We will see, however, that the problem is not endemic to the Democrats so much as it is to anyone who is out of step with dominant media logic at the time. Before offering our alternative explanation of the media's impact on political behavior, we must take a brief look at the way the media covered the media, through the tenets of media logic, of course!

Media on Media

One of the most innovative twists of media coverage of politics was apparent during the 1988 campaign when the process and technique of media coverage began to receive a lot of attention. Lichter et al. (1988:36) estimated that "one out of every twenty election stories dealt extensively with the media's campaign role." Media on media. The media logic had itself been encapsulated within the logic of media coverage. It became known as the "media angle" in which the substance of politics, which had increasingly become more obscure and less available to anyone not drowning in media logic, could comment, often flippantly, on the role of the media in what we were reading, seeing, and hearing. These included several Public Broadcasting Specials from which we have selected materials for this book, and several books published in time for the election market. What is common to these is an excited awareness of the role of media logic in constructing messages.

A number of stories, for example, dealt with "sound bites," those 15 to 30-second statements, photo opportunities, and "actual" instances of something, which were being recognized as ordering press conferences, on the one hand, and what the journalists would report to the audience, on the other hand. Of course, academics became more aware of this timely rhythm of political communication. Kern's (1989) work on "30-Second Politics" shows the relevance of sound bites for constructing the symbols in political advertising. This notion, along with reports about "photo opportunities," were intended to suggest to the audience, in an ironic sort of way, that even though the journalists sort of realized that messages and scenarios were being crafted for the journalists—and therefore, were less "real," more contrived, and were intended to help manipulate the audience—that the journalists would continue reporting the organizationally mediated and controlled messages anyway. Except now, the audience was let in on a piece of the secret, an omission that the journalists, with some exceptions, had not developed a vocabulary for in previous elections. What is most important for the significance of media logic is that even this mode of delegitimating and challenging some of the politicians' statements was still reported within acceptable guidelines and formats for crafting a report. It was as though most of the messages said "this is what they say happened and is important except that we have every reason to doubt them because they were adjusting to our logic of work and presentation so that we will be assured to always present something, even this." An interesting problem, isn't it?

The point, then, is that the routine journalistic practices were not significantly altered by the awareness that politicians and others were increasingly aware of media formats and were using them; the message was still presented, except the audience became more adroit at recognizing elements of the communication process that were heretofore protected by news sources and news reporters. Even though we think that this increased awareness is quite good, all indications are that the rationale for including them by news agents was to have a different kind of story rather than alter reporting formats that continue to restrict the nature and extent of journalistic reporting about politics.

Media logic was sustained and reinforced. One temporal feature of political reporting that did change was "exposés" and "insider" accounts of the news process as well political decision-making. Until 1988, most insider accounts followed the election; in 1988, they were published in order to enhance buyer interests and increase sales, as well as influencing the election outcome. The other payoff was that the general news media would have another source and theme to discuss in its political coverage. Thus we had reflections and reports by journalists about either journalists or some politician (or event) that would then be "publicized," discussed, and evaluated by other journalists, and would even be included in future press conferences (cf. Mayer and McManus 1988). In turn, answers to such queries would permit journalists pursuing an additional angle for their future reports. For example, Lichter et al. (1988:17) note that many journalists felt that the media overplayed the "character issue" we discussed above:

> Many journalists themselves took issue with the media' emphasis on character, and the television news coverage reflected their ambivalence. Nearly two-thirds (64 percent) of the sixty-seven sources with a clear opinion argued that the media overplayed this issue. But most of the debate about the media as "character cop" took place in 1987. In fact, we recorded no viewpoints on this theme after the Iowa caucuses. Despite dire predictions

of a camera in every bedroom, the issue evaporated quickly after the primary season got under way.

An excellent example of media-on-media to come out of the 1988 presidential campaign was Mark Hertsgaard's *On Bended Knee: The Press and the Reagan Presidency* (1988). Drawing on interviews with some journalists and Reagan staff members, this 31-year-old son of a former Baltimore news anchorman presents an argument that has been well documented by others about presidential candidates, namely that Reagan received a "friendly press," and that the key White House advisors worked hard, and were apparently quite successful, in managing the news about their candidate, including providing scenarios and opportunities that fit the dictates of news formats, e.g., photo opportunities, sound bites, and additional subsources and minor themes. In other words, wrote Hertsgaard, the press and politicians were involved in a process of symbolic interaction, which belied traditional notions (but perhaps not actual practices) that the candidate would do or say something for some other reason besides communication opportunities, and then the press (and TV) would come along, ask or find out about it in some way, and then probe the event until it became a story. As we have stressed in this book, things have not really been done this way for at least 30 years, and most journalists are well aware of it. So there was not a lot of news here, except that the routine newsworking conditions and procedures were explicated, and the politicians' advisors have become more candid about their acumen at directing the camera's gaze, the reporter's cursor, and the editor's criteria of interest.

The book was released in September, in time for Hertsgaard to appear on numerous talk shows, express concern about press manipulation, and for numerous journalists to follow with columns and/or review pieces on these claims. Journalistic reflection is important and we have urged this for some time. But what is easily overlooked is that this kind of reporting fits the media logic of "interesting" political reporting; it personalizes the "discovery" by the young journalist, and names the offenders, e.g., Michael Deaver, Richard Darman, (Frank 1984) and David Gergen, of the Reagan administration, who freely explained to Hertsgaard that they always tried to provide ample photo opportunities and sound bites that would portray their candidate in a favorable light. One small but important thing to writers who are outside of the media inner circle is that these points had been made years before by us and other observers of the election scene. Although serious scholars recognize the contributions, virtually no attention has been given to those works by popular writers like Hertsgaard even though the work offers a more informed context for understanding the tactics rather than suggesting that the tacticians are evil people. But, we, along with other researchers, are pleased that the format features that underlie the substance and form of official information officially have been made "public." There is still far more to understand political decision-making. We now focus on an interactive emotional and communicative perspective for understanding political communication.

Part II

Time to Take Stock

At this point we must digress briefly to set up the complex and unique argument about the impact of TV on politics, everyday life, and how voting choices may be understood within the context of mediated experience. Although our general approach to understanding the media effects on social life are now widely acknowledged, it is very significant that the nature of the impact has not been well understood by political analysts. Part of the problem is that our slant on these major issues includes the communicative act, which involves a symbolic statement, a medium, a context and previous experience of an audience member, and, of course, that audience member's interpretive scheme. These elements are complexly related and are joined in the concept *format*. We give considerable weight to the manipulative talents of imagemakers, but our theoretical argument does not stop there; that is, it is not enough to just describe the manipulative process, condemn the manipulators, and then realistically expect that the problem will be solved if only reforms are enacted. That will help, but it is not nearly enough, because the audience familiarity, context and context of mass mediated experience, discourse, and logic engulfs any particular message. Most media analysts have missed this point, largely because their focus is limited only to the message construction scenario.

Successful political campaigns must make people feel that they can identify with the "candidate who feels and thinks like me." Increasingly, it is the producer's values and skills that essentially define the candidate's message. Nesbit (1988:19ff) observes:

> Affective strategies are extremely common and used throughout the campaign. If the truth of the ad is in the feelings evoked, then all commercials, to some extent must evoke emotions. In most cases, even the predominantly cognitive spot will contain some affective elements.

And

> The presentation of self in video-style involves large, heterogeneous audiences and rapid and simultaneous message transmission; it also empha-

sizes the candidate's and producer's abilities to anticipate audience
reactions. While candidates generally exercise the right to veto certain
"presentations of themselves, "the spots that are aired are steeped in, and
clearly reflect, the producer's philosophy. (p. 150)

Kern's (1989:1–2) study of campaign ads includes ample supporting
materials for this point of view:

> Personal issues are thus squarely at the heart of politics and increasingly
> personal ways are being found to present the candidate as a leader who
> will address them. . . . In the 1980s fatherhood staged a comeback not only
> on the Bill Cosby show but as a key ingredient in candidate messages. . . .
> Framing a message so as to relate to voters' personal lives, whether it in-
> volves a teary-eyed reference to one's father in a presidential nomination
> acceptance speech or an appearance at a day-care center, is essential to the
> language of politics in the 1980s.

Democratic presidential candidates have, with varying degrees of "expertise," succeeded in convincing people that they are unlike the majority of voters! How has this been accomplished?

Political reality in the postmodern world is mediated reality. In our
age this is television. But we are saying far more than what is obvious,
and what we stated over 10 years ago: We are not merely stating that a
candidate's image and ads must be "quality TV." *We are also stating that
the scenarios and meanings must be capable of being interpreted by the TV viewers
in a manner that is consistent with how they experience and interpret other TV
images.* People are viewers and experts with media logic and formats
before they are voters. They apply the criteria, discourse, and logic of
the media to the images and messages. In this way the viewer–voter acts
like all audience members in actively participating in the construction
and interpretation of messages. Voters take for granted that the candidate's logic will reflect the logic of the medium through which they
experience the candidate's symbolism (the candidates themselves are in a
minority of TV ads) (cf. Cook 1989).

We believe that the mediation of political experience by TV also
explicates an apparent anomaly that has been noticed by numerous
political analysts, including Seymour Martin Lipset (1989:25):

> Americans voted for the *status quo* and continued divided government on
> November 8, 1988. A solid majority, 54 per cent, cast their ballots for
> George Bush for President. But a slightly larger one, 55 per cent, sup-
> ported Democratic candidates for the House of Representatives, where
> the party increased its majority by three seats to 262–173. The Democrats
> also improved on their Senate advantage by one to 55–45 and gained a
> state house. They now hold 28 of the 50 governorships. They retain an
> overwhelming lead among members of state legislatures. Over three fifths
> of the 7368 are Democrats including a gain of 29.

Why would Americans vote for one "symbol" of Presidential leader-ship—Republican, but another one for Congressional action—Demo-cratic? Lipset, with little consideration of the media's role, essentially provides the following explanation. By interpreting survey data and some "exit poll" interviews to impute a rather complex array of mean-ings to voters, he argues that enough of the electorate view the Presi-dency as different from the "local" Congressional elections. Thus they associate the Presidency with some kind of national issues:

> The office is inherently linked to nationalism and religion in a county [which] . . . is more patriotic and orthodoxly devout than any other eco-nomically developed democracy. Democratic liberals look weak in this con-text. Reagan and Bush appear strong. Congress, on the other hand, is the place where cleavages get fought out. Members perform services, act as ombudspeople, and represent interests. They appeal narrowly, rather than broadly. And the Democrats with links to mass groups and popularly based interest organizations are in a better position to fulfill these func-tions. (Lipset 1989:37)

Lipset further argues that Americans are in general "Democratic" on economic and welfare policies, e.g., state provided health care, but "Re-publican" on social issues, e.g., national defense and crime control. Since it is social issues that tend to be pushed by Presidential candidates, any-one who differs from the "status quo" on these concerns is likely to be suspect.

> Still the data reveal that Republicans and Bush supporters were very much more likely than their opponents to mention crime, abortion, and defense spending as among the issues which mattered most. (Lipset 1989:35)

Moreover, those concerns tend to be associated with income and ideol-ogy, Lipset argues, so that voters who are wealthier and better educated tend to support the Republican position. There are several problems with this structural explanation.

One is that there are numerous exceptions and shifts. For example, the occupational categories "Professional or Manager" and "White-col-lar worker" did tend to vote for Bush, but fewer did so than in the previ-ous election. Conversely, more people in the "Blue-collar worker" category voted for Dukakis than in the previous two elections. Relatedly, (62%) "Unemployed" people (only about 5% of the total vote) cast their lot with Dukakis, but this was 5% less than in 1984! Lipset (1989:35) seemed to sense part of this problem when he wrote,

> It is difficult to draw any definite conclusions from these results, particu-larly since the responses on a number of them, such as liberal views, de-

fense spending and abortion, could be mentioned by people holding sharply contrasting opinions on the issues.

Indeed, the 1988 election wrecked havoc with a number of theories about political behavior, including the role of the mass media. One political scientist, Michael J. Robinson, wrote:

> 1988 is confounding almost all the political wisdom we had built up from 1976, 1980, and 1984 . . . We thought momentum was everything and it turned out to be ephemeral, if not meaningless. (quoted in Lichter et al. 1988:109)

Although we think that even these "answers" are insufficient for a full understanding of the political participation process, plausible accounts for the differences in Congressional campaigns seem to be lacking. The general problem with Lipset's analysis of why voters select their "local" representatives involves the different meanings of a party label like "Democrat" throughout the congressional districts between states as well as within states. Any one familiar with their own state politics can readily attest to the problems associated with any general statement about the meaning of Democrat or Republican as worn by particular representatives! If straightforward structural "variables" were ever adequate to account for voting behavior, it is clear that they cannot do so today. Still the question of why different party affiliations have different outcomes in Presidential and Congressional forays remains (cf. Vermeer 1987).

Our answer to this query is different, albeit tentative, but we regard the theoretical foundation we have set forth in this work as essential for any coherent theory of voting behavior and political change. This is our answer, and we will explicate it below as we relate it to the foregoing analysis: What we find to be lacking in Lipset's and similar analyses of political outcomes is an awareness of the *communication and the sense making process that informs how people identify with individuals and party platforms at all "local" and "national" levels. Election outcomes are informed less by objective indicators such as "income," than by the communication process joining meaningful experience, credible symbolic definitions, and individual identity. It is the voters' association of an individual candidate with the voter's salient meaningful experience that is central in the voting decision. As we have stressed, much of this experience is mass mediated.*

Mass-mediated criteria, logic, formats, and emphases are altering experiential criteria for voters, who, as we have stressed, are viewers before they are voters. The mass media can be said to have an effect on the voting process. When the mass-mediated experiences are more salient for the interpretation of how a candidate's position fits with one's own identity.

Fortunately, there is some interesting information available about the role of the mass media in Presidential, House, and Senate elections (cf. Vermeer 1987). The nature and impact of mass communication vary in Presidential, House, and Senate campaigns because the *interpretive frame-work* of the voter is different. In general, ideology and specific issues are more significant in Presidential elections than for House and Senate races; incumbency and name recognition counts for more in the House and Senate campaigns; "valence issues" such as "supporting the family" and "the American way of life" are relevant for both.

Consider a few points about the 1988 presidential election. Some major issues for the Bush supporters were patriotism, national defense, and crime control. (Paradoxically, the Republicans mentioned foreign policy issues four times as often in their primary campaigns as the Democrats! (Lichter et al. 1988:19ff). Very importantly, it was the underlying values associated with these positions that resonate more through national than "local" election campaigns: trust, integrity, protection, and justice (criminal justice, that is). Indeed, most of the nonvoters indicated that they would have supported Bush even though they were younger and poorer than those who voted! (Lipset 1989:38).

One big difference between the Presidential race and the others is that policy implications are stressed more in the former. One study indicates that House incumbents are not well known for their issue positions, and can "hide their issue positions unless they encounter newspaper coverage of these positions or unless they themselves interpret their positions on paid television" (Simmons 1987:68–69).

Ideology is less variable in recent Presidential and House and Senate campaigns. Indeed, to run on an "ideological" platform suggests differences with the status quo, a threat and challenge, and something to be feared. During the 1988 campaign Michael Dukakis stated that the contest was about "competence" and not "ideology."

Nowhere is the demise of ideological rhetoric more evident than in the virtual disappearance of the mention and meaning of liberal, "the L word." The Bush campaign, along with several decades of big time politics, succeeded in drawing on viewers mediated and other experiences to symbolically define their protection as "someone who is not a liberal." Bush never pushed himself as a "conservative," "reactionary," of "conspirator," even though he was implicated in the Iran-Contra dealings long before the election was held. What mattered was the label, and who it was applied to—Michael Dukakis! The most important thing about Bush in the 1988 campaign, then, was what he was not, and, which of the voters' experiences (mass mediated and otherwise) were commensurate with this nonidentity.

Data from analyses of House and Senate campaigns during the past 20 years reveal that candidates systematically have refrained from identifying themselves with liberal ideology and programs. These findings provide at least a partial explanation of Lipset's quandary about congressional and presidential outcomes. For example, Raymond Vermeer's (1987:21ff) study of campaign pamphlets of 137 candidates in 1978 shows little difference between Republicans and Democrats on all issues, extent of vague proposals or solutions, or stressing of valence issues and personal values, e.g., support for the family. They are about equally likely to stress their opposition to government spending, inflation, taxes, and social security.

> candidates' partisan identification has limited explanatory power. Evidently what issues candidates choose to discuss will be determined more by their perceptions of the electorate's policy concerns than by their party affiliations.

Political advertising stresses individual rather than group-issue concerns.

> political advertising, like its commercial counterpart, now appeals to the individual in his or her own right, not as a member of an economic or social class, a political party, or other institution above the family level. (Kern 1989:212)

Joslyn's (1987) study of 131 TV ads of liberal House and Senate incumbents in 1984 shows the systematic avoidance of liberal symbols. Only 16 percent had "definite liberal content," 14 percent had "possible liberal content," but 47 percent contained "nonideological content." Joslyn's (1987:46) interpretation bears noting:

> Apart from the belief in preserving social security and Medicare benefits, and opposition to wasteful defense spending, Liberalism offered little else to the 1984 congressional election. Absent are traditional liberal concerns with the regulation of unfair business practices, the protection of vulnerable wage earners, the assistance of workers in their struggle with management, the advancement of consumer interests and civil liberties, the reversal of environmental degradation and the role of government in overcoming social and political inequalities.

These data clearly indicate that liberal House and Senate candidates did not promote themselves as standing for clear policies, especially alternatives. And they were the incumbents! If we consider the mass-mediated messages of such campaigns to constitute part of the explicit political awareness and experience of voters, it is clear that voters are not "experiencing" a range of alternatives. This was part of the Reagan legacy.

The Bush campaign built on the Reagan legacy of opposing new social programs, which at the national level translate into poverty programs, keeping a strong national defense with no additional tax revenue, and being tough on crime. These campaign characterizations were incorporated with Bush's identity through the magic of media logic in particular, the televised debates, and TV commercials, in particular. For example, Bush challenged explicitly and implicitly Michael Dukakis' patriotism! He associated this with visuals of American flags waving in the background. Regarding crime control, Bush's media contingent produced a brilliant commercial visually depicting criminals going through a revolving door, into prison and back onto the streets, to commit more crime. This spot came to be associated with the celebrated case of a man, Willie Horton, who had been paroled and committed a brutal crime during Dukakis's term as governor of Massachusetts. Kern (1989:210) nicely connects the thematic emphasis on crime with an individual transformed through TV formats:

> Issues are now personified through the use of visual and aural effects. For example, the crime issues *becomes* Willie Horton, and it is with this personified entity that a candidate is linked.

Whether such images would stick with a viewer–voter will depend on the voter's range and depth of personal and mass-mediated experiences on such issues. What is important, however, is that political advertising is produced on the basis of the considerations we have stressed. However, it must also be remembered that there is a relatively small percentage of voters who make a difference in outcomes. During Nesbit's (1988:104) study of three senate campaigns, one producer explained his rationale:

> If you look at any given campaign in almost any situation, you have those who aren't registered, so you don't have to deal with them at all. They're women, minorities, and the unemployed. It's sad, but true. You have 40 percent who are for you because you're a Democrat, or they're for the incumbent because he's the incumbent. The campaign battle is over 20 percent that you're trying to divide . . . what I call the "visceral vote." There's a lot of move to that vote. They tend to be the most influenced by a campaign to begin with, particularly media campaigns.

These people are the main targets of political advertising and, if such ads and any related news reports have an impact on voters, it will be with this group or "undecided" swing voters. Moreover, this group is becoming larger and more important as traditional voting membership

blocks disappear. With these qualifications, we can continue to understand some mass-mediated features of voting patterns. Even though national election data are constituted through the perspective of survey
research and are therefore quite inadequate to answer systematically the
kinds of questions we are posing, we can use the available data to ask
some relevant questions about the experiences of certain voting groups.
Bush received 59 percent of the white vote, but only a fraction of the
Hispanic vote (30%) and the black vote (12%). Clearly, for most Hispanic and black voters, the campaign rhetoric and ads were less compelling compared to their other personal as well as media experience.
Available data suggest that they were prone to view the Presidential campaign in terms of certain social and economic programs, rather than
crime, fear, and patriotism. This is not surprising when we consider that
the Democratic supporters tend to live in large cities, while the Republican supporters live in the rural South, small towns, small cities, and sub-
urban communities. As suggested by analysts of House and Senate
campaigns and candidates (Goldenberg and Traugott 1987:129),

> It also underscores the need to account for the information environment
> when analyzing the strategic behavior of candidates and the electorate's
> response to their campaigns. Where you live makes a difference in what
> you know about politics, candidates, and issues; and it affects how attitudes
> and levels of information change across the campaign.

The rhetoric, the ads, and the thrust of the Republican campaign were
geared primarily to whites, most of whom were Protestants and funda-
mentalists (66% and 81%, respectively, voted for Bush). As Arthur
Vidich (1990) has cogently argued, even Bush's running mate, Dan
Quayle, was from the Midwest and represented the values of small town,
business, tradition, and individual initiative. Though Quayle was much
maligned by the national media for poor college grades, reluctance to
fight in Vietnam, and skilled at golf and business lunches, he resonated
certain clear values of the heartland.

> Quayle, who the Eastern liberal journalists mercilessly hounded, criticized
> and mocked, represented powerfully middle-western conservative, popu-
> list values, almost all of the values antithetical to those of Eastern Seaboard,
> considered by some Mid-Westerners as an almost foreign country popu-
> lated by radicals, Jews, aliens and communists . . . Quayle's mediocre re-
> cord as a student and his preoccupation with gold more accurately
> represent a national norm and qualified him as a non-intellectual, a legiti-
> mate businessman who takes his gold seriously and conducts his business
> on the golf course. The Eastern journalistic establishment criticized
> Quayle precisely on those of his attributes that in many parts of the coun-
> try have a positive value. (Vidich 1989:21–22)

Professor Vidich could have added poor urban blacks to his list, the epitome of crime and fear, symbolized by the Willie Horton ad in the Bush campaign.

Conclusion

The critical question for us, then, in our efforts to make sociological sense out of political outcomes concerns experience. *What experiences do people identify with, what do they see as threatening that identity, and where do they derive those experience?* Campaign ads are significant if they are consonant with values, images and accounts that sustain identity. Indeed, we are arguing that as people across a spectrum of educational, occupational, and income groups share more of these mass-mediated experiences, the media become a competitive arena for salient meanings and identities that can inform voting decisions. We find Lipset's (1989:43) explanation suspect that elections "are largely affected by the macrosocietal and economic developments, and/or unanticipated crisis—like a great depression or a lost war." At one level this is a non-sequitur—of course this matters. *But at the level of sociological theory, it is more accurate to say that it is the claims, definitions, symbols, and identities that are negotiated and associated with a range of meaningful experiences that are critical in election outcomes. If the mass media contribute to the form and content of such negotiations and interpretations, then those media are a major force in voting behavior.*

We are suggesting, then, that the content and form of TV-mediated experience is implicated in voters' choices. When it is recalled that only 15–20 percent of voters need to be influenced by such messages to affect the result, and when one reflects on the number of evocative ads presented (along with news reports, which often support and sustain the general definitions contained in the ads), the body of literature that suggests that mass-mediated experiences do make a difference gains further credibility (cf. references in Kern 1989; Nesbit 1988; Vermeer 1987). As we have attempted to show, however, the ads are consequential within an interactive context involving previous media experiences, the viewer–voter's own preferences and emotional identification with particular issues.

The programming logic of getting viewers is paramount in the programming logic for successful candidates, i.e., those who win elections. The reason is complex, but can be simply stated: Interpretation and sense-making occurs through a narrative process, in which one point or fact is related to a temporal story line. In other words, facts and claims are relational, and second, these relational terms are experienced as typical, most apparent—because they are most familiar—or as novel. In this sense, the narrative form of knowing (Richardson 1990) is taken for granted and is nondiscursive. In a strict sense, then, we do not derive meaning as "processing bits and pieces together," but rather, as scenarios, scripts, and story-lines.

When more of the content and format of such scenarios are both derived from and participated in as we interact with a medium like television, *we become extensions of TV-mediated discourse.* Such extensions may include the main elements of format including grammar, rhythm, pace, images, and symbols.

The world of television includes its content, but this too is contingent on audience participation through certain communication codes or formats. Even though several generations of viewers have learned these codes from TV, we now expect them to be there. Thus we have producers of entertainment and news shows justifying their programming decisions on the basis of "audience demand," and "how the people are voting" by their viewing choices. In our language, formats have been learned, adopted, and appropriated as media logic by viewers, who in turn expect to see experiences reproduce such logic. Thus, as we argue in the sports chapter, the "game in person is not as interesting as seeing it on TV," or "he looks better on TV."

It should be apparent at this point that content and form are not distinctive, although we must discuss them this way in a print medium such as this book. The content of TV is unambiguous, quick, dramatic, visual, and familiar. With some exceptions, this is true of how we identify and understand the kind of show we are watching (news or a soap opera), the character (villain), emotion, credibility, and truth (evocative and expressive rather than discursive), and "real" program or commercial (rhythm, tempo).

It is not the literal translation of a TV message that is meaningful, but rather its emotive and relational meaning. How does this relate to politics? Viewers realize that political messages are commercials and that all commercials are produced and packaged to persuade them. What they like to do, however, is interact with the commercial, setting forth their expertise that "it is a commercial," and then playing with it by second guessing it, and if they are with other viewers, actually arguing aloud.

But commercials are not to be automatically disbelieved just because "they are trying to convince us." Commercials are "played with" to demonstrate the competence and ability of viewers to decipher the "true messages." What is also significant about political ads on TV is that they are produced to evoke an emotional attachment to the symbol portrayed in the message. The easier it is for the viewer to make this relational connection to a taken-for-granted narrative form or scenario, the more the message will be interpreted as something familiar and plausible, or as something that is just a "commercial."

The Democrats' problem is that their messages have not resonated through their candidates as something that is familiar, credible, and consistent with mediated reality. The candidates as "challengers," to a reality represented by the other party, have had to take TV images of the background of problems and issues and make them the problems. Stated differently, content and format of most TV programs do not deal with problems such as poverty, health care, and urban settings, but instead deal with those as mere backdrops or contexts for setting up individual actions involving humor, heroic deeds, crime fighting, and when tragedy is presented, it is usually as a prelude to overcoming tragedy. Stated differently, it is the way in which conventional mass-mediated story telling is produced and organized—its formats—that provides the content. One searches in vain for heroes of a TV drama who are ensconced in poverty and the day-to-day struggle to survive. Although we do have sitcoms, soaps, and dramatic portrayals of health care providers, it is hard to conceive of placing people who do lack health care—and attempt to receive it—in a TV format.

TV news does deal with some of these topics, but as we have already seen, the news formats and themes prevent long-term and systematic treatment of these as anything more than "problems," usually relevant for a minority of people. These are the same "people" who form the backdrop of the action-packed crime dramas. Thus poverty and a number of social problems are passed through TV and occasionally documentary formats as transitory, brief, and nearly insurmountable experiences. There are not the programming, viewing, and logics available to apply in the same way that, say, police are routinely shown to solve crime, battle corruption, and protect us from the threats evocatively played to by ratings-hungry news organizations and political advertising. As Kern (1989:210) cogently predicts,

> It is clear from this research that negative advertising and what may be termed Ronald Reagan's brand of emotional advertising have become nearly indispensable in competitive races. Few can argue with the success of Roger Ailes's effort in these areas on behalf of George Bush on the presidential level.

This is what the Democrats had to contend with since President Carter. And it is what American citizens and political analysts must understand in order to contend with media logic during the next half century. We are a media civilization. There will be no going back, but we can understand it and make appropriate adjustments in our expectations, evaluations, and conduct.

The Conclusion is George Bush, Drugs, and the Invasion of Panama

We are not out to bash the Republicans because the problems we identify transcend conventional boundaries of ideology, hegemony, (Lee
1980) and social control. The mass media involvement in our everyday
lives is not due to some conspiracy, cooptation, or any direct or indirect
manipulation of media personnel, organizations, or channels by any
person, political party, or economic interest. All have been implicated
in our current situation, but it has been the emergence of technology,
communication formats, and logic that has contributed to the present.

In 1979, we made several predictions. Virtually all have come true,
and, indeed, have surpassed our expectations. Several of those claims
involved the engulfing of public life and issues with media logic, including political claims, outcomes, problems, issues, and strategies. The first
year of George Bush's term in office illustrates the future. We will note
briefly only two events: His address to the nation on September 5, 1989,
and the invasion of Panama. Both were media related.

During the President's first address to the nation, he stressed the need
to intensify the "war" on drugs at home and abroad. In carrying over
the Reagan administration's bid to define the major problem in the
United States as drugs, and in particularly, "crack" cocaine, Bush
pledged more support for drug enforcement, including targeting users
and low-level dealers, rather than putting more effort into education
and rehabilitation. Not since the Nixon administration's efforts to manipulate the American citizens—with the complicity of the major TV
networks—about the "scourge of heroin," had such an outcry been
heard, broadcast, replayed, and heralded across the land (cf. Epstein
1977?).

In making his nationally televised point about the availability of
"crack" cocaine, the President produced a packet of "crack" cocaine that
was "seized a few days ago in the park across the street from the White
House . . . It could easily have been heroin or PCP" (Arizona *Republic*
September 22, 1989:A5). The entire scenario was contrived and scripted
for television. Bush staffers had requested that officials with the Drug
Enforcement Administration (DEA) try to arrange a buy very close to
the White House because, "Evidently, the president wants to show it
could be bought anywhere." What followed was great television. *Washington Post* reporter, Michael Isikoff, gave the following account (Arizona *Republic* September 22, 1989):

> But obtaining the crack was no easy feat. To match the words crafted by
> his speech writers, Drug Enforcement Administration agents lured a sus-

pected Washington drug dealer to Lafayette Park four days before the speech so they could make what appears to have been the agency's first undercover crack buy in a park better known for its location across Pennsylvania Avenue from the White House than for illegal drug activity, according to officials familiar with the case.

In fact, when first contacted by an undercover DEA agent posing as a drug buyer, the teen-age suspect seemed baffled by the agent's request. "Where the (expletive) is the White House?" he replied in a conversation that was secretly tape-recorded. "We had to manipulate him to get him down there," said William McMullan, assistant special agent in charge of the DEA's Washington Field office. "It wasn't easy."

The invasion of Panama less than a year (December 20, 1989) into Bush's term is another prime-time example. This was a symbolic spectacle for George Bush and his administration to demonstrate evocatively that he was not a "wimp," and could be decisive. The media portrayals of the Panamanian leader, Manuel Noriega, as a lunatic, philanderer, follower of voodoo, and drug runner helped dramatize evil and tied Noriega–Panama to the fears of many Americans about drugs, crime, and foreigners. To make matters easier for Bush, Noriega suffered from an acute acne problem, and his photos were far from flattering. He become "pineapple face." The invasion by some 35,000 American troops certainly did defeat the Panamanian resistance, and also resulted in the deaths of some 25 American soldiers, reports of more than a 1,000 Panamanians, and billions of dollars in damage to homes and stores in a country that was already one of the most impoverished in the Western hemisphere.

As we noted in the chapter on entertainment, the main goal of capturing Noriega was not immediately accomplished as he ran for cover, eventually taking sanctuary in the Papalnuncio. Rather than honor the sanctity of embassies, which we had so long condemned "barbaric" countries, like Iran, for violating, we blared rock music throughout the compound. Finally, after several days of "heavy metal," and delicate negotiations that included clear U.S. ultimatums about directly or indirectly seizing the Papalnuncio, Noriega emerged and was deported to the United States to stand trial for drug dealing. With that action, the U.S. chapter on Noriega was partially closed. That chapter includes paragraphs about Noriega: the man our own CIA put in office, the man who sheltered the Shah of Iran, who had met with George Bush—as Director of the CIA and as Vice President—and the man who was instrumental in the illegal arming of the Contras in Nicaragua.

There was virtually no news media reflection or criticism of this operation. There has never been such media silence on a U.S. operation! No opposition leader made any major statements questioning the wisdom and the strategy of this use of brute force. Nearly a month would pass before a handful of columnists began reflecting on the social and economic costs, especially since it was widely known that Noriega's contributions to the drug scene in the United States were quite minimal. Bush's opinion poll popularity went into orbit. Citizens who wrote letters to editors of local newspapers challenging the use of our military in such a barbarous way were chastised, and, in some cases, threatened. The country was united behind George Bush.

All this occurred within weeks of the fall of the Berlin Wall, the domino-like capitulation throughout Eastern Europe toward Democracy and away from armed violence. Even the Soviets were suggesting that they had made mistakes, that it was time for a change. East German border guards who had previously riddled teenagers with bullets who sought freedom in Berlin, now offered directions to the latest hole the people had dug through the wall. It was a time of worldwide rejoicing of epic proportions, but Bush invaded Panama. What a show it was. TV was there, live in hotel rooms, capturing street fighting, "bang-bang" as the journalists call it.

Then there was the return of some of the troops. In a carefully choreographed way, the lives of the troops who survived Panama were again put at risk as some 1,900 army paratroopers "filled the sky with green parachutes . . . as they floated earthward on their triumphant return home after invading Panama" (Arizona *Republic* January 13, 1990:A20). It was great television, and led the evening newscasts. Only four soldiers received minor injuries. Clearly, a different kind of "highway to the danger zone."

7

Media Ministry

In the 1979 edition of *Media Logic* (Altheide and Snow 1979) our discussion of religion and media focused on the emerging media ministry in evangelical religion and the general role of media in the religious revival of the 1970s. We pointed out that religious activity was rapidly becoming a significant part of that segment of American culture being created and presented within and through the mass media. Furthermore, religious experience inside traditional churches was becoming similar to watching prime-time television. In other words, the format strategies that were currently in use in television were borrowed by the clergy to attract larger congregations. The new breed of televangelist took this approach a step farther and turned the TV studio into a church and produced a private religious service for the home. From our point of view evangelical television was becoming popular with the TV viewing public because media ministers employed the same formats to present religion that network television used to present typical prime-time programs. Consequently, it was no surprise to us when on November 11, 1989 Reverend Billy Graham was awarded the 1,900th star on Hollywood's Walk of Fame (Murphy 1978). Appropriately, the press photo of the ceremony shows Graham kneeling by his star in the sidewalk and a bystander behind him wearing a Batman T-shirt!

Following the publication of *Media Logic,* a number of works on "televangelism" drew similar conclusions on the impact of media on religion and religious experience. Examples include *Electronic Christianity: Myth or Ministry* by Donald Oberdorfer (1982), *Religious Television* by Peter Horsfield (1984), *God-in-a-Box* by Colin Morris (1984), *Televangelism* by Razelle Frankl (1987), and numerous magazine and periodical articles. Encouraged by these works, the following discussion focuses on the religious trends during the 1980s, the manner in which media have presented the topic of religion during this decade, an analysis of televangelism as "media culture," and the broader issue of television's impact on religious practice and experience.

Recent Trends

All too often, the scribes of history and political/economic movements tend to ignore the role of media or relegate it to minor importance. This is particularly true in chronicles describing the early development of the modern era. It is commonly accepted that at the core of the modern age was the conflict between secular political and economic centers of power and the ecclesiastic authority of the church. At the same time, scientific rationality was replacing theology as the dominant knowledge framework. In this grand process modern media are given credit as the means used by the middle class in Western Europe and America to secularize society according to rationalistic criteria. But what is often overlooked is the fact that mass media emerged as the arena in which the major institutional norms and values of modern society were discussed, shaped, and enforced. Even discussions of morality shifted from the church to media. Therefore, recent trends in religion will parallel recent trends in media. A brief overview of the past four decades in American culture will illustrate this point.

The 1950s were years of optimism and stability in every institutional domain. The economy was stable. Trust in government was strong. Science and technology guaranteed a bright future, and education was the ticket to successful upward mobility. In this relatively unproblematic environment, home, work, and church were the simple staples of life, and for the most part television was a leisure time novelty. One exception was the popular half-hour weekly television lecture delivered by a smiling but pious catholic priest—Bishop Fulton J. Sheen. Dressed in formal vestments, he stood almost motionless before a single black and white television camera and delivered a paternalistic lecture on Christian duty to consistently large interfaith audiences. Although organized religion during the 1950s remained a matter of traditional teachings and clear social class and ethnic boundaries, Bishop Sheen was a harbinger of things to come.

1960 is being credited as a turning point in American culture—the beginning of the postmodern era. At the heart of this process is television. In 1960 Americans elected the first television president on the strength of a short series of television debates. At the end of those debates a political unknown became an instant media personality. As Marshall McLuhan noted following those debates, Jack Kennedy was completely consistent with the unique requirements of television; Richard Nixon was not. Following Kennedy's narrow victory, unbridled optimism continued for two short years and television became another example of an expanding and wondrous technology. On Saturday and Sunday evenings television even produced the appearance of America as a mass and happily united society. But as McLuhan warned, television also brought us unpleasant and dangerous views of the world. The graphic pictures of Kennedy's assassination, his funeral, and Oswald's murder were presented to a stunned and horrified mass audience that has never fully recovered from those scenes. With the war in Vietnam expanding, news on television showed a nation in turmoil. American servicemen were once again dying on foreign soil, but this time it was on television and it was not glorious. Perhaps for the first time in history, the young people who would fight the war saw what it was like before hand. In any case, the dancing and carefree youth culture that began to form in the 1950s jelled into what Theodore Roszak (1969) aptly described as a "counter culture." By the mid 1960s rigid lines were drawn between angered youth and the so-called "establishment," which youth claimed had become immoral.

The morality play came on so suddenly that everyone was caught off guard. Establishment religion made feeble attempts to entice youth back to the church through folk music and words about harmony, but in 1968 young people felt that the "Woodstock Nation" represented a more relevant religious community. For the Woodstock generation, the church stood as a symbol of a corrupt and failing social order. On the other hand, the rock concert was "community." Moreover, it was an electronically amplified community with instant emotional gratification and catharsis. Youth literally "turned off" the church scene as they would turn off a boring radio station. By the late 1960s, introductory sociology courses responded to the ratings by ignoring the topic of organized religion in the classroom. Religion did not seem relevant.

In contrast to the emotional fervor of the late 1960s, the early 1970s seemed flat. People talked of dissolution, cynicism, minimal involvement, and coping strategies. Commitment to social causes and social activism declined sharply. Young adults turned toward a more personalized and less abstract religious experience. The "Born Again movement" and the "Jesus freaks" epitomized the desire for a belief system that was simple, unambiguous, and personal. To the reborn believer, Jesus was not just a symbol of Christianity, he was "the way." Bringing this personalized approach down to earth, Billy Graham, the Hare Krishna, and Reverend Moon captivated loyal followers in search of leaders or a movement that seemed to "make a real difference" in everyday life.

The religious fundamentalism that emerged during the 1970s had little to do with theology or religious truth. People were returning to religion to achieve a sense of personal identity and social security. Tangible, in-the-flesh leaders, such as Reverend Sun Myung Moon, the 14-year-old guru Mahariji, and even the ill-fated Jim Jones provided an emotionally stable personal and community life. In this context religion became a pragmatic way to deal with problematics of everyday life rather than a philosophy for the future. Pop culture and "new journalism" reporter Tom Wolfe described the period as a "The Third Great Awakening" (1976). According to Wolfe, this was the "me" generation, and religiosity was now being achieved through such profane actions as psychotherapy, sensitivity groups, long distance running, and even "liberated" sex. Although others observed only the rejection of personal commitment and ambivalence toward social issues, Wolfe saw that people were reaching for intimacy, but not at the price of vulnerability. Rather than defining this phenomenon as a religious awakening per se, it was a groping for social security.

What Wolfe and others were observing was a fundamental change in religious orientation. The distinction between sacred and profane had disappeared. Religious ritual was no longer necessary, as it was enough to utter phrases that could be read on bumper stickers at 35 MPH. Religion as well as other institutions were being redefined in terms of immediate pragmatic concerns. Although pragmatism has always been an essential element in the fabric of American culture, the new pragmatism was in the form of "instant gratification" and as a self-aggrandizement consumption strategy. The gloomy and cynical outlook of the early 1970s was being replaced by a "present-oriented" and "consumption-oriented" social character. Worrying about the future was a "downer" in the face of the good life constantly portrayed in mass media. Style, as something instantly consumable, replaced the concern for "substance." The brief periods of nostalgia witnessed during the late 1970s and early 1980s were generated for the purpose of recapturing the style of earlier times, rather than the cultural norms and values of those periods. Whereas the youth of the 1950s were "at play," and the youth aristocracy of the 1960s created cultural independence, the youth of the 1980s become consumers of style.

How religion serves this age of consumption, style, and leisure may, in part, be understood through David Riesman's (1950) conceptualization of the "other directed" social character. Since people in a consumption-oriented society worry more about being socially accepted, they are unlikely to turn to abstract ideas or principles, such as theology or religious dogma, to find social security. Following Riesman's argument, being "God-fearing," the "Protestant ethic," and doing religious duty involves a framework that is incompatible with the consumption-oriented social character of today. On the other hand, in today's world the church could serve as a place for social activity particularly if formal ritual and theology were deemphasized. And as the mid 1980s census revealed, the traditional church organizations declined in membership while the nondenominational and fundamentalist operations increased. Religious fellowship became more salient in the lives of churchgoers than religious duty. Or, as Robert Fulghum humorously notes, it may be remembered as "The great hugging plague" (1990:127)

In addition to Tom Wolfe's observations, others, including Christopher Lasch (1979), Philip Slater (1970), and Arthur Brittan (1977), argue that current trends in urban American society include an elimination of the distinction between public and private spheres of life, as well as a turning inward and/or avoidance of intimate commitment to others. Although each of these works and ideas is slightly different in scope and argument, we feel they forecasted one common feature of the 1980s. In the urban and media environment of the 1980s there is heightened sensitivity to potentially adverse social encounters. Consequently, people seem to be more guarded, more self-indulgent, and less willing to risk personal identity in problematic interpersonal encounters. In this environment it is possible to give the appearance of social involvement without seeking and demonstrating commitment to particular others. Consequently, vicarious involvement with media (through soap operas, talk shows, etc.) has become an acceptable social activity for many, and a preferred social reality for some. In this context, a person can either thumb their nose at society through the drama of defiance commonly depicted in the heavy metal rock music videos of 1988, or they can turn to the safety and security of the familiar and enjoyable social world in television. Either alternative affords a defense against social vulnerability. Moreover, this media world is simple, entertaining, convenient, and moralistically clear.

Religion in Media

As television became the medium of choice during the 1970s, religion became a subtle but integral part of both the structural form and substantive content of television. In the 1979 edition of *Media Logic* we observed that prime-time television was loaded with moral messages, and that media created the impression that some sort of religious revival was under way. As stated earlier, the prime-time strategy of TV networks was described as following an LOP (least objectionable program) principle in order to attract the largest possible audience. Since norms, such as fairness, justice for all, virtue, respect for authority, and so forth represent what Americans idealize about their collective moral conscience, it stands to reason that prime-time television would use ideal norms as a strategy for detering potential criticism at a public or mass audience level. Even a cursory glance at typical prime-time fare supports this point. The popularity of "The Cosby Show," "Family Ties," "60 Minutes," and even "Dallas" rest on the audience's belief that morality and justice must be served. Appeals to religious ideals on talk shows invariably receive applause from a studio audience. News programs carry at least a subtle if not clear message of humanitarian compassion, especially in crisis situations, as witnessed in the 1988 "save the whales" effort when four humpbacked whales were trapped in an ice pack off the Alaskan coast (cf. Rose 1990). This morality play is subtle religion to be sure, but religion nonetheless. In following this LOP or ideal norms strategy, television has become a voice of rather traditional morality in American society.

Although morality is embedded in television format strategy, organized religion is also a topic for the content of television—particularly television news. However, as a program topic, religion is vulnerable to existing format strategies, such as confrontation, entertainment, simplification, and the big story syndrome. When the Pope visited the Western Hemisphere in 1988, complaints arose that news media simply described the Pope's arrival, places he visited, any protests that occurred, and his departure. Very little was said about why he was here or what his visit may have achieved. Instead, the news was restricted to events that photographed well and conveyed an instant symbolic recognition of piety. Similarly, in the sex and financial scandal of Jim Bakker (1987) the dominant symbols were Jim and Tammy Faye's kewpie appearance, and their lavish life-style. The Heritage USA Christian theme park scam, which eventually led to Jim Bakker's conviction on criminal fraud charges, was also a major story, but the content of that story always seemed to be overshadowed, literally, by Tammy Faye. As the Bakker's drama unraveled from March 1987 into 1989, the spotlight was constantly on a willing and very emotive Tammy Faye. She, and her eye makeup, rather than televangelism, had become the big and most enduring story.

At the same time that religious activity provided visually exciting and profitable news stories, televangelism provided paid for programing for the previously unprofitable Sunday morning hours in local television stations. During the late 1970s the paid programs from Oral Roberts, Robert Schuller, Rex Humbard, and others quickly replaced the community service religious programs offered both locally and nationally. Although this new religious programming did not constitute an increase in broadcast time allocated to religion (Horsfield 1984:88–99), it served to legitimate televangelism as a viable religious entity and at the same time exaggerate its importance as a cultural phenomenon in American religious and political life.

The success of televangelism as a commercial enterprise was due almost entirely to the adoption of entertainment formats, such as the talk show, soap opera, variety show, news format, and even cartoons and music video. The more traditional panel or interview format is still being used by local stations, but this intellectualized approach to religion primarily serves an FCC community service commitment and is relegated to the lowest rating periods. As dull but also inexpensive television, these panel discussions pay lip service to mainstream religion and social awareness, but do little to promote either one. By contrast, the low key Johnny Carson or Oprah Winfrey style talk show format in religion effectively uses entertainment to capture a revenue-generating audience. A young priest adds his guitar and folk hymns to an informal discussion with young people. A husband and wife team imitate the physical staging used by Carson to present a question and answer program using letters from viewers. Two evangelists interview each other in a conversational manor on a studio set designed as an ice cream parlor or living room. Viewers are encouraged to feel at ease, and the potential status and authority distance between religious authority and audience member are eliminated.

In arguing that television has become an integral part of the strategy of presenting religion to the public, several points need to be emphasized: demographic change and television consciousness. The critical demographic changes are obvious. The postwar baby boom is entering middle-age, and people are living longer. Although the elderly are singled out as a heavy television viewing audience, it is safe to say that in the 1980s the entire American population is a television age society. Even people who do not rely solely on television are still being exposed to television format criteria. Today all media are infused with TV formats. Television is no longer viewed with suspicion or alarm, rather, it is embraced. For a person to become a leader or influential public figure in any field, they must possess a significant amount of what may be called "television appeal." In turn, the physical staging and ritual character of an event will be enhanced to the degree that it imitates television format criteria. Consequently, a great many people are seeing and participating in religion through a new framework, and they are calling for changes in their neighborhood church services that make them livelier, more visually dramatic, and more germane for the pragmatics of everyday life. In response, enterprising clergy in mainstream Christianity, such as the College of Preachers (an Episcopal institution in Washington D.C.), have organized training workshops on dramatizing sermons.

An extreme example of the entertainmentized church service occurred at the Phoenix, Arizona First Assembly of God church led by

Pastor Tommy Barnett. The amphitheater style building seats 6,500, and Barnett's illustrated "Sunday Super Bowl" services (as he calls them) are usually enjoyed by a packed house. A broad professionally lighted stage features ample space for Barnett to move about while acting out a sermon. At the rear of the stage is a curtained platform for a 20 piece orchestra. Behind the orchestra is another curtained platform that seats a choir larger than most church congregations. A drum roll signals the beginning of the service and the curtains revealing the orchestra and choir are raised in succession. As everyone in the congregation sings loudly and sways to the beat, the decibel level and excitement approaches rock concert proportions. The music director shouts "Are you happy to be here?" and people respond with "Amen" and "Praise the Lord." "Let's just give God a round of applause," he adds, and God receives a half dozen standing ovations.

After this warm-up Barnett appears and begins his sermon from a prepared text and referenced in a traditional manner to a particular bible passage. But five minutes into the sermon he suddenly departs from the text and appears to ad lib the remainder of an emotion-packed, visually dramatic message. In one fairly typical service, Barnett used two 15-foot live trees (one dead and the other lush in greenery) on the stage and proceeded to prune the limbs of the dead tree while making the sermon's points. He began with a small pruning saw for the small limbs, progressed to a bow saw for larger branches, and then to the delight of the audience he took out a 4-foot axe and chopped away at the dead trunk. But this was not enough. For a grand finale he fired up a chain saw. Preaching at the top of his lungs and with the chain saw roaring and ripping through the trunk, the tree crashes to the stage. At that dramatic moment he paused, leaned toward the hushed, ecstatic crowd and reverently asked, "Do you want to live spiritually or do you want to dry up spiritually, wither and die?" He then burst into song and with everyone around the alter to end the service (Simpler 1986).

Barnett's First Assembly of God church is Pentecostal, and critics would quickly point out that this in no way represents a typical Sunday church service in middle-class America. Although this is certainly true, several points need consideration. First, the Pentecostal services of today are more like television entertainment then the "hell fire and brimstone" tent services of decades past. Pentecostal services have changed as the major media formats in American culture have changed. Second, mainstream church services have also changed to fit media formats, although they are not as extreme as a flamboyant Barnett service. And yet, when the Pope visited Phoenix, Arizona in 1987, he delivered a visually dramatic televised mass at the Arizona State University football stadium. An altar was erected on the field with a gleaming high tech backdrop depicting Arizona's most familiar environmental symbols—the Grand Canyon and a Saguaro cactus. Through the stadium lights the scene to the television audience was ethereal, and the Pope looked properly saintly in his white vestments. But the visual topper came as the Pope made his exit following his solemn and emotionally moving mass. Although he apparently had not been forewarned, a fireworks display exploded over the stadium and became the grand finale for the television audience. But to the stunned parishioners in the stadium it was confusing. Why would a mass end with fireworks?

Televangelism as Media Culture

By the late 1970s it was clear that a marriage of television and religion would be very successful, although it seemed limited primarily to evangelists and neopentecostal pastors and organizations. At that time evangelists, such as Pat Robertson, Jerry Falwell, Oral Roberts, Jimmy Swaggart, and others were following the lead of Reverend Billy Graham by expanding their broadcasts to audiences nationwide and to a few foreign countries. At the same time, religious networks, such as the Christian Broadcasting and Trinity Broadcasting networks, were developing into bonafide businesses in their own right. Between 1978 and 1988 the number of TV stations devoted exclusively to religious programming had increased from 25 to 100 (Schultze 1988). By the mid-1980s, media ministers, such as Jimmy Swaggart and Oral Roberts, were claiming audiences in excess of one million households in 140 TV markets during any given week. The public joked freely when Oral Roberts pleaded for 8 million dollars by March 31, 1987, or "God would call him home." To the surprise of those unfamiliar with the power of televangelism, he made his literal deadline with the help of a $1.3 million dollar contribution from a Florida Dog Track owner the last week in March. Even after the sex scandals of 1987, the empires built by Swaggart, Falwell, the Bakkers, Schuller, and others were exceeding annual revenues of $100 million. Although this astounding achievement was initially due to appeals through television, the ability to extract revenue from viewers was based on a direct mail strategy, and these religious entrepreneurs found that "crisis begging" for small donations provided the capital required for continued expansion of their personal empires.

It is easy to become sidetracked in the dramatic numbers story of televangelism during the past decade. Indeed, the penchant for big numbers (as news criteria) has had an impact. In 1976, *Newsweek* magazine called the evangelist movement "the most significant and overlooked religious phenomenon of the 1970s." The *Wall Street Journal* stated on July

11, 1980 that televangelism was reaching an estimated 128 million viewers each week. But as several researchers have demonstrated, these
figures were grossly overestimated (Horsfield 1984:79; Schultze 1988:
18–23). Put bluntly by William Martin in "The Birth of a Media Myth"
(1981), the televangelist movement was an exaggerated television phenomenon. In actual percent of followers, the fundamentalist and evangelist movement is no more powerful or extensive today than it was in
the pretelevision era (Schultze 1988:20). Regardless, televangelism in
the mid-1980s became an important segment of media culture, as it
blended perfectly with the visually dramatic criteria of contemporary
commercial television. And this television reality (mythical or otherwise)
has taken on a life of its own that exceeded the actual numbers of viewers and contributing followers.

As a media culture phenomenon the evolution of televangelism is
essentially a story of theatrics and charisma in which the church has
become a theater, the preacher a consummate actor, and the congregation an attentive audience. Although the performance of religious ritual
has always been richly theatrical, there are major differences between
the way in which televangelism employs theatrics and the performance
ritual in mainstream church services. That difference is the elimination
of a status and ecclesiastic authority dimension between church symbols
and the preacher vis-à-vis the audience. The televangelist show is a
theatrical production in which the audience becomes emotionally involved in the play. Moreover, the actors on stage play to the needs or
desires of the audience, effectively creating the impression that the
audience is being served. The audience or congregation does not listen,
watch, or perform ritual for sacred duty. They are emotionally captivated and become united reciprocally with the charismatic leader. This is
not simply the result of a leader's magical charismatic ability, it is the
result of establishing the definition of "theater" rather than "church
service." And in the American popular culture of the 1980s, theater
means television theater with its accompanying secular and informal
intimacy.

In 1979 we reported on the prototype of today's televangelism production, noting how ordinary secular symbols were used to develop a
television church. In the early 1950s a church called Soul's Harbor
began telecasting services from an old meeting hall near downtown St.
Paul, Minnesota. The minister wore a captain's uniform and preached
from a pulpit decorated with nautical artifacts. Although, the respect-
able middle class paid little attention, Soul's Harbor became a success.
Soon the established denominations were televising their services, but
the difference was great. Soul's Harbor adapted to the format of television, whereas the established churches did not. In the established
churches there were problems with acoustics, busy color backgrounds

that affronted the eye on black-and-white television, bad camera angles, and the solemn air of the service. In addition, the established churches lacked the single most important ingredient in television—entertainment. In a sense, Soul's Harbor did "shtick," and the viewers loved it" (Altheide and Snow 1979:202–203)

Shortly after Soul's Harbor debut, Robert Schuller founded his Garden Grove Community Church (1955) in Orange County, California. Today he delivers his edited "Hour of Power" television program from Garden Grove's spectacular, 12-story-high "Crystal Cathedral" sanctuary with its dancing fountains, mammoth alter/stage, plush seats, and of course its professional lighting and sound system. The Crystal Cathedral is not a church in the usual sense, it is Schuller's stage and the embodiment of Schuller himself. He, as well as other successful televangelists, have become media personalities in preacher-centered religious operations. Schuller symbolizes a church, just as Jerry Falwell, Rex Humbard, Jimmy Swaggert, and Oral Roberts symbolize churches.

Several years ago Robert Schuller demonstrated his persona at church in a July 4th celebration in which his message was "I am the American Flag" (Horsfield 1984:37–38). A uniformed military band played patriotic selections to an applauding audience. Accented by background strings and brass, Schuller painted word pictures of America's glories past, present, and future. Flags were paraded up and down the aisles culminating in the grand finale in which a gigantic American flag was stretched from floor to ceiling, draping the alter to symbolize the unity of God and the American flag. Although Schuller is dwarfed by the flag, he is the humble but powerful servant who orchestrates the spectacle; who at that moment represents the triumph of the American way through Christianity. The message is clear; the response is intensely exhilarating. Millions of TV viewers in over 150 television markets witness a polished and professionally edited visual masterpiece of television production billed as "The Hour of Power" staring Robert Schuller. In 1990 he took his show to the Soviet Union.

Whereas Schuller ensconces himself in a dazzling crystal sanctuary, other televangelists do not bother with an independent physical structure. They situate themselves on a television studio set that is designed to accent their personality. Jimmy Swaggert employed a tiered, red carpeted stage with a plain altar, and moved dramatically about to draw his audience into his persona. There were no props to distract the viewer. Swaggert's powerful and animated impression management was more than enough to hold an audience's attention through an hour long discourse of folksy stories, testimonials, song, and prayer. The production values in lighting, sound, camera work, and editing on the Swaggert program easily met the standards of network television. Furthermore, camera movement served to draw the viewer into a degree of intimacy that was almost uncomfortably close, as experienced by viewers when Jimmy repented on camera following the first disclosure of his sexual activity with a prostitute. Even the cynical viewer would be hard-pressed to avoid at least a few moments of captivated attention.

In contrast to the emotional intensity of Swaggert's approach, the Praise the Lord programs are carnivals of hope, joy, and thanks. They are similar to the informal afternoon television variety hour, or talk show, but have the pizzazz for a prime-time schedule. With a rousing introduction using computer graphics, hyped voice-over, snappy musical theme, and camera zooms, viewers are whisked off to several hours of a "joyful praise and prayer gathering." The set design blends symbols of traditional Americana with an idealized goodness of simple but prosperous christianity. In 1988 the TBN (Trinity Broadcasting Network) "Praise the Lord" program used a set design that combined traditional church architecture (stained glass gothic windows) and a palatial estate living room with curved marble staircase, large crystal chandelier, eighteenth century paintings, elegant period chairs, fireplace, lush plants, a large world globe, the ever-present red carpet, and a white grand piano used to accompany professional evangelist recording artists (who often give testimonials during the program). A typical program led by the Southern California based Paul and Jan Crouch follows a well-timed schedule that begins with a few announcements, an opening prayer, a musical selection, one or more interviews with guest evangelists, more music, prayer for the unfortunate, prayer for a personal cause of the evangelist (tied to a call for contributions), more music, and so on. All the while prayerline telephone numbers flash at the bottom of the screen, and periodically we see prayer partners taking prayer calls in call booths away from the main set.

Husband and wife teams on the various programs are interchangeable and often take turns hosting the program (not unlike Carson's guest hosts). Perhaps not surprisingly, these teams all look and sound alike. Both husband and wife have full heads of thick well coifed hair. Men wear light suits; women wear conservative high neck ruffled blouses or dresses. Affluence is openly displayed in jewelry and cosmetics. The wives are "stand by their man" arch types. As we stated in 1979 (Altheide and Snow 1979:210) they reminded us of Merv Griffin and Dolly Parton—models of humility and success.

To the casual observer the immediate question is "How could these people become religious figures?" Who could take them seriously? The answer lies partially in the context of white lower middle class bible belt culture that rejects urban sophistication, promotes religious fundamentalism, and glories in the sense of community afforded by Sunday afternoon family "socials." Most important, they are admittedly oriented toward friendship with people "just like themselves," as opposed to being authoritative theologians. These evangelists create the impression that the Bible speaks for itself, and they are simply facilitators in a Christian calling. Jim and Tammy Bakker were considered good neighbors doing God's work. At the same time, mixing religion and entertainment was never considered sacrilegious, and displaying affluence, even in a garish manner, is a demonstration of God's rewards in this world. As Reverend Jerry Falwell once remarked, "Material wealth is God's way of blessing people who put him first" (Woodward 1980:35). One of these rewards was created by the Bakkers in the form of a leisure resort hotel complex known as Heritage Park, a place where good Christians could socialize together and celebrate Christian/American values. In a parasocial sense, the Bakkers, Crouches, and other evangelists developed extended families or communities that promised social security and righteousness.

Consequently, the impact of televangelism is not simply the ability of particular evangelists to attract a following. Rather, televangelism has become a cultural form (media culture) in which the distinction between religion and television has disappeared. Moreover, this cultural form has become a social context in which people focus and live their lives. The new televangelists do not link viewers to local churches, they promote their own form of religious community. Since their goal, as stated by Paul Crouch on a program broadcast January 4, 1989, is to establish television stations in the Trinity Broadcasting Network, their missionary work is to entice people to watch television—specifically televangelism, and to make contributions that continue that effort.

The criteria of this new form of media culture are primarily visual. Although this may sound absurdly self-evident, consider the factors that are relied on to create acceptability and a sense of legitimacy for any media subject. In radio, voice quality and audio rhythm and tempo are everything. By contrast, Hollywood movies constructed a visual grammar that emerged during the silent picture days. Television borrowed the grammar of Hollywood film and added a dimension of everyday life familiarity and routine interpersonal intimacy. For televangelism, Billy Graham was the transition. He had a deep resonant radio voice and a visual continence for television. But today, voice quality is relatively unimportant, as demonstrated by Jim Bakker and Paul Crouch. What is important about voice in today's televangelism is timing, specifically the ability to speak slowly and succinctly. What is essential now in a televangelist's message is the visual cue for the viewing audience, just as it is on soap operas. In terms of syntax, the visual cue leads the auditory, as it has on visual media since the silent film era. Eyes brighten, sadden, and plead; smiles click on and tears of sorrow flow as cued by well-planned scripts. And with deft camera work the viewer is drawn into an approximation of a close interpersonal relationship with the person on the screen—a larger than life and yet intimate visual encounter.

As televangelists have become more knowledgeable about visual media (their telecommunications studies probably surpass any other non-media professional), they have altered their television strategies to underscore the visual character of religious experience with positive results from viewers. Of course, visual dramatics are nothing new in religious ceremony. Any ritual designed to promote an intense emotional state may profit from dramatic visual and auditory stimuli. Our point, in part, is that the new visual and auditory religious formats are drawn from the familiar formats of television, and during the 1980s these evangelists have become even more polished in current video skills. In fact, the visual impression management techniques of the televangelist in the late 1980s have reached the point that it is impossible to distinguish between the theatrics of the staged performance and what the televangelist may be off stage. As Tammy Bakker said on the December 19, 1988 "Sally Jesse Raphael Show," "What you see is what you get!" However, when Bakker apparently suffered a nervous breakdown during his trial for embezzlement in 1989, a court appointed psychiatrist ruled that he was sane enough to stand trial.

The difficulty in distinguishing between televangelism as video theater and televangelism as religion is what has made televangelism a consummate form of media culture. This is not simply religion being telecast to a viewing audience, it is a new form of religion—a televisionized religion in which religious experience as a cultural phenomenon is "informed" by television format criteria. Remove television and no doubt the Bakkers of this world would virtually disappear. But does the impact of television on religious experience go beyond the confines of televangelism? Evidence, such as Reverend Tommy Barnett's First Assembly "Sunday Super Bowl" services and the staging of the Pope's mass on his American visit, suggests that media culture is indeed informing religious practice and experience outside the confines of television itself.

Religious Practice and Experience

In 1979 we concluded the chapter on "Media Ministry" with this statement:

Religion, projected by electronic media, is presented through an entertainment perspective and an ideal-norms format which simplifies it according to an LOP principle. In turn, the institution of religion has been altered. Religious movements have taken a "back to basics" approach as witnessed with the Born Again Christians, among others . . . Consequently, and to a significant extent, the meanings of religion and religious experience in contemporary society are developed through a media consciousness. (Altheide and Snow 1979:216)

In the decade since that publication, we believe the argument is even more salient. Certainly the recent history of televangelism demonstrates that when religion is presented through television formats, the substance of religious practice and experience changes. Based on his doctoral dissertation on religious television, Peter Horsfield (1984:43) states:

> The dominant functions of television, combined with the pressure on stations to maximize their audience, has shaped television programming in America in several characteristics ways: it has led away from in-depth demanding analyses to an oversimplification of issues and their solutions; it has fed the desire for instant gratification of needs rather than disciplined resolution; and it has tended toward the sensationalization of events and experiences. Each of these results has had a marked shaping effect on religious programs as well, particularly those programs that have placed themselves in a situation where their continued existence depends on their successfully competing within this system.

Although Horsfield's conclusions and most of our earlier statements were directed primarily to the impact of television on religious programming, we also argue that religious practice and experience outside of media are changing as a result of the general media or television consciousness (logic) that pervades American culture. What Allan Bloom (1987) laments about American education, and many observers lament about Presidential politics, Harvey Cox (1979) laments about Christianity in America. Our restatement of Cox's concerns is that the lessons of the Christian gospel are being altered and eliminated through the logic embedded in a media consciousness. Although television is not the only factor in this web of cultural change, it stands as the primary mover and shaker in the decade of the 1980s.

A brief examination of recent religious movements, such as the Unification Church under Reverend Moon, Jim Jones' People's Temple, the commune of the Bhagwan Rajneesh in Eastern Oregon, and even the followers of Ramtha, demonstrates a shift away from the importance of abstract theology and ultimate salvation of the soul to a more concrete experience involving religious personalities and immediate solutions to everyday life problems. Followers in these groups seek social security in this world as opposed to a salvation of the soul in the hereafter. Extending this reasoning to the Born Again Christians, it seems reasonable to suggest that displaying the sign of the fish on store fronts, automobile trunk lids, and business cards is a strategy of social networking as much as it is a statement of religious belief.

Although religious communities have always provided a significant degree of social comfort or at least explained why the social order is as it is, the difference more recently is the deemphasis of abstract principles in favor of everyday life pragmatism. And although American culture has always been intensely pragmatic, and more recently oriented to instant pragmatic solutions, television encapsulates and intensifies those cultural characteristics. The compelling question is, "Was religious practice and experience different before the television age?" Sociologically, religion has been conceptualized as the institution that clearly distinguishes between the sacred and the profane, and between what should be valued for the sake of social order and personal grace, as opposed to what is of immediate and practical value in the secular profane world. At the very least, religious ritual reminds us of what is right and good, while at the same time affecting an emotional state of religious experience. Until recently, modern society protected religion from the profane, or at least it has maintained a sufficient degree of sacred stature for religious activity. To put it bluntly, church was church, and business was business. However, as our participation in various institutional realms, such as religion or politics, occurs more and more through media, the various institutional criteria or normative frameworks have been replaced with media, namely television, criteria. Consequently, effective politics is recast as effective use of television, and religion is being evaluated by parishioners according to television format criteria.

The major cultural change is essentially a matter of practicing and experiencing religion and morality through the formal properties of television as opposed to the traditional formal properties of the church and ecclesiastic organization. It is not stretching the point too far to state that today television "informs" the church, and in some cases it is the church. As such, religious experience in this current television age seems to be quite similar to political experience. In both, the emphasis is on visual dramatics, simplicity, and instant gratification. Perhaps this explains in part the popularity of Ronald Reagan's presidency, and his perceived association with Reverend Falwell's moral majority in 1984. On the one hand it could be argued that they used each other. It may also be argued that both were products of the same process—they were, first and foremost, media personalities.

8

Media Sports

Over the last three decades, organized sports and television have become inseparable. With the possible exception of politics, no other institution in American society has been so clearly dominated by media logic. Operating through an entertainment perspective and other media formats, sports have undergone major changes in fundamental characteristics, such as rules of play, style of play, stadium theatrics, economic structure, media markets, and hero construction. Together, these changes have produced a new media sports culture built on the keystone of television (Duncan and Brummett 1987). As articulated by one of the architects of modern media (Roone Arledge, ABC TV) "So many sports organizations have built their entire budgets around network TV that if we ever withdrew the money, the whole structure would collapse" (Arizona *Republic* December 27, 1978). Although the economic structure of sports has become dependent on media, so has nearly every facet of what constitutes sports culture. From the character of the new athlete to how a game is watched, sports culture today is media culture (cf. Bogart 1956).

Prior to the television era, print and radio carried sporting events to fans in a fairly matter-of-fact manner without altering how the game was played or viewed by the fan. Certainly these media provided a degree of hype and hoopla, glorifying the sports hero and exalting the ideal of fair play and rivalry, but they had very little impact on the economics of sports, and made no effort to create an audience. Basically, print and radio served the fan. Today, television dominates sports and the situation is no longer a local or regional phenomenon. At present, mass audiences view sports from the perspective of television entertainment, which essentially means that sports events became athletic spectacles (Stone 1971), and sports audiences now consist of TV viewers as well as die-hard fans. In effect, TV has created a whole new sports experience through the entertainment perspective.

Consider the following example as you reflect on the rest of this chapter. A 1989 movie, *Field of Dreams,* was about an Iowa corn farmer who hears voices and is motivated to build a baseball field in the middle of his corn field. On completion, he is visited by great baseball players from the past, many whose dreams were cut short, e.g., Shoeless Joe Jackson, who was implicated in the famous Black scandal in 1919, and was subsequently banned from baseball. All are dead. This includes his father, a minor league ball player whom the farmer never really knew. It is a wonderful movie, emotionally rich in its ability to strike a chord in viewers. But there is more to it. The man who actually built the field on his farm for Universal Studios to use in making the movie reports that more than 10,000 people from all over the world have visited the field, and many have left notes, like the following: "Thanks for sharing the dream and keeping it alive" (Arizona *Republic* April 6, 1990).

Sports in American Society

When the firing of a sports announcer (Brent Mussberger—April 1990) is front page news across the country, the importance of sports and television's involvement in sports has moved into a new dimension. Since the end of WW II, the development of sports as an institution in American society has been phenomenal. Behavioral science began paying attention to this phenomenon in the late 1960s and discovered the interdependence of sports with the rest of society (Luschen 1967; Sage 1970; Stone 1972). By the 1990s it was clear that sports intersect with other institutions to the degree that if sports were withdrawn, organizational activity in business, education, politics, health (insurance), family life, and even religion would be significantly altered. Sports can no longer be thought of as an escape into leisure, or time away from the more serious pursuits of the work-a-day world. For many people sports replaces work as a major source of existential meaning in life, as that's where the action is. David Riesman had it right 40 years ago when he said that avocations would replace vocations as a major source of personal competence in life (1950:290–301). At present both participant and spectator sports constitute primary avocations for the modern urbanite. Furthermore, sports symbolizes personal integrity and courage as well as any other set of institutional symbols in American society. Indeed, sports resonates with the primary values and moral fabric of American society (cf. Durkheim, 1961). At present, the most positive public opinion indicator of community well-being seems to reside in sports.

An illustration of the importance of sports occurred in our back yard on March 13, 1990. The home of the Phoenix Cardinals (Sun Devil Stadium on the Arizona State University Campus) was selected to host the 1993 NFL Super Bowl, and a month later we heard stories that officials for World Cup Soccer were looking at the same stadium for several of the 1994 games. According to one report (Beard and Novotny 1990), the Super Bowl alone would mean an estimated $200 million for local business. But that might be minor compared to the profits and tax revenue over the long run that could be generated in business deals struck during the event or through networks established as a result of the event. Politicians will be on parade in the national limelight, and whomever is Governor or Senator will get a considerable degree of free media exposure. Phoenix and the specific site (Tempe) will receive worldwide attention. Families will be reunited with friends and relatives they have not seen in years. And individuals living in Phoenix will bask in the glory of major league status. With the World Cup, this status would move up a notch, as the international audience would number in the billions. On the strength of these factors, it may be suggested that sports are the last bastion of community in American society. World fairs were once the means of achieving world class status for an up and coming city; today it is hosting the Super Bowl.

On an everyday life and interpersonal level, sports has become so pervasive that it is difficult to listen to a conversation without hearing sports imagery, lingo, or metaphors (cf. Wenner 1989). World leaders talk about game plans, and cheap shots, business leaders refer to being "players," and individuals talk about "striking out," "touching base," or "being in the ballpark." In other words, sports is commonplace in everyday life. There is more news on sports in the newspaper than any other single topic, and it is often read first, at least by men. However, with the increase in co-ed and women's organized athletics, sports is no longer the exclusive domain of men. In fact, we feel that in modern urban life, with its high degree of uncertainty and ambiguity, sports offers one of the most concrete (unambiguous and stable) activities a person can partake in either as a spectator or participant. Games are won and lost, the rules are clear, the players intent and affiliation are never in doubt, and the emotional gratification or expression is immediate. Furthermore, the basic moral fabric of society is deeply embedded in sporting activity. In the minds of fans and players, justice probably wins out more often in sports than any other institutional activity.

In the more routine aspects of everyday life, sports provides something to look forward to in the immediate future, as well as a means for bracketing periods of time and creating seasonal rhythms. Whether it is the game this weekend or the coming of baseball in Spring, sports provides substance for anticipation—a future orientation—a rebirth of spirit. When someone yells "play ball," winter is officially over, and when the first regular season kickoff occurs, Fall has begun. If this seems overly romantic, read almost any popular book on one of the major sports, such as Roger Kahn's "The Boys of Summer." As a friend of ours once remarked to a nonsports fan, "You must remember, most Nobel prize winners would give up that distinction if they could play second base for the "Cubs." If this does not ring true, further argument on our part is fruitless.

Finally, a brief word about sports as small talk. Everyone understands that small talk is a social skill necessary for maintaining civility and sociability during awkward moments. Small talk keeps things going, and, for several reasons, sports are a very common small talk topic. Like weather, sports are immediate and ever present. There is always some sports topic to discuss, and it aids in establishing a sense of involvement in current affairs. Unlike politics, sports can be argumentative without threatening the identities of the participants, and, therefore, the immediate social encounter. To be trite about it, sports are safe social intercourse.

Putting the characteristics just mentioned together, sports appears to be one of the more powerful components of personal self-esteem and social stability in everyday life. On a community level sports represents community identity and moral order. On a societal level, sports are sacred in the value system as religion. Given these characteristics, sports are fertile ground for exploitation by the media.

The Marriage of Media and Sports

The first sporting event ever televised was a baseball game between Columbia and Princeton in 1939. With one camera following the flight of the ball from pitcher to batter to fielder, an audience of 400 sets was tortured with a barrage of blurred images. Today, eight or more cameras and instant replay machines feed a plethora of information to millions of viewers watching on giant screens or mini-portable sets. Although television no doubt recognized the potential for profit in sports coverage early on, numerous obstacles had to be overcome. Cumbersome camera and broadcasting equipment made it difficult to televise any event that did not approximate studio conditions, such as wrestling and boxing. Fragile equipment failed so often that it became the butt of humor in comedy skits by Milton Berle and Sid Caesar. Obviously, advertisers were reluctant to pay the price, particularly when there was no guarantee of a specified number of ads. After all, who could predict how long a contest would last, whether it would be exciting enough to stay tuned to the end, and how many minutes would be available for commercials. Until the development of video tape, advertising was too risky on any program where commercial breaks could not be preplanned, and the only fans who would watch the event on TV were those who could not get to the game. Prior to the 1970s, watching the game from the stands was still preferable.

During those early years (1950s and early 1960s), sports coverage was similar to news coverage. The camera was aimed at the action and the audience interpreted what it saw. Play-by-play announcing seemed inappropriate, and commentary was sparse. Compared to radio broadcasts of baseball and football, television was boring, particularly in black and white. And then came color, both on the screen and from the announcer's booth. It began as the coach-as-expert on Saturday afternoon college football games. Famous coaches (often retired) were asked to explain strategy, which provided the viewer with something the fan in the stands could not obtain. This evolved to the former star, such as Tom Harmon, who could give the viewer the player's viewpoint. In some cases, the coach and player were one in the same, such as Bud Wilkenson. Nevertheless, it was still essentially a news rather than entertainment format. We are reluctant to say that Howard Cosell was the first of the sports entertainer announcers, but he certainly made a gigantic impact in developing this format. Although he claimed to "tell it like it is," he actually became one of the protagonists in the contest. He was the television referee, the gadfly who injected controversy, and, aided by an astounding memory, he tossed out trivia for the viewer to play with. Cosell made the fan pay attention to television, not just the game, and this was the new departure that "Monday Night Football" brought to professional sports.

Meanwhile, television obtained league permision to get special advertising breaks during the games. Video tape enabled advertisers to bring entertainment formats to their advertisements; no longer were they dependent on play-by-play announcers who read ads like news bulletins. A parade of color commentators filled dead air, and play-by-play announcing returned. A rival professional football league (The American Football League) was developed primarily as a television venture and an effort to crack the monopoly held by the NFL owners. It proved beneficial to all, particularly when Joe Namath and the New York Jets defeated Johnny Unitis and the invincible Baltimore Colts in the 1969 Super Bowl. From then on, anything could happen in professional football—"on any given Sunday." As color broadcasts became perfected and dependable, and as big league sports expanded to new cities in new TV markets, ratings for nearly every sporting event increased. By the mid 1970s sports of almost any kind was a sure winner on television, particularly if the sidelines proved entertaining, such as the Dallas Cowboy cheerleaders, the Laker Girls, or the San Diego chicken. By the mid-

1970s, sports and television were inexorably tied together in a business and cultural relationship.

Media Logic and Sports

As discussed earlier, one of the characteristics of media logic is that television creates events that have a high probability of attracting large numbers of viewers. In other words, television programs are commercials for commercials, and viewers are packaged for advertisers. Nowhere is this process more apparent and clearly illustrative than with sports. Unlike most other audiences (politics, religion, etc.) the sports audience is not only predictable in terms of what it will watch, it also has steadily expanded in numbers. One reason for the appeal of sports is that in urban America, sports constitutes one of the stable or dependable aspects of everyday life. Politicians, cars, and even jobs come and go, but Chicago Cubs baseball and New York Giants football are perennial. Combining this dependability with the increasing popularity of entertainment TV, networks outdid each other in outrageous bidding wars to land exclusive rights to broadcast professional baseball, basketball, and football. In fact, the most recent negotiations (1990) between the NFL and five television networks produced a 3.56 billion dollar deal for the league over four seasons. It might seem preposterous that advertisers would support that kind of investment, but recent history shows that advertisers will pay whatever the networks ask. Sports are a seller's market in America, and all the networks need is assurance that games will be played. Entertainment television delivers entertainment sports, and "the show" is better than ever. Even if advertisers do not come through with the needed money for these outlandish network contracts, the networks have a guaranteed mass audience for promoting other television programs.

Entertainment. Sports not only fit the format requirements of entertainment television, they do a better job than most other kinds of programs with the possible exception of award spectaculars and some situation comedies. Over the past decade, the highest rated single program each year has been the NFL Super Bowl. When ABC decided to put professional football in a prime-time slot on Monday night, the trend toward imposing an entertainment format on sports events went into high gear. Specifically, this meant tailoring the event according to the current format criteria for entertainment, such as rapid tempo, an emphasis on visual glamour, and the importance of ideal norms. In fact, almost everything discussed in Chapter 2 on entertainment applies to how sports is presented in the 1990s. "Monday Night Football" was not a program designed to appeal to dedicated football fans, it was an attempt to create viewers, and that meant "show business." As play-by-play announcer Frank Gifford explained:

> We don't want to televise a game that's going to be 48-7. Quite frankly, in the prime time area, you can't put on a game with a team that's not going to be competitive with the other team because people won't watch it. They might watch it once, but they won't watch it again. (Los Angeles *Times*, January 23, 1977)

Howard Cosell's (1973) account of reaction to "Monday Night Football" by executives from other networks was:

> It's entertainment shouted Bill MacPhail and Carl Lindermann, the respective heads of CBS and NBC Sports, it's not football . . . if we wanted that kind of stuff, we'd put Jack Benny, Don Rickles and Bob Hope in the booth. But we're not going to sink to that. We're not running a comedy hour . . . We don't need to bother with any of that junk that Cosell and his buddies are hanging out. (p. 343)

But as Cosell goes on to explain, if NBC and CBS were to compete in the ratings with their respective sports coverage, they would have to change. And they did. In the spring of 1973, Carl Lindemann utterly recanted. He was saddled with 15 Monday nights of major league baseball and he knew he had to attract enough viewers for those games to induce advertisers to pay enough money to recapture the very costs of carrying the package. And so, Curt Gowdy and Tony Kubek, the regular announcing team, would be joined in the booth each week by a different personality from show business. Dinah Shore one week, Bailey another. Maybe Woody Allen a third. Maybe even Howard Cosell (Cosell 1973:344).

Since the apparent rhythm and tempo in a sports event are normally tied to the closeness of the contest, television must create the illusion that action exists when things are actually quite boring. ABC realized this early when a Monday night pro football game was so lopsided that nearly everyone left the stadium and the cameras were left with nothing interesting to photograph. Although recent rule changes almost guarantee that one-sided games are a thing of the past, it occasionally happens, as with the 1990 Super Bowl. Now, there are contingency plans, including other games that can be cut to, media personalities that visit the booth, stories from roving sideline reporters, graphics, statistics, biographical sketches, predictions for next week or next year. Last but not least are the zany costumes of fans who want to get on TV.

Following the early success of "Monday Night Football," the networks followed their standard procedure of working a winner until it collapses. During the 1970s this ranged from the development of sports anthologies, such as "Wide World of Sports," to the creation of "made for television" tournaments in boxing, tennis, and golf. This eventually proliferated into arm wrestling, bubble gum blowing contests, and the ludicrous "Battle of the Network Stars," in which entertainers battled it out in a series of playground events for the distinction of "being number one." These "not quite sports" events seemed to have run their course by the early 1980s, although one semi-sports event has endured—wrestling. During the early days of TV it was Gorgeous George. Forty years later the clone was Hulk Hogan. Andre the Giant replaced Yukon Eric, and "The Crusher" evolved into Randy "Macho Man" Savage. Women's wrestling became GLOW (Gorgeous Ladies of Wrestling), and we cannot forget those timeless favorites, tag teams, mud wrestling, and the "no-holds barred-fight-to-the-finish." Everything is the same except the costumes, which are brighter, bolder, and more erotic.

As contrived entertainmentized sports wore thin with television viewers, the networks returned to the big three of baseball, basketball, and football, and lengthened the seasons, scheduled more games during prime-time, and expanded the playoffs. By the end of the 1980s one could legitimately argue that the regular season in most professional sports was simply a preseason for the playoffs, and very few teams were excluded. The result is that playoffs and the championship finals have become television spectacles that have been so successful in ratings that the process has extend to the college ranks. The NCAA has realized that big money could be made in playoffs, hence the NCAA basketball playoffs and the current talk of a national football playoff. What began as statistical rankings a few years ago has turned into television playoff events that earn high Nielsen ratings. The next step in this evolution is in high school where national rankings recently emerged in football and basketball. USA Today carries the super 25 high school rankings along with profiles of prep stars, and these rankings are the basis for nationally televised basketball tournaments, such as the Las Vegas Holiday Prep Classic.

The sports spectacular has become so glorious and glamorous on television that for a time during the late 1970s and 1980s, people seemed to prefer the televised event to the stadium. The response was to turn the stadium into a giant television studio, a strategy that solved two problems simultaneously. First, the new domed stadiums were built for easy access by TV cameras and optimum broadcast values. Of course, the dome also keeps out inclement weather, ensuring that broadcast schedules can be maintained. Second, the new stadiums provide television for the fan in the seats. What began as a giant TV-like scoreboard run by computer graphic software has become giant television screens placed for easy viewing by everyone in the stadium. Now the stadium fan can see the same instant replay, and something entertaining to look at during breaks in action. All the visual technology available for broadcast can and is brought to the stadium. Another advantage of instant replay is that it also serves the advertising game. When sponsors put their logos on uniforms, hats, and even bottoms of shoes they are aware that these may be noticed in "real time," when the action originally occurs, but more importantly, during replays, often in slow motion. This time adds up. For example, Maxfli golf balls received more than $800 thousand worth of free exposure during the 1989 Masters telecast, while Coca-Cola generated more than $62 thousand worth of exposure as rain fell on Coke umbrellas for 22 seconds during the same golf tournament (*USA Today*). Not surprisingly, the major TV networks are monitoring this "new" form of exposure.

As stadiums became theaters, replacing the opera house as a symbol of cultural class, athletes became actors, especially in costuming expertise. It began with baseball players tailoring their uniforms to emphasize a svelte look (the TV camera puts weight on). Then came the perm, the gold chain, stylish footwear, gloves, glasses, Florence Joyner's designer costumes for the 1988 Olympic games, and the latest wrinkle, the shaved hair design on the scalp. The new athlete is costumed for capturing the camera during breaks in the action. Uniforms are still symbols of team identity, but they are brighter, bolder, and sexier than they were several decades ago, and, whether it is Jim McMahon's head band, or Florence Joyner's harlequin tights, the effect is one of emphasizing individual style. Several decades ago kids would mimic the playing style of their favorite player. Today kids copy the costume, and fashion designers are commissioned by high schools to design team uniforms.

Turning to the grammar of prime-time entertainment, most sports events easily fit the inflection requirements of prime-time television. Specifically, this means visual appeal, rapid tempo, and the periodic crescendo. In other words, anything that produces accent, rhythm, and tempo qualifies. For example, beginning in 1990, ESPN will have telecast capability in every major league ballpark, enabling them to cut live from the game being telecast to any park where a major event, such as hitting streak, no-hitter, or other big play is taking place. This constant action capability should produce a rapid tempo and give the viewer a sense of up to the minute headlines, much like network news. Big plays will be relayed numerous times, expert commentators will flood the screen with diagramed strategy and computer graphic statistics, pre-taped interviews, humorous inserts, and, of course, advertisements, which always conform to the inflection criteria of entertainment television.

In addition, since television became a major economic force in major sports, the rules of play in the games themselves have changed in order to meet television format criteria. Television demands games that are faster, higher scoring, and more exciting. Die-hard fans may prefer defense, but viewers and fair weather fans want offense, and everyone wants big plays. As a result, we have slam dunks and three point shots in basketball, longer kickoff returns and long threat passing attacks in football, and more home runs in baseball. Even women's tennis is now a serve and volley game. Read through a list of rule changes in the major sports and it is difficult to find a recent change that has not made the game more consistent with the current grammar of prime-time television. Baseball has the designated hitter, a smaller strike zone to encourage more hitting, a livelier ball, umpires who keep games moving at a faster pace, and fast artificial turf in most parks. Every park also has lights for night (prime-time) broadcast. Football has undergone so many changes that it is not uncommon for a game to be decided by a field goal during the final seconds. During the 1980s basketball changed from a big man's inside game to a running and outside shooting game.

New sports, such as arena football, indoor soccer, world basketball, and indoor lacrosse are all examples of faster paced, offense-oriented colorful contests that televise easily and provide a more intimate spectator experience. Arena football is played in a hockey rink with artificial turf with eight players on a side, and all but the quarterback and kicker play both offense and defense. Games are high scoring, and scores often come in bizarre (entertaining) ways. World basketball began with players no taller than 6′4″, who generate a fast-break offense and spectacular (Michael Jordon style) dunks. Tie games are decided in sudden death by the first team to score seven points. Lacrosse is probably the most physically violent game of the new breed, and indoor soccer the most absurd. All are exciting, but none has a history or firm identity that fans can associate with beyond the dimension of entertainment. On the other hand, entertainment may be enough, especially if the action, drama, and attractive body parts are prominently displayed, as in TV coverage of surfing competition! (San Diego *Union* July 20, 1989).

Ideal Norms. An aspect of the entertainment format for sports that needs special attention is the extent to which the ideal norms framework has been imposed on professional sports. Although some critics of sports decry the amount of violence on the playing field, these critics must be unaware of the pre-television history of professional sports. A quick newspaper content analysis of football, hockey, basketball, boxing, and even baseball will demonstrate that violence on the field and in the stands has decreased since pro sports moved into prime-time. In brief, the argument made in Chapter 2 on entertainment applies to anything broadcast during prime-time, whether it is football or a sitcom. One of the first sports announcers to make this clear to the television audience was Frank Gifford when he stated repeatedly on "Monday Night Football" that "Violence has no place in this game." That comment must have produced some laughs from members of the old Giants, Packers, and Colts. By the late 1970s things had changed. During an NFL playoff game, "Mean" Joe Green of the Steelers was caught on camera punching an opposing lineman in the stomach. The announcer remarked "the refs may have missed it Joe, but millions of people saw what you did." This practice has continued in part to show the deviance, but it is invariably accompanied with a disclaimer from the announcers that the game should always be clean. To reduce violence, rules and penalties have become more stringent, even to the point of suspending athletes from play and prosecuting them in criminal court.

An extension of the ideal norms requirement concerns the athlete as a role model. Baseball great Reggie Jackson said in 1978 that "Being a pro athlete is one of the most difficult things in the world. Realistically it's not realistic" (Arizona *Republic* December 22, 1978). Today those words are even more poignant. By 1990, athletes were expected to make public pronouncements on drug free living, make promotions for charities, such as the United Way, demonstrate adherence to traditions, such as family life, and live a clean and healthful life by rejecting tobacco and steroids. Random drug testing was required of athletes and stiff penalties were imposed. Even heroes of gigantic proportions, such as Steve Garvey, Wade Boggs, and Pete Rose, were not immune. It is not difficult to speculate on what would happen to Babe Ruth if he were playing in today's television era.

Another point about ideal norms and sports concerns the underdog, or "Cinderella finish." Americans root for the underdog in nearly everything, and when the Cinderella phenomenon can be captured on television it is a sure ratings winner. It is most likely to occur during the NCAA basketball tournament, as it did in 1989 when two underdogs (Seton Hall and Michigan) weaved through their respective divisions to face each other in the championship. The Chicago Cubs have the enviable status of perennial underdog, and receive appropriate attention whenever they occupy first place. Of course, the Olympic games are usually the best bet for a David vs. Goliath showdown, as these contests celebrate courage and perseverance better than most other sports events.

One aspect of television and sports that runs tangent to the ideal norms format criterion is the role of television as legitimator. As discussed earlier, television has become a powerful source of legitimacy, as just being on television establishes self-worth in the eyes of the public. This, together with the notion that the camera is objective, has established television as the ultimate referee. For years, television replayed close plays for home viewers and debated the judgment of referees on the field. The problem became so intense that former NFL commissioner Pete Rozelle commented in 1977 that officials not only are being second-guessed in the media, but the league office is flooded almost every week with letters about officiating. Everyone today is a television referee by virtue of the television replay. In the name of objectivity, the National Football League eventually bowed to TV pressure and decided to use television replay tapes to make decisions. What is interesting about this is that objectivity via television was considered more important than maintaining the flow of the game. In this sense, the view from television had become the most important and most legitimate view, and, for controversial calls, fans were willing to wait for television to make a decision. The wait did not bother home viewers, as they benefited from color commentary from the network broadcast team. To appease bored fans in the stadium, television runs the replay until a decision is made and the game resumes. As this process becomes normalized by viewers, we can expect that it will soon appear in basketball and baseball. No doubt it will be infused with a little entertainment as well.

Impact of Television

Economics

Everyone familiar with sports in America today understands that there is too much money in the games. During the late 1970s, a pro football team received six million dollars a season from television revenue alone. The contract for 1990–1994 will net each team $32 million each season through contracts with five broadcast and cable networks. On top of that there are local media deals, playoff extras, and revenue that comes from ticket sales, parking, beer, soda, and popcorn. The same story holds true for baseball and basketball. NBC outbid CBS for NBA basketball to the amount of $600 million, and CBS outbid NBC for baseball. The National Basketball Association received an enormous jump in TV revenue beginning in 1990. Each team increased from $2.8 million to $7.5 million over the old contract. The baseball deal ($1.4 billion over four years) adds ESPN, which will air Sunday Night Baseball in prime time. Each baseball team will receive $16 million per season from national television. Teams in strong local media markets, such as the Yankees and Dodgers, can add another million on top of that. Is it any wonder that players ask for astronomical salaries even for mediocre performance levels? Is it any wonder that every city would like an NFL franchise, and will promise the moon to get it? Although the number of major league franchises in baseball, hockey, basketball, and football have more than doubled during the last 15 years (Johnson 1971:57), it has not moved fast enough for business interests in a number of cities despite astronomical price tags. In 1981 the Seattle Mariners were purchased for what many thought was an inflated price of $17 million. They were resold in 1989 for $77 million! During the mid-1980s Phoenix, Arizona was testing the water to obtain an NFL expansion franchise and some people wondered whether the backing could be obtained to post a $100 million bond to show good faith to the league. The business community's response was almost a chuckle. In Oakland, California, a city with desperate social problems and a bankrupt school system, community leaders and city officials offered to guarantee Raider's owner Al Davis a renovated sold-out stadium for the next 15 years if he would return the NFL team from Anaheim. This meant the city would pay for all unsold seats, which would overcome the league blackout rule for local TV and boost local advertising. Eventually the city came to its senses and withdrew the deal, particularly in light of negative press given Oakland's inability to solve other problems.

As mentioned earlier, television recognized the profit potential in sports from the beginning. The promise of lucrative TV money actually led to the creation of the American Football League, when in 1959 ABC paid the AFL $1.7 million for exclusive broadcast rights for a 5-year period. The ante increased steadily, and by 1970 team owners realized that a merger between the NFL and AFL was a lucrative proposition in terms of television receipts alone. Owners were convinced by the argument that television markets in certain AFL cities were expanding. That is precisely why traditional NFL strongholds such as Baltimore, Pittsburgh, and Cleveland decided to realign with the American Football Conference. According to one observation:

> For better or for worse an entire sport had been bought by the television industry. Things would never really be quite the same again. Everybody, including the fans, soon recognized—and quite docilely accepted—the fact that whatever professional football did in the future, the decisions would have to be made in terms of the economic needs of commercial television. (Johnson, 1971:136)

The same has held true for pro basketball and baseball. The only complaint owners have left is stadium renovation to permit expensive sky boxes. Fan support in terms of filling seats is almost irrelevant.

Another way to examine the importance of television revenue to professional sports is to note the failures. The World Football League got off the ground with direct seed money from television, but floundered when that support was withdrawn. The American Basketball Association struggled for several years, but failed without television support. The same held true for "World Team Tennis," and the hockey-like version of indoor soccer. In television entertainment, shows are not given much time to build an audience, and in the above examples the ratings never met network criteria for success. On the other hand, those early failures occurred prior to the rise of cable subscriptions, which rose exponentially during the 1980s. With cable in 55 million homes in 1990, ESPN and several other major cable systems have moved from strictly entertainment (often bizarre) sports to the major college and professional leagues. In 1979 ESPN carried 158 college events. By 1988 that figure has risen to 723, including 325 nationally telecast basketball games. Beginning in 1990, ESPN will pay $110 million to the American Football Conference for major college football over a 5-year span. That rivals a $170 million deal between ABC and the AFC. And with the ESPN major league baseball contract, it is obvious that cable no longer takes what is left over after the networks finish business. All-in-all, the appetite for sports among television viewers seems to be insatiable. According to Seth Abraham, HBO's sports director, "Program tastes come and go, but sports is always constant. More is never enough" (Zoglin 1990:66). It may well be that Spring and Summer football will be successful after all.

Although major league sports has profited emensely from TV, the minor leagues have struggled. Instead of watching the local "town" team, people sit home and watch the majors on TV. Attendance at minor league baseball games began to drop around 1950 when television began regional and national coverage. In 1949 there were 59 minor leagues in baseball, with 448 teams and 42 million fans (*Time* June 23, 1975). In 1974 there were just 18 leagues, with 145 teams and 11 million spectators. Although part of this decrease may be due to the major league expansion and the increase of college baseball, the difference is still considerable. As Gary McCune, general manager of the Knoxville (Tennessee) Blue Jays said:

> What's going to happen when some guy has to decide whether to drive 10 or 20 miles across town in traffic on a muggy night to watch a minor league game in our old park, when he can sit at home and watch major leaguers like Canseco and Mattingly? (*The Show,* Spring, 1990:5)

What McCune may be missing in this equation is that minor league ball does not have the media culture quotient that television provides. Certainly big league stars make a difference, but they also do it within a format of television pizzazz. The television-oriented fan watching a minor league contest may not recognize big league skill or potential without the trappings that television provides. Regardless, the fact is that most minor leaguers play in nearly empty stadiums.

An illuminating case history of the association between TV and sports economy is provided in boxing. In the early 1950s, as the number of boxing matches on television increased, attendance at live boxing matches decreased. As former middleweight champion Gene Fullmer put it:

> Television made fans but it also killed boxing. The small clubs couldn't exist anymore and colleges dropped the sport. Television didn't put any money into developing boxing and amateur programs just fell apart. (Los Angeles *Times*, September 14, 1975).

Even the fight center of the world, Madison Square Garden, suffered greatly. Its average attendance of 10,000–12,000 spectators every Friday night in 1948–1949 dropped to 1,200 by 1957 (Johnson 1971:93). The number of smaller clubs in the United States was reduced from 300 to fewer than 50 between 1952 and 1959. The reason for the disparity between increasing numbers of TV fight fans and decreasing number of supporters for local clubs is tied to the logic of television. TV promotions were geared to the top contenders, especially the champions. As Chris Dundee, a boxing promoter, explained:

> Look, TV definitely hurt boxing bad. The big thing you were up against is that there had to be a loser, you know? And you couldn't bring a loser back on TV. The sponsors didn't want losers, just winners. And let's face it, sponsors called the shots during the TV age in boxing (Johnson 1971:92)

In addition, it must be pointed out that the ideal norms character of prime-time TV made boxing unacceptable to prime-time audiences. In fact, there were numerous attempts to ban boxing during the late 1990s and 1970s. Boxing is just too violent (too realistic) for prime-time television.

By the 1980s, television network control of the audience was strong enough that advertisers no longer call the shots, they stood in line to get on TV. A humorous illustration of this turnaround occurred prior to the 1990 Super Bowl. A well known manufacturer of sports shoes made an ad featuring the voices of Dick Enberg (NBC), Marv Albert (CBS), and Al Michaels (ABC). With NBC broadcasting the Super Bowl, CBS objected to using the ad on the grounds that Marv Albert's voice should not be associated with NBC. The shoe manufacturer agreed to pull the ad stating "We are a major advertiser, and we don't want to be in an adversarial relationship with a major network" (Cohen 1990:E5).

Although sponsors once had a powerful voice in television, the corporate structure of television networks began taking control of scheduling, promotions, creating tournaments, and even buying teams and player contracts (CBS owned the Yankees and ABC had boxers Leon Spinks and Ray Leonard). In 1967 ABC established its own heavyweight boxing tournament for its "Wide World of Sports." This was followed successfully by other "created-for-TV" events in tennis and golf. However, this process went too far when ABC essentially rigged the heavyweight boxing ratings so that Spinks could get a title match on ABC TV. Rival networks curtly pointed out that television should not create its own world, and yet that is precisely what has happened.

ABC demonstrated the power of network TV during negotiations with the NFL for the four year contract beginning 1990. When it complained about not receiving enough for its $900 million for Monday Night Football and one Super Bowl, the NFL agreed to add two more teams to the playoff (now 12 teams) and add two more weeks to the season in 1992. In addition, the NFL guaranteed three additional 30-second advertising spots in 1990 and two more in 1992. Similar TV economics is being experienced in college athletics. ABC negotiated a five year $210 million deal with the American Football Conference, only to have Notre Dame do an end run and sign a separate deal with NBC for exclusive rights to its 30 home games. This raises numerous questions, not the least of which is the ability of governing organizations, such as the NFL and NCAA, to control individual teams and schools. The golden egg that television offers may be too much temptation for anyone. At the very least, sports seems willing to trade the time, place, and duration of events for the riches available from television.

Player Salaries.   During the 1980s the most dramatic illustration of the relationship between TV money and sports was the astounding increase in player income. In the three decades prior to the 1980s, team owners complained that TV money was desperately needed just to make a modest profit. With the quantum leap in profits during the 1980s, players demanded and received mind boggling deals. In 1977 there were 10 major league baseball players making more than $250,000 a year, four made more than $350,000, and two had contracts in excess of $2.5 million spread over 4–5 years. Twelve years later premier players, such as the Yankee's Don Mattingly, were getting nearly four million per season. At the end of the 1989 season Oakland A's Rickey Henderson signed a four year contract for $12 million. The following summer teammate Jose Canseco received a $23.5 million over five years. Bargain basement pitchers were suddenly worth over a million, and weak hitting infielders were in the half-million range. In 1977 the average player in the National Basketball Association made $109,000, and pro football players earned an average of $40,000. By the late 1980s top players in all sports were getting comparable salaries rank for rank. In 1990, Buffalo Bills quarterback Jim Kelly signed a $20 million seven year contract, and Super Bowl winner Joe Montana was looking forward to surpassing Kelly by renegotiating his five-year $10 million deal (*Sports Illustrated*, Aug. 13, 1990).

Although fat salaries are a direct result of television, an additional dimension of this phenomenon bears scrutiny. What has gone almost unnoticed in recent years is that the public no longer seems concerned about the money ballplayers receive. Perhaps the size of salaries have become just one more part of the giant spectacle of television sports. A decade ago Pete Rose was razzed by fans for holding out for the big bucks. In 1990, Minnesota Twins fans were happy to have Kirby Puckett remain with the team at any price. Kansas City fans were pleased to see Cy Young winner Mark Davis leave the San Diego Padres to join the Royals despite a $3 million per season salary.

Another point of interest on ballplayer salary is the status accorded the high figures. As quarterback Jim Kelly stated after inking his $20 million deal, "I just want to be considered up in the elite, whether I was the highest-paid player or the sixth-highest-paid player." Similarly, Rickey Henderson responded to teammate Jose Canseco's contract noted above by saying, "If what I'm hearing is true, I am going to feel underpaid." These superstar athletes have forged a new criterion and class of symbolic membership in which athletic performance is an indirect factor. Earning big money is "proof" alone of one's outstanding ability, and to earn less than the big-money players is to be second class. Therefore, when one player hits a new high in salary, others (via agents) make similar demands. In fact, it is as much an agent's game as the players. As stated by Mark Langston's agent (after signing with the Padres), "We wanted to at least get the same deal as Dwight Gooden got with the Mets."

To expand on the change in criteria, what seems to be occurring is that box office draw (stadium and television ratings) is at least as important as athletic skill if not more so. As George Steinbrenner commented after offering a fat contract to first baseman Don Mattingly, "he'll bring people to the ballpark." In other words, people will pay to see money play. And the new play ranges from theatric skill in executing plays, such as the aerial acrobatics of basketball star Michael Jordan or back flipping shortstop Ozzie Smith, to the showboating of former Jets' defensive lineman Mark Gastineau. Every team seems to have its showboat, and if it does not, there is usually a clown mascot that does the job. Anyway you look at it, the athletic performance is infused with showbiz, and agents who negotiate player salaries use the showbiz quotient indirectly to get fat contracts. They understand that fans and spectators want to see the superstar more so than the team or a contest. The impact on player's style and skills is obvious. Agents now tell players who have been thought of as defensive specialists, such as shortstops, to practice their hitting. The real money is in offense, and the big money is in offense and theatrics. Once players achieve that level, they can create their own show or their own telephone "hot line" such as baseball player Jose Canseco (1-900-432-JOSE).

The Rise of the Sportscaster

The role of the sportscaster became more important as the pressure to entertain a mass audience grew. All was predicated on obtaining good ratings. Indeed, even the abilities of skilled players would be called into question: they would be ridiculed to promote the sportscaster's verbal skill. Cosell (1973:343) gave the following account:

> The game between the Oilers and the Raiders may live in memory as the classic football telecast. Never has a worse game been played. Oakland won it 34–0, and Oakland didn't even play well. But the Houston performance was a catastrophe. I threw the game to the winds. . . . At one point, after a series of pitiful turnovers, I said, "I think we better get the game films this Wednesday, Giff, and take them around to local high schools to encourage the youngsters. There's no way they can be this futile." . . . By the fourth quarter Chet Forte was desperate in the truck [control]. . . . Chet decided to show that the people in the stands felt the same way. He panned around, catching the backs of people leaving. Then he zoomed in on a gentleman who apparently was asleep. But this particular spectator sensed the camera upon him and woke up. He looked directly into the lens and made what is known in polite circles as an obscene hand gesture. When he did this, I stopped in the middle of a sentence, aghast. But not Dandy (Don Meredith). He jumped right in and said, "Ha'hrd, he means we're Number One." . . . Dandy had made us immortal.

The rise of the sportscaster as a TV personality followed logically from the role these "play-by-play" and "color" people performed in translating games into mass entertainment. They are now celebrities, selected primarily for their appearance as much as their knowledge of the game, as much for their reputation even to "mix it up" on the screen, to argue with players and managers—in short, to actively participate in the contest they present. They have become the new players. One observer assessed how star pitcher Tom Seaver would complement Howard Cosell as they teamed up for ABC's coverage of the 1977 World Series:

> Tom Seaver . . . will try to out-expert Cosell. That confrontation, alone,

> between the scholarly and erudite Seaver . . . and pitchman Cosell should attract many viewers, in addition to the great excitement that always surrounds a World's Series. (Los Angeles *Times* October 9, 1977)

Not only was Cosell's name a household word among millions of sports fans during the 1970s, but he was more well-known than the players. He was in demand to make speeches, appear on talk shows, and even appear in movies and TV sitcoms (Cosell 1973). Eventually, as with most television personalities, Cosell wore out his TV quotient and was replaced by a new set of personalities, such as O. J. Simpson, Dan Diedorf, and John Madden. They have all followed in the entertainment mold, which is to say they are funny, fairly quick witted, confrontational, decisive, and have a voice quality that may be described as crisp and climactic (almost breathless, e.g., Al Michaels). A good illustration of the new sportscaster is Jon Miller of ESPN, who is known as the Rich Little of baseball announcing due to his mimicry of other well-known announcers and sports personalities. He fills dead air with media trivia as well as baseball trivia.

In addition to the sportcaster as entertainer, they have also exerted influence on player popularity. In reassessing Cosell's influence on "Monday Night Football," Pat Stabler, former quarterback with the Oakland Raiders, commented that

> Monday night football can do a lot for a player both ways. If Cosell says someone is good, a lot of people watching think he is, even if he isn't. The same goes for someone he knows. That can have an effect on sportswriters who don't see the Raiders play. They vote for all-pro teams and it might be because of what Cosell said rather than how good a player really is. That's the bad part of it. (Stabler and O'Connor 1977:157)

Regardless of Cosell's actual influence with viewers, the fact that a player is singled out for attention, or a team receives more TV exposure than another will have an impact with viewers. Players with teams that receive more exposure have a better chance being selected on allstar teams and becoming media personalities in their own right. Given two players with identical playing skills, the team will keep the one with greater television appeal, hence box office appeal. Conversely, players who are constantly in trouble with the media may be in constant trouble with the front office. Bad press used to mean box office receipts. Today it means trouble in television ratings. Before television, the aging player might finish up a career with a minor league team. Today, if that player is a media personality they go on to a career in media, or they stay with the team as media PR person. The aging player with no media personality simply disappears.

Television sportscasters, or more accurately television format, have also influenced sports writers in print media. Since sports as news has been replaced with sports as entertainment, print reporters must focus on the behind the scenes approach to tell what may have happened in the locker room, the courtroom, the boardroom, and the bedroom. Racism, drugs, sex, religion, gambling, exploitation, psychology, cheating, feminism, dress styles, violence, antitrust legislation—all these subjects, and many more, have been explored in detail on the sports pages in recent months. Even the most *avant garde* sportswriters admit that in their zeal to eschew the old scores-and-statistics approach, they often have overreacted and provided a surfeit of offbeat, interpretive, sociological stories at the sacrifice of solid news and analysis of daily happenings in the sports world (Los Angeles *Times* February 7, 1972).

The impact of such reporting on public information about sports, especially the individual players who are written about, cannot be understood without realizing that the sportscasters and writers have changed. Media not only exert influence over the public perception of players and teams, but also may serve as intermediaries between a player and the team.

Joe Kotarba's study of major league baseball players illustrates this delicate interaction. Two players on an east coast team explained how the general manager (GM) could promote a player to the press and the public. "[He] had a lock on official knowledge. His definitions of good and bad, lazy and hustler, were immediately bought by the press. This was really true with _____ . [GM] builds a case against a player, using the press as an organ that players really don't have access to," [personal communication].

Indeed, several players insisted that their boss even influenced the official scorer! All of this places greater pressure on players, many of whom are not highly educated or articulate. Some players we have talked with will no longer speak to anyone from the press, and a few even have personal managers and agents who do their talking for them. We have come full circle: Sports reporters originally oriented to keeping the fans abreast of the games, the respective teams, and the abilities of particular players are now confronted by "handouts," public relations statements, and disgruntled players.

Update

During the 1980s a trend that we were concerned about in the late 1970s was reversed. As the money factor in sports became more prominent during the 1970s, fans, sportswriters, and league officials began to worry that rich teams could buy championships. This is particularly true in baseball, where ranking teams by total salary and comparing how they finished in league standings showed that in 1977 the top three teams in salary in each division were also three of the top four in standings. Indeed, the success of the New York Yankees seemed to be a sign of things to come. They were not developed from a farm system, they were just a complicated business merger. A $3 million pitcher here, a $2.9 million outfielder there, a $1 million shortstop on top, and presto! Instant World Champions. An article in the Los Angeles *Times* (November 20, 1977) stated that the pennant will be decided in a countinghouse in November, not a playing field in October.

However, during the 1980s this trend began to reverse, and low budget, low glamour teams rose to become contenders and champions. What happened is not entirely clear, but one scenario may be that big money and the new individualist athlete works against the "team" concept, and teams that play like teams can outplay teams of individual stars. Perhaps a more realistic view is that owners got together to protect their investments and reduced the bidding wars for premier players. This coincided with the rapid increase in revenue from television, which made every club rich. Ironically, TV money may haved produced a leveling effect during the 1980s in professional sports. By contrast, the situation at the college level has remained one of inequality and considerable disparity in team quality. During the early 1980s, it was primarily the rich schools who also enjoyed continuous Bowl appearances that, in turn, produced effective recruiting campaigns. As television money increased, those schools that aggressively pursued the riches of a major league schedule and bowl appearances began to compete with the big name schools, such as Notre Dame, UCLA, and Penn State. The new kids on the block, such as Florida State, Oklahoma, and Miami, quickly learned what TV revenue and exposure could do for a football program. Athletes who aspire to the pro ranks have also become very savvy as to which schools hold the best promise for an eventual professional contract. Not surprisingly, the recruiting process now begins in Junior High School, especially for basketball. This phenomenon raises several questions regarding sports culture for the 1990s and beyond.

The notion that professional sports careers may begin at the junior high school level will most certainly raise the ire of those concerned about sports exploitation. Although we do not wish to diminish the importance of that concern, there is another matter that might miss attention. As media attention focuses on career lines that begin in prep sports, and as media accents particular sports models, the distinction between amateur and professional sports becomes blurred. Even the casual observer recognizes that college sports has the look (style and rules) of professional sports, and that athletes at the college level are treated like professional sports celebrities. This blurred distinction is also evidenced in rule changes at the college level, making college athletics look like professional games, particularly in terms of action and big plays. In our estimation, this illustrates the development of a homogenized sports culture in which the action looks much the same regardless of the game or whether it is amateur or professional. Indeed, baskets are lowered so that 10 year olds can compete in "slam dunk" contests!

Moreover, the homogenized sports culture tends to be ahistorical. Television tends to run the cultural history of every corner of society together in a lump sum, rather than emphasizing lineal development. In television, the temporal order is "now," and the longest wait is to the weekend. Perhaps as a result, fans grow impatient. Not too long ago it was common to expect rebuilding periods for both professional and amateur teams. Teams would develop around a core of athletes, and when they graduated or grew too old, the process would begin again. Fans were willing to endure lean periods in anticipation of rebuilding a new championship. Today, fans know that money is available, and that aggressive recruiting will produce quick results. Even geographic, ethnic, and racial prejudice is suspended in favor of continuous winning. In addition, the morality of respecting and maintaining a culture of amateur athletics is being discarded in favor of one sports culture operating according to media culture criteria. High School, college, and professional sports are becoming one show, and the only difference between the ranks is level of performance.

This homogenized media sports culture may help explain the emergence of another phenomenon recently recognized by coaches, sportswriters, and even a few television commentators—the "new athlete." These individuals, and that is exactly what they are vis-à-vis team players, are so common in sports today that it is difficult to find an athlete that does not fit this new image. In a most general sense, they play for the sake of the "show," as opposed to gritty head to head competition for its own sake. In social psychological terms, the significant other for the new athlete is the crowd, the statistic in the record book, and the media story. The old nonmedia culture athlete was oriented more to other players, and they were not accustomed to being evaluated by the media, especially off the field. At best, they were heroes and legends, not celebrities. The important criteria was in the particular game, and the game was everything. Certainly they wanted to make a living, but if that could be accomplished, they would endure considerable hardship just to play. This distinction is much the same as David Riesman's "inner" and "other-directed" social character (1950), and to that extent the distinction is not exclusively a television phenomenon. Still, there are a few sports where the "new" athlete is not the rule (horse racing, soccer, rugby), and there are a handful of older style athletes in every sport (lately referred to as blue-collar players). Where television enters the description is with the economics of big money, the elite status as legitimized through media, the entertaining style of play that captures viewer attention, and that rare ingredient, media charisma. Thirty years ago a premier athlete did not need charisma. In the television era, media charisma is necessary to achieve the status of superstar. Magic Johnson has it; Larry Bird does not. Joe Montana has it; John Elway does not. Muhammad Ali had it; Mike Tyson never came close. Although each of these athletes demonstrated extraordinary ability and outstanding performance, there was a difference that television paid attention to, and the person with television charisma received more attention and higher status in sports media culture. Today, kids in junior high school are not only aware of great athletes, they are aware of the television factor. As they might say, "Bo knows television."

Conclusion

Our intention in this chapter was to make a general clarification of the influence of media logic on sports. Unfortunately, a number of examples of media influence were of necessity omitted, or were given only brief mention. However, the evidence presented makes a strong case for the influence of media logic on sports, and most of the trends we identified during the 1970s are continuing into the 1990s. In fact, a case could be made for the claim that sports media culture is the most prominent form of media culture in America, and is beginning to spread worldwide. Perhaps one of the reasons for the huge sums of money paid by networks to professional sports is that the networks are preparing for worldwide sports culture control. Test marketing has already begun.

9

Conclusion: Our Media Condition

Throughout these pages we have argued that American society is ordered largely through the sense-making strategies developed in mass media, particularly television. In part, this argument draws from the work of sociologist Georg Simmel, who observed at the turn of the century that people create their culture within the strategies of abstract social forms, such as work, play, art, and institutions, such as the family, education, and religion. To this category we add modern mass media, and argue that it is the dominant social form in American society today. Indeed, we have argued that so powerful is the media logic that it has effectively terminated journalism as an effective representation of independent events and meanings.

The mass media are a major social influence because their logic and formats have become incorporated within the logic of social institutions. Media logic and the formats it has created are important because they are *nondiscursive and taken for granted.* They precede the discourse and communication content usually associated with "mass communication." This can be seen in the approach and style of various news sources as well as activities that have changed as a result of mass mediation (Ferrarotti 1988). In 1979 we argued that mass media have risen to a dominant position in the institutional network of society primarily because various institutions follow a media logic in the definition and solution of problems. This process has resulted in the construction of a media culture—a cultural content that emerges from acting through specific media formats. The entire process is best understood as an interaction among the various participants rather than as a one-way form in which media dictate definitions of reality. However, existing media logic is so incorporated into contemporary urban society that media professionals and the public take for granted that "seeing" social phenomena through media logic is "normal." To this extent media logic "cultivates" a media consciousness as well as a media culture (Gerbner et al. 1973:560ff; Snow

1983). Existing media logic may be altered, but this awaits both a recognition that such a logic exists and a desire for change.

We have illustrated this perspective with materials from entertainment, news, politics, religion, and sports.

This logic also flourishes in the academic world. It is an embedded communication order that has contributed to the transformation and the overall cheapening and devaluation of the educational process noted by Bloom (1987) and others. Ideas and the very nature of the university itself are subject to fads steeped in a media logic utilized by publishers, interest groups, administrators, the professors who teach, and the students who study. Intellectuals and university administrators are media-wise and help connect news reports with curriculum and, in many instances, hiring policies. We will take a brief look at the faddish nature of some university offerings, to be followed by an overview of how numerous academic organizations rely on media logic for legitimacy.

Marketing and communication are joined through the medium of books, which in turn is tied to an interactive communication context featuring TV news reports about the topic, movies playing the theme, etc. Increasingly, ideas and their acceptance are driven by markets for books that promote such ideas. Publishers play to and often promote the "most recent" hot item because they know that if it can be sold as "the coming thing," then they will sell a lot of books. Numerous professors who want to be current with new developments will then look to book advertisements as an indication of what is "new" and what they should read and discuss.

This process is not to be mistaken for innovative ideas or the support of creative inquiry by the publishing industry. To the contrary, unless you are an established scholar, it is quite difficult for merely a "new idea" to be cast in print. The risk of not selling enough books is too great, and that would be bad business. However, if the "new thing" can be combined with a market that can be constructed and then delivered by the sales department, then the production process will take over.

In *Media Worlds Postjournalism,* numerous ideas and courses of study are temporally linked to the current news emphases. And we know that news of world changes according to the "good organizational reasons" discussed throughout this work. This is why the intellectual scene in the United States and Western Europe is so prone to new topics and fads. During the last few decades in the United States we have seen emphases, books, courses and entire programs develop around various ethnic, racial, and religious "studies." Most of these do not last very long because few intellectual fads survive sustained intellectual scrutiny, but also because the very process that produced the "latest hot topic" is working on another. Most of those that originated during the last two decades have either been partially integrated within existing curriculums or dropped altogether, usually with far less fanfare than they were greeted by university administrators eager to show potentially powerful interest groups that they supported them. There is a similar story with varieties of women's studies, feminism centers, and in some cases, men's studies.

The university and "higher education" has truly become part of the marketplace of ideas! Like most good communication products, these media topics are in competition and do not easily coexist. For example, various ethnic studies programs seldom survive women's studies. However, the process also depends on agents promoting certain interests. The major focus and support behind the ethnic/racial studies programs in the 1960s and 1970s were white faculty and students. There were—and still are—very few racial and ethnic minority faculty members who are from the major impoverished groups. Racial and ethnic minority students came and went, and relatively few entered graduate school to become professors. It is this factor, which contributed in part to the successful rise of women's studies programs.

The situation is much different with women's studies programs that are primarily oriented to work and competitive occupational opportunities with men. Their major focus and support is derived from upwardly mobile white women, who combine their concerns with the plight of the most recently defined aggrieved group(s) with their own career potential and professional identities. Thus, they argue that when members of their ethnic/racial/gender status are not proportionately employed, tenured, promoted or salaried when compared with others, it is due to implicit or explicit discrimination. Since many of these supporters, both men and women, work within the university settings, they are and will remain not only a significant part of the university work force, but a formidable political force for years to come. With some exceptions, the most appropriate metaphor is "unionism." They exert tremendous pressure on university administrators, who in turn are oriented to keeping the favor of this powerful interest group so that their own career paths will not be jeopardized by charges that they did not do enough for the poor, dispossessed, and disenfranchised.

The politics of modern universities are closely tied, then, to the underlying media logic which drives the nearly instantaneous development and transfer of scarce resources into such programs in order to buy-off potential adversaries, and make a public (read, a mass mediated) statement that the university is sensitize to the plight and supports such efforts. Thus, because the current lineup of racial/etnnic/gender workers are part of the organization undergoing change, they will not be easily moved off center by another interest group seeking to capture the publishing and university attention.

Professional academic organizations also celebrate media logic. As we have argued, it was the recognition of the significance of communication process that led to the emergence of widespread interest in culture and "cultural studies." Culture is now quite popular—it is "intellectually in"—and the same theorists and theory-groups that previously celebrated "social structure" (à la Marx, Durkheim, and Parsons) are now on the bandwagon. (A good example is a collection of essays edited by a proponent of neo-functionalism, Jeffrey C. Alexander, *Durkheimian Sociology: Cultural Studies* (1988)! In short, the recent celebration of culture is itself a feature of the media logic that has pervaded Western culture. Indeed, the significance of "media legitimacy" for academic careerists is apparent as social science associations like the American Sociological Association publishes a newsletter, *Footnotes,* which includes a "Mass Media" section (quoted in the media). No kidding! Scholars who have earned their Ph.D. stripes and are widely published, now compete with each other to see who can claim the most prestigious mass media citations! The process then comes full-circle, as a few of these people are circulated through various mass media outlets, as "expert sources" to comment on numerous topics that they often know little about, for two sentences or 15 seconds. As their visibility and name recognition increases, they may then be sought out by publishers and other entrepreneurs to help legitimize another media logic product!

It is no longer the case that the mass media merely "transmit" certain "biased" and ideologically informed messages about news and politics. Of course they do this, and social scientists have known and documented this process for some 50 years! (Hughes 1940; Park 1940). That is no longer scientific news, even though numerous social scientists continue to promote their own ideological agendas by claiming that "they have found yet another example of media (ideological) bias!" As we have stressed, this earlier mode (especially Phase 3) of media criticism presumes that a few structural and ideological changes in the "news channels" could alter the significant messages (the content). These critiques are content based, but they are not informed by a thorough-going theory of the mediation of all experience, and especially the workings of media logic and formats. This is what we have been attempting to delineate.

The most significant media effect on social orders throughout the world is the folding in of media logic and perspectives into the daily routines and expectations of everyday life. The communication formats that mark off the time, place, and manner of social meanings, definitions, and activities constitute the taken-for-granted and largely nondiscursive features of everyday life (Altheide 1985c; Meyrowitz 1985). The media perspectives comprise the context and discourse through which the mundane and extraordinary events of our public order take place. We identify the grammar of mass media and treat it as a logic employed by both media professionals and audience members in making sense of events and media experience. These media and attendant logics do not determine the specific events and outcomes, but they do set the stage, comprise the rules of communication for establishing agendas and issues, and provide the discourse and frameworks to interpret and reflect on events. However, we emphasize the indeterminacy of this process and place responsibility for meanings in media experience squarely on the audience. In our mind, media do not shape the audience against their will. We treat the medium or media as a pervasive and encompassing social form that must be analyzed in terms of its properties of form more so than its content. Similar to Simmel, Whorf, and McLuhan, we argue that content emerges through form. However, it should be clear to the reader by now that we have radically expanded this perspective into the constitutive processes of interpretation, definition, and meaning. This has led us to assert that form constitutes, guides, and essentially becomes the most significant content. We argue that television has accomplished just that, and, furthermore, we insist that public social order now reflects this process as millions of human beings reflexively reify the media logic and worlds in the time, place, and manner of their conversation, memories, dress and style, problems, hopes, fears, and solutions (cf. Lyman and Vidich 1988).

Conceptualizing form in media into something observable, we identify various formats, or presentation and interpretation strategies, such as news, entertainment, sports, and talk shows. This is not to be confused with genres, which are categories for organizing content, such as philosophies, ideas, values, fears, and historical experience. Fundamentally, formats are grammatical devices for ordering action and events, establishing accent and pace, and constructing symbols to represent phenomena and convey emotion. In this sense, our use of the term format is consistent with the way it is used by media professionals, although media professionals see it as a logic for making sense of experience to the degree that format makes the experience legitimate. Newspapers now must look like *USA TODAY*, television news requires an anchor person and visuals, sports must have instant replays, and political campaigns must have one-liner slogans and quips. Increasingly, six-column newspapers, black and white TV, a movie with an intricate plot, and a news magazine without photographs have all been relegated to the media archives. They look quaint and even boring by comparison to today's dazzling visual wizardry.

In comparing our approach to other current theories and models, several points should be reviewed. First, our concern is not with who does what to whom, rather it is with the construction of meaning through media formats. Who controls the purse strings of media empires may be important for selecting the content of television, newspapers, and movies, but this agenda setting still rests on the design and use of various formats. The impact of television entertainment as a format strategy has been, in our estimation, more fundamental and pronounced than attempts to inject ideological or commercial bias into content. If anything, the audience is less concerned with content regardless of ideological bias, and more concerned with whether the format is right. In fact, this may be far more insidious than deliberate attempts at bias. As we argued in earlier chapters, youth do not merely listen to Michael Jackson, they watch him. Voters in 1980 and 1984 did the same with Ronald Reagan. *Time* magazine could change its politics tomorrow, and few readers under age 40 would notice as long as the new 1980s style format was maintained. On the other hand, this raises another question, that of subtle or subliminal persuasion.

The question of encoding messages in the minds of an unsuspecting audience has fascinated sales people, religious leaders, and assorted tyrants for centuries. If subliminal suggestion or various so-called propaganda techniques really generated behavioral consequences at the will of the sender, we would be aware of it by now. Like it or not, the evidence from numerous studies over the past 50 years demonstrates convincingly that people cannot be persuaded to violate firmly held beliefs, or stop using products that serve a person's sense of self, such as being "a Ford man," or "a Chanel woman." Brainwashing is a misnomer at best, and when conversions do occur, they are usually wrapped in a highly dramatic and emotional experience that cannot be challenged by mere rational procedures. In short, people do not change easily, and when they do the change is accompanied by changes in identity and conceptions of self. Slight of hand may dazzle the viewer in a magic show, but everyone knows it is just that—slight of hand.

From our view, one of the most recent approaches in communication theory, semiotics, is similar to the hidden message approach and the hypodermic needle logic of behaviorism. Obviously, this is also true of any argument based on the "power of the image." As we noted in some detail, images are constructed and interpreted through an active process, which involves relying on other contexts of meaning. In arguing that meanings are embedded in symbols, the semiotics approach simply avoids the arduous task of ascertaining what the audience has in mind, and, unfortunately, a number of very talented observers have made the mistake of simply deducing the members' understanding and involvement with certain symbols from the analysts' own point of view. This is one of the shortcomings of the otherwise very encouraging perspective of "cultural studies." Indeed, one of the most gifted social analysts, Peter

K. Manning (1988), has argued that semiotic analysis should never be divorced from a solid ethnographic awareness of the situations in which the symbols appear to the members. However, as we demonstrated in our statements about the mass media's impact on voting behavior (Chapter 6), general consensus on the meanings of various symbols may exist, and in a given situation audience response is highly predictable. But this cannot be extended to argue that symbols generate meaning regardless of social context or without regard to the identities of the interacting parties. We agree with the best social researchers that it is of little value to do a content analysis of symbols without placing these symbols in a viable social context. It is even more difficult to develop a list of symbols on a hierarchy of power to subvert the audience. In certain contexts, even sex in advertising can be ignored or rendered absurd by the viewer. Our own studies have led us to develop innovative quantitative approaches to content analysis—which we call "ethnographic content analysis"—in order to better understand and avoid some of these problems (cf. Altheide 1987d).

In fairness to many people who use semiotics, particularly those concerned with popular culture, it is interesting to note the rejection of the neo-Marxist approach that consumers are being shaped or managed by particular sectors of the economy or pop culture industry. They have correctly recognized that in today's pop culture world, the term that best describes consumer activity is anarchy. In clothing, anything goes, and that includes violating all the rules of color, shapes, and whatever. The rule is to be as outrageous as possible. However, what tends to be missed in the semiotics of the current pop culture world is that for more than 30 years, the affluent youth of American society have been generating a rich consumer culture based on play and acted out largely through the technology of video. In short, what is passing for postmodernism is largely a act of "playing with visual imagery." It is the age of the costume, not the uniform, and to impute a causal relationship between embedded symbolic meanings and behavior is to miss the theme of play in this whole process. As Simmel might say, the relevant social form is play not work.

It seems that sociologists in general and Marxists in particular have great difficulty accepting the significance of play and the increasing merger of work and play. This is largely because the "big two" for establishment sociology's focus continues to be social stratification and organizations. The concern with "hierarchy" and the training of most social scientists in a modern period when communication technologies and logics had not obliterated age-old time–space barriers continue to fuel the quest for any data to indicate that conventional "variables" can explain behavior and perceptions. Thus the kind of jobs people get means something different for the social analyst than it does for the people seeking them, largely because more and more people have expanded their job-preference criteria to include "quality of life" features that go well beyond dollar-per-hour considerations. People play at work and expect to do so. Often this involves communication media. Fun, play, and work are less distinctive temporal features of everyday life.

On the other hand, Neil Postman (1984) warns us that we may be "Amusing Ourselves to Death," and Mitroff and Bennis (1990) caution that the mass media and the rest of the "unreality industry" are leading us to "trivialize" and "fantasize" too much. How awful, suggest these authors and scores of elitist fascists of the minds, that the "masses" are immersing themselves in media culture, when they could be doing something else. And what impact is this having? Sure enough, "bad" examples can be found, e.g., we do not focus as much on "truly important social problems." Ironically, we have critics like this who routinely are churned through the cycle of mass media "talk shows," proclaiming the stupidity of the American people and shouting Hossanah for Western culture. The critics seem to suggest that if people are watching and laughing and enjoying and talking about this stuff, then it will be directly transferable to other situations, without further reflection or adjustment. No wonder, such critics claim, young people do not read as well today (on the basis of mind-numbing standard test scores). Who in the world will save us from our sins! Does this sound familiar? These critics and the disciplines they represent are out of time!

The major problem, of course, is that you want to see some data to support their views that somehow the United States and much of western civilization is going down the (cathode) tubes. The productivity of the world, especially those countries enmeshed the most in media culture, does not seem to be a casualty (e.g., Japan). But a more fundamental problem is the inability of conventionally trained social scientists to adapt to new ideas about situation and context. Much of social science has been built on a very shaky models of learning, cognition, meaning, and behavior. When, for example, modern educators decry the inability of students to do well on math tests in school situations, they are playing to the model that suggests that what is learned and applied is meaningful regardless of the context or situation in which it occurs. In other words, if you cannot do math in a classroom, you cannot do it on the job. Have you heard this before? Indeed, we have all heard it, but what only a few of us have done is to actually check it out, which is what scientists are supposed to do. For example, a recent study by Jean Lave (1988) shows that meaning is processual and situational. Lave actually followed people around to see how they solved certain practical math problems, such as shopping for groceries and preparing diet meals. She found that people who had trouble with math in the classroom did quite well in specific contexts because math at the desk and the supermarket is different; there is a different logic at work. Shoppers are not automata guided by their habitus as suggested by Bourdieu and other postmodern critics who, essentially, base their work on the semiotic perspective noted above, but rather, they are "creative problem solvers." Thus, what is done, watched, reproduced, spoken, enjoyed in one context does not determine what is done and accomplished in another context. It is this realm of "tacit knowledge," according to Altheide and Johnson (1990), that is brought to bear on a specific situation and provides contexts of meaning for meaningful and often innovative conduct. It should be apparent to the reader that this is precisely the kind of argument we have been making about how people incorporate media logic and formats within their own lives and situated activities. When these are routinely pursued by thousands of actors in the course of their daily negotiations of definitions of situations, we have the institutional effects contained in the previous pages.

In contrast to the media bashing and harbinger of doom approaches, we agree with the like-minded theory of Anderson and Meyer (1988) called "Accommodation Theory." Based on two axioms, the social construction of reality (Berger and Luckmann 1977), and the situational character of meaning, which have also informed all of our previous work, Anderson and Meyer bring a host of empirical work to bear on current models, and come away with a convincing argument that to understand media in today's world we cannot analyze media messages independently from the audience and their situational context (Berman 1987). This makes it tough to do research, but there is no alternative.

In Anderson and Meyer's model, we would like to emphasize a point we have made earlier, the emergence of a media consciousness as a result of adopting the format strategies of the major media. In the abstract, the general social form of television seems to have become a general consciousness and even an environment in the sense that it is pervasive across the institutional spectrum and ubiquitous in everyday life. This is why journalism is dead, and has been replaced by what we tentatively term "information mechanics." Much of what we have discussed in previous pages illustrates this notion, but several additional illustrations may aid in clarification.

As a dimension of temporality, or rather as a means for conceptualizing time in this so-called postmodern age, television has become relatively nonlinear. In terms of the syntax of many types of programs, such as sitcoms, television format follows a linear development of identifying a problem and ending with a conclusion. However, a television season is no longer a clear linear development from a beginning to an end point in the Spring. Reruns are interspersed throughout the year, and syndication occurs on independent channels. Sitcoms and other dramas seem to blend into one another both in overlapping characters (e.g., "Golden Girls" and "Empty Nest") and the general themes (e.g., single parent families, the trials of youth or single life) that may prevail. A result is that chronology tends to disappear and history becomes a mixed bag of events that lacks unifying or integrating threads. Moreover, there does not seem to be any particular reason to be historical in a linear manner. Today's sophisticated television viewer recognizes that people seldom pay attention to history in order to learn and avoid repeating earlier mistakes. Everyone seems to get the opportunity to make their own mistakes, or reinterpret their own history to suit themselves. The relativism that Allen Bloom (1987) decries in "The Closing of the American Mind" seems to hit squarely on that point. Television paints rather wonderful pictures of the past, and when they are not so wonderful they at least look visually interesting. Besides, when we watch television we are not concerned with history, we are concerned about killing time.

Killing time and being concerned about the moment or present have become the primary temporal orientations in today's consumer society. The temporal dimension of social behavior has seldom been examined by serious social scientists (Zerubavel 1981; Maines 1987), although we learned that we must do so some time ago (cf. Snow 1983; Altheide and Snow 1988). There are many facets to this phenomenon, but the practice of killing time through watching television is crucial to our notion of the television environment. On the one hand people talk about buying time, and there were some humorous advertisements about buying minutes, hours, and days like one would buy fast food. Certainly people feel hurried and stressed out. By contrast, television is an escape from work-a-day time and from the hurried pace and commodity approach to time. Of course, television time is also commodified, with commercial and quick-paced formats intended to attract and hold the viewer's attention for a moment as it contrasts a faster rhythm with conventional programming. It is not innocent, but like any routine interaction, has a logic of its own.

As a temporal environment, television is one of the few waking hour environments in which the individual can control time to his or her satisfaction. In "Time Wars," Jeremy Rifkin is concerned over our hurried pace and our artificial sense of time. What he overlooks is the possibility of controlling time through the very artificial means that he laments. On the other hand, this method of control would not be to the liking of the modernist who lives by linear rationality, progress, and the belief that structural change is the only hope to building a better society. As we suggested above, this is where most media critics are coming from.

We ended our concluding chapter in 1979 as follows:

> Whereas Karl Mannheim (1936) alerted us to the significance of political ideology and utopian thought as forms through which knowledge was constructed, we urge researchers to recognize the role of a highly rational and bureaucratized media logic in transforming and shaping the meanings of knowledge of social institutions, including politics. We believe this approach will not only demystify and delegitimize the media culture being produced but will once again elevate relevant decisions to the respective institutional arenas.

More than two decades of observations and additional study of the role of media logic in daily affairs and particularly public life have led us to modify our position. We were wrong in 1979 about the possibility of altering media culture. It is us, and this is how we live. We are not merely in a vestigial stage of civilization that can be redirected by moral (or intellectual) reformers. We do not advocate changing the "medianess" of our social order, and we could not possibly hope to do so even if we dishonestly claimed to have a better alternative. No, we will not insult the reader with a host of throwback ideas to a "previous golden era" when individuals and publics possessed certain things they no longer have; nor will we whine about the evils of capitalism or communism, and hope to invoke conventional academic "story telling" rhetoric to convince the reader that the "evil media formats and logic" can be somehow conquered, that things can be set "right," and that we can return to a golden age when the form of communication did not dominate content and discourse. There never was such a golden age, and we cannot return to it. To argue otherwise is to be "hip and relevant," but also out of time.

The social world has changed because of the way we interactively impress our ideas and definitions on our environments and experiences. Of course, not everyone has equal opportunity to impose their criteria and definitions. That is the long and short of technology. The modern world (and its postmodern inhabitants) is a communicative order that is no longer oriented to nonmediated tasks. Experience is mediated, we learn the rules and logics of mediation, and we are in turn self-mediated.

It is time that researchers position themselves within the flux of their media culture and help articulate how these formats and logic actually operate, and what consequences they have. Indeed, much of our own work has been dedicated to showing the consequences of certain formats on social life, and proposing alternative ones. Journalism, as we know it, cannot be salvaged; it must be replaced with a different expectation and a different format that will permit independent representations of culture, events, and issues. But we urge our readers to reject all claims by others—and us—that focus only on the inappropriateness of media culture for our lives. It just is, that's all. We know how it got that way and we are still learning how it works. But we are fools if we commit the error that chroniclers of any age almost always commit: evaluating their age by the standards, criteria, logics, and rhythms of another era. We are in a media era. We cannot return to the time when the dominant discourse was the spoken word to be heard by those within earshot, or several thousands of years later, the written word to be read by those who were interested in becoming familiar with the claims.

Our view is that a new analytical perspective must be adopted if we are to understand the process of media logic and consequent media culture. Traditionally, media have been analyzed as devices that facilitate information flow. This approach focused attention on the nature of the information passing through media. Studies emerged that found bias in news reporting, harmful effects of television violence, and adverse socialization conditions. Although these studies were of value in understanding some media effects, they did not lead to an understanding of how communication occurs or why mass media are such a pervasive force in urban society. Utilizing a behaviorism framework, many observers simply assumed that media constituted a powerful stimulus in producing behavioral effects. Our point is that media are powerful because people have adopted a media logic. Since people perceive, interpret, and act on the bias of the existing media logic, that logic has become a way of life. Consequently, media should not be viewed as just another variable in the process of social change. Nor should media be considered just one of many factors that may be plugged into a sophisticated structural model. To follow this approach is to miss the pervasive influence of media. Social change occurs and is recognized through communication forms and logics. Since media are essential to the process of nearly all social life, urban society cannot be understood apart from media. Mass communication and attending media logic are at the very heart of the collective consciousness that binds society together.

How significant the media presentations of reality are for the historical process remains an open question, but one that must be carefully considered on a case-by-case basis within and between cultures. Indeed, we are both fascinated and chagrined at the potential for a dominant media logic to transform the historical process worldwide (Tunstall 1977; Schlesinger et al. 1983; Altheide 1985c). Although the events in China and Eastern Europe in 1989–1990 were not caused by the media order, there is no question that they were strongly influenced. Although these important questions are just being formulated, we believe that contemporary society manifests a media consciousness. Everyone touched by media logic becomes another agent, and social reality is being "produced" through a major institutional inversion that we are now only beginning to understand.

The media logic that was perfected with the mini-invasions of Grenada, Panama, and that was brought to bear on the Chinese student movement, continues to flourish and define situations. As this work goes to press, the United States and some of its United Nation's allies are toe to toe with Iraqi and other Arab forces in the hellish desert sands that foretell Armageddon. Following Iraq's invasion of Kuwait and posturing to annex Saudi Arabia, President George Bush drew a line in the blowing sands and staked his claim with the largest buildup of firepower in history. During these tense times, several US network news anchor persons raced for "on the scene" reports, including CBS's Dan Rather's "scoop" interview with Iraq's leader Saddam Hussein. Ted Koppel was there for "Nightline" reports, and thousands of video-cameras were sent to GI's so that they could record their experiences. Bush complained that he did not have the same access to the Arab people as Hussein did to U.S. news watchers, although Bush would accept Hussein's invitation to give an eight minute taped statement to the Iraqi people; Hussein would request equal time; and comedian Jay Leno would opine during the 1990 Emmy Awards (for television) that the war was being fought through television! Indeed! Organized journalism covered it all, and some of the best known journalists denied that they were major players! As the United Nations imposed a deadline of January 15, 1991 for Iraq's withdrawal of Kuwait approached, a local Phoenix TV news program captioned its news, "Countdown to Conflict," and CBS's Dan Rather proclaimed "7 Days to Confrontation." It was theater of the most deadly sort, directed, produced and criticized through media logic.

The United States of America bombed Baghdad, Iraq, on January 16, 1991. Americans watched it on television. Billy Graham spent the night at the White House.

References

Adams, William and F. Schreibman (eds.). 1978. *Television Network News: Issues in Content Research.* Washington, D.C.: George Washington University.

Adams, William (ed.). 1981. *TV Coverage of the Middle East.* Norwood, NJ: Ablex.

Ailes, Roger. 1988. *You Are the Message: Secrets of the Master Communicator.* Homewood, IL: Dow Jones Irwin.

Alexander, Jeffrey C. (ed) 1988. *Durkheimian Sociology Cultural Studies.* N.Y. Cambridge Univ Press.

Altheide, David L. 1976. *Creating Reality: How TV News Distorts Events.* Beverly Hills, CA: Sage.

————. 1977. "Mental Illness and the News: The Eagleton Story." *Sociology and Social Research: An International Journal* January:138–155.

————. 1978a. "RTNDA News Award Judging and Media Culture." *Journalism Quarterly* Spring:164–167.

————. 1978b "Newsworkers and Newsmakers: A Study in News Use." *Urban Life* October:359–378.

————. 1980. "Learning from Mistakes: Toward a Reflective Journalism." *Gazette: International Journal for Mass Communication Studies* 26:111–120.

————. 1981. "Iran vs. U.S. TV News! The Hostage Story Out of Context." Pp. 128–158 in *TV Coverage of the Middle East*, edited by William Adams, Norwood NJ: Ablex.

————. 1984a. "Media Hegemony: A Failure of Perspective." *Public Opinion Quarterly* Summer, 48:476–490.

————. 1884b. "The Media Self." pp. 476–490 in Andrea Fontana and Joseph Kotarba (eds.), *The Existential Self in Society.* Chicago: University of Chicago Press.

————. 1985a. "Symbolic Interaction and 'Uses and Gratification': Towards A Theoretical Integration." *Communications: The European Journal of Communication* 11:73–82.

————. 1985b. "Impact of Format and Ideology on TV News Coverage of Iran." *Journalism Quarterly* Summer, 62:346–351.

————. 1985c. *Media Power.* Beverly Hills, CA: Sage,

————. 1987a. "Formats for Crises." *National Forum* 68:12–14.

————. 1987b. "Media Logic and Social Interaction." *Symbolic Interaction* 10:129–138.

————. 1987c. "Format and Symbols in TV Coverage of Terrorism in the United States and Great Britain." *International Studies Quarterly* 31:161–176.

————. 1987d. "Ethnographic Content Analysis." *Qualitative Sociology* 10:65–77.

———. 1988. "Computer Formats and Bureaucratic Structures." Pp. 215–230 in David Maines and Carl Couch (eds.), *Communication and Social Structure.* Springfield, IL: Charles C Thomas.

———. 1989. "The Elusive Mass Media: Franco Ferrarotti's 'The End of Conversation: The Impact of Mass Media on Modern Society.' " *International Journal of Politics, Culture and Society* 2:416–421.

———. 1990a. "Controlling the Urge for a Central Sociological Concept: A Comment on Gibb's, 'Control as Sociology's Central Notion.' " *The Social Science Journal.* 27:69–77.

———. 1990b. "The Culture of Electronic Communication." *Cultural Dynamics: An International Journal for the Study of Processes and Temporality of Culture.* 2:62–78.

———. 1990c. *Gonzo Justice.* Presented at the Stone Symposium, St. Petersburg, FL., Jan. 25–28.

——— and John M. Johnson. 1990. "Tacit Knowledge: The Boundaries of Experience." Presented at the Annual Meeting of the Society for the Study of Symbolic Interaction, Washington, DC, Aug. 12–14.

Altheide, D. L. and Robert P. Snow. 1978. "Sports versus the Mass Media." *Urban Life* July:189–204.

———. 1979. *Media Logic.* Beverly Hills, CA: Sage.

———. 1988. "Toward a Theory of Mediation." pp. 194–223. in J. Anderson (ed.), *Communication Yearbook 11.* Beverly Hills, CA.: Sage.

Anderson, James A. and Timothy P. Meyer. 1988. *Mediated Communication.* Newbury Park, CA: Sage.

Anson, R. S. 1978. "The World According to Garth." *New Times* October 30:18–27.

Aronson, James. 1970. *The Press and the Cold War.* Boston: Beacon Press.

Barnouw, E. 1975. *Tube of Plenty: The Evolution of American Television.* New York: Oxford University Press.

Batscha, R. M. 1975. *Foreign Affairs News and the Broadcast Journalist.* New York: Praeger.

Beard, Betty and Jean Novotny 1990. "Economic Bonanza." *Arizona Republic* March 14: A-1.

Becchelloni, G. 1980. "The Journalist as a Political Client in Italy. In A. Smith (ed.) *Newspapers Democracy.* Cambridge Mass: M.I.T. Press.

Bell, Q. 1978. "The Riddle of Fashion." *Human Nature* December: 60–67.

Bennett, W. Lance. 1983. *News: The Politics of Illusion.* New York: Longman.

Bensman, Joseph and Robert Lillienfeld. 1973. *Craft and Consciousness: Occupational Technique and the Development of World Images.* New York: John Wiley.

Berger, Peter and Thomas Luckmann. 1977. *The Social Construction of Reality.* Garden City, NY: Anchor.

Berman, Ronald. 1987. *How Television Sees Its Audience.* Newbury Park, CA: Sage.

Billy Graham Evangelical Association 1977. Report to Minnesota Securities Department (Corporation Balance Sheet).

Blanchard, R. O. 1974. *Congress and the News Media.* New York: Hastings.

Bloom, Allan. 1987. *The Closing of the American Mind.* New York: Simmon & Schuster.

Blumer, Herbert. 1969. *Symbolic Interactionism.* Englewood Cliffs, NJ: Prentice Hall.

Bogart, L. 1956. "Television's Effects on Spectator Sports." Pp. 386–396 in *Sport in the Socio-Cultural Process,* edited by M. M. Hart. Dubuque, IA: William C. Brown.

Bonafede, D. 1978. "Uncle Sam: The Flimflam Man?" *Washington Journalism Review* April/May:65–71.

Boorstin, D. J. 1961. *The Image.* New York: Harper & Row.

Boot, William. 1990. "Wading Around in the Panama Pool." *Columbia Journalism Review* March/April:18–20.

Bourdieu Pierre and Jean-Claude Passeron. 1990. *Reproduction in Education, Society & Culture* Newbury Park, CA: Sage

Braestrup, Peter. 1978. *Big story: How the American Press and Television Reported and Interpreted the Crisis of Tet in 1968 in Vietnam and Washington.* Garden City NY: Anchor.

Brissett, Dennis and Charles Edgley. (eds.) 1990. *Life as Theater.* New York: Aldine de Gruyter.

Brittan, Arthur. 1977. *The Privatised World.* London: Routledge & Kegan Paul.

Bronk, C. Anthony. 1987. *A Horse of a Different Color: Television's Treatment of Jesse Jackson's 1984 Presidential Campaign.* Lanham, MD: University Press of America.

Burns, T. 1977. *The BBC: Public Institution and Private World.* London: Macmillan.

Cantor, Muriel. 1980. *Prime-Time Television: Content and Control.* Beverly Hills, CA: Sage.

Carey, James (ed.). 1987. *Media, Myths and Narratives.* Newbury Park, CA: Sage.

Carlson, Timothy. 1990. "Beauty and the Beast: The Show that Wouldn't Die and the Fans Who Wouldn't Let It." *TV Guide* January 13:2–6.

Chesebro, James W. and John D. Glenn. 1982. "The Soap Opera as a Communication System." pp. 250–261 in *Inter/media,* edited by Gary Gumpert and Robert Cathcart. New York: Oxford University Press

Cicourel, Aaron. 1968. *The Social Organization of Juvenile Justice.* New York: John Wiley.

Clift, Eleanor. 1987. "The Legacy of Larry Speakes." *Columbia Journalism Review* March:40–44.

Cohen, Akiba and Charles R. Bantz. 1989. "Where Did We Come From and Where Are We Going?" *American Behavioral Scientist* 33:135–143.

Cohen, Bob. 1990. *Arizona Republic,* January 28, p. E5.

Cohen, Stanley and Jock Young. (eds.). 1973. *The Manufacture of News.* Beverly Hills, CA: Sage.

Combs, James. 1984. *Polpop: Politics and Popular Culture in America.* Bowling Green, OH: Bowling Green University Press.

Comstock, George. 1980. *Television in America.* Beverly Hills, CA: Sage.

———. (ed.). 1989. *The Evolution of American Television.* Newbury Park, CA: Sage.

Cook, Timothy E. 1989. *Making Laws and Making News: Media Strategies in the U.S. House of Representatives.* Washington, D.C.: Brookings Institution.

Cosell, Howard. 1973. *Cosell.* New York: Pocket Books.

Couch, Carl. 1984. *Constructing Civilizations.* Greenwich, CT: JAI Press.

Couch, Carl. 1990. "Mass Communication and State Structures." *The Social Science Journal* 2:111–128.

Cox, Harvey. 1979. "Bad News for the Good News." *The American Baptist* January:2–3.

Davis, D. E. and S. J. Baran. 1981. *Mass Communication and Everyday Life.* Belmont, CA: Wadsworth.

DeFleur, M. L. and S. Ball-Rokeach. 1975. *Theories of Mass Communication.* New York: David McKay.

Denisoff, R. S. 1975. *Solid Gold: The Popular Music Industry.* New Brunswick, NJ: Transaction.

Denton, Robert E., Jr. 1988. *The Primetime Presidency of Ronald Reagan: The Era of the Television Presidency.* New York: Praeger.

Desmond, R. W. 1978. *The Information Process: World News Reporting to the Twentieth Century.* Iowa City: University of Iowa Press.

Duncan, M. C. and B. Brummett. 1987. "The Mediation of Spectator Sport." *Research Quarterly for Exercise and Sport* 58:168–177.

Dunn, D. 1969. *Public Officials and the Press.* Reading, MA: Addison-Wesley.

Durkheim, Emile. 1961. *The Elementary Forms of Religious Life.* NY: Collier Books.

Edelman, Murray. 1989. *Constructing Political Spectacles.* Chicago: University of Chicago Press.

Elliott, P. 1972. *The Making of a Television Series.* London: Constable.

Entman, Robert M. 1989. *Democracy Without Citizens: Media and the Decay of American Politics.* New York: Oxford University Press.

Epstein, Edward J. 1974. *News from Nowhere.* New York: Hastings.

———. 1975. *Between Fact and Fiction: The Problem of Journalism.* New York: Vintage.

———. 1977. *Agency of Fear: Opiates and Political Power.* New York: Putnam.

Ericson, Richard V., Patricia M. Baranek, and Janet B. L. Chan. 1987. *Visualizing Deviance: A Study of News Organization.* Toronto: University of Toronto Press.

———. 1989. *Negotiating Control: A Study of News Sources.* Toronto: University of Toronto Press.

———. *Acknowledging Order.* forthcoming. Toronto: University of Toronto.

Ewen, Stuart. 1988. *All Consuming Images: The Politics of Style in Contemporary Culture.* New York: Basic Books.

Fang, I. 1968. *Television News.* New York: Hastings.

Featherstone, Mike (ed.). 1988. *Postmodernism.* Newbury Park, CA: Sage.

Ferrarotti, Franco. 1988. *The End of Conversation: The Impact of Mass Media on Modern Society.* Westport, CT: Greenwood Press.

Fishman, Mark. 1980. *Manufacturing the News.* Austin, TX: University of Texas Press.

Fiske, John. 1984. "Popularity and Ideology: A Structuralist Reading of 'Dr. Who.'" Pp. 165–198 in *Interpreting Television: Current Research Perspectives,* edited by W. D. Rowland, Jr. and B. Watkins, Newbury Park, CA: Sage.

Fiske, John. 1987. *Television Culture.* New York: Methuen.

Frank, Thomas M. 1984. "Michael Deaver Rates the President's Press." *Washington Journalism Review* 6:23–25.

Frankl, Razelle. 1987. *Televangelism.* Carbondale, IL: Southern Illinois University Press.

Freund, C. P. 1978. "Remembering Newspaper Row." *Washington Journalism Review* January/February: 62–65.

Friendly, Fred. 1967. *Due to Circumstances Beyond Our Control.* New York: Vintage.

Fritz, Noah and David L. Altheide. 1987. "The Mass Media and the Social Construction of the Missing Children Problem." *Sociological Quarterly* 28:473–

Fulghum, Robert. 1990. *It Was on Fire When I Laid Down on It.* NY: Villard Books.

Gans, Herbert. 1979. *Deciding What's News.* New York: Pantheon.

Garfinkel, Harold. 1967. *Studies in Ethnomethodology.* Englewood Cliffs, NJ: Prentice-Hall.

Gentry, James K. and Barbara Zang. 1989. "The Graphics Editor Takes Charge." *Washington Journalism Review* January/February: 24–28.

Gerbner, George and W. H. Melody (eds). 1973. *Communications Technology and Social Policy: Understanding the New "Cultural Revolution."* New York: John Wiley.

Gilbert, R. E. 1972. *Television and Presidential Politics.* North Quincy, MA: Christopher Publishing.

Gitlin, Todd. 1980. *The Whole World Is Watching.* Berkeley: University of California Press.

———. 1983. *Inside Prime-Time.* New York: Pantheon.

Glasgow Media Group. 1976. *Bad News.* London: Routledge & Kegan Paul.

———. 1985. *War and Peace News.* Milton Keynes, England: Open University Press.

Goffman, Erving. 1959. *The Presentation of Self in Everyday Life.* Garden City, NY: Doubleday.

———. 1967. *Interaction Ritual.* Garden City, NY: Doubleday.

———. 1974. *Frame Analysis: An Essay on the Organization of Experience.* New York: Harper & Row.

———. 1981. *Forms of Talk.* Philadelphia, PA: University of Pennsylvania Press.

Goldenberg, Edie N. and Michael W. Traugott. 1987. "MassMedia Effects on Recognizing and Rating Candidates in U.S. Senate Elections." Pp. 109–159 in *Campaigns in the News: Mass Media and Congressional Elections,* edited by Jan Pons Vermeer. New York: Greenwood Press.

Golding, Peter and Graham Murdock. 1979. "Ideology and the Mass Media: The Question of Determination." Pp. 198–224 in *Ideology and Cultural Production,* edited by M. Barrett et al. New York: St. Martins.

Goldman, Kevin. (1990) "Was Today' Mess Just a Plot to Make Jane Pauley a Star." *Wall Street Journal,* March 12, p. 1

Graber, Doris. 1984. *Processing the News: How People Tame the Information Tide.* New York: Longman.

Greenberg, B. S. 1976. TV for Children: Communicator and Audience Perceptions. Pp. 29–44 in *Children and Television,* edited by R. Brown. Beverly Hills, CA: Sage.

Greenfield, P. M. 1984. *Mind and Media: The Effects of Television.* Cambridge, MA: Harvard University Press.

Gronbeck, Bruce E. 1988. "Symbolic Interactionism and Communication Studies: Prolegomena to Future Research." Pp. 323–339 in *Communication and Social Structure,* edited by David Maines and Carl Couch Springfield, IL: Charles C Thomas

Gronbeck, Bruce E. 1990. "Popular Culture, Media and Political Communication." Pp. 185–222 in *New Directions in Political Communitcaion: A Resource Book,* edited by David Swanson and Dan Nimmo Newbury Park, CA: Sage.

Gunter, Barry and Mallory Wober. 1983. "Television Viewing and Public Perceptions of Hazards to Life." *Journal of Environment Psychology* 3:325–335.

Haddix, Doug. 1990. "Alar as a Media Event." *Columbia Journalism Review.* March/April: 44–45.

Hall, John S. and David Altheide. 1990. "Leadership in Context: Some New Realities." Pp. 130–159 in *New Directions for Arizona: The Leadership Challenge,* edited by Ron Melnick and John Stuart Hall. (56th Arizona Townhall). Tempe, AZ: Morrison Institute for Public Policy, Arizona State University.

Hall, Peter M. 1988. "Asymmetry, Information Control and Information Technology." Pp. 341–356 in *Communication and Social Structure,* edited by David Maines and Carl Couch (Eds.), Springfield, IL: Charles C. Thomas.

Hall, Stuart. 1973. "A World at One with Itself." Pp. 85–94 in S. Cohen and J. Young (eds.), *The Manufacture of News.* Beverly Hills, CA: Sage.

Harris, Mark, 1974. "The Last Article." *New York Times Magazine* Vol. 6, 20–25.

Hart, Roderick P. 1987. *The Sound of Leadership: Presidential Communication in the Modern Age.* Chicago: University of Chicago Press.

Haas, C. 1978. "Invasion of the Mind Snatchers." *New Times* July 24:31–36.

Hearings Before the Committee on Governmental Affairs, United States Senate (1977). Matters relating to T. Bertram Lance, Volume 1 (January 17 and 18); Volume 2, Part 1 (July 15 and 25); Volume 3, Part 3 (Appendix, September); Volume 4, Part 4 (September 8–19). Washington, D.C.: U.S. Government Printing Office.

Herman, Edward S. and Noam Chomsky. 1988. *Manufacturing Consent: The Political Economy of the Mass Media.* New York: Pantheon.

Herman, Edward S. and Gerry O'Sullivan. 1989. *The Terrorism Industry: The Experts and Institutions That Shape Our View of Terror.* New York: Pantheon.

Hertsgaard, Mark. 1988. *On Bended Knee: The Press and the Reagan Presidency.* New York: Farrar Straus Giroux.

Horsfield, P. 1984. *Religious Television.* NY: Longman.

Horton, D. and R. R. Wohl. 1956. "Mass Communication and Para-Social Interaction: Observations on Intimacy at a Distance." *Psychiatry* 9:215–229.

Hughes, Helen M. 1940. *News and the Human Interest Story.* Chicago: University of Chicago Press.

Jackson, Russell. 1990. Department of Broadcasting, Palomar College, Vista, CA (Personal Interview).

Jamieson, Kathleen Hall. 1988. *The Interplay of Influence,* 3nd ed. Belmont, CA: Wadsworth.

Johnson, W. O., Jr. 1971. *Super Spectator and the Electric Lilliputians.* Boston: Little, Brown.

Joseph, Greg. 1990. "Anthony Quinn Lifts 'Old Man'." *Arizona Republic: Television,* March 25, p. 3.

Joslyn, Richard A. 1987. "Liberal Campaign Rhetoric in 1984." Pp. 31–49 in *Campaigns in the News: Mass Media and Congressional Elections.* New York: Greenwood Press.

Katz, Elihu and T. Szecsko. (eds.). 1981. *The Mass Media and Social Change.* Beverly Hills, CA: Sage.

Katz, R. 1978. "The Egalitarian Waltz." *Human Nature* April:76–82.

Kern, Montague. 1989. *30-Second Politics: Political Advertising in the Eighties.* Westport, CT: Greenwood Press.

Kinsella, James. 1990. *AIDS and the American Media.* New Brunswick, NJ: Rutgers University Press.

Klein, Paul 1975. "The Television Audience and Program Mediocrity." Pp. 74–77 in *Mass Media and Society,* edited by A. Wells. Palo Alto, CA: Mayfield.

Kroeber, A. L. 1919. "On the Principle of Order in Civilization as Exemplified by Changes of Fashion." *American Anthropoligist* 13:235–263.

Kurtz, Howard. 1990. "Dr. Whelan's Media Operation." *Columbia Journalism Review* March/April:43–47.

Lang, G. E. and K. Lang. 1977. "Immediate and Mediated Responses: Reaction to the first Ford–Carter debate." Presented at the Annual Meeting of the American Sociological Association, Chicago.

Lang, Kurt and Gladys E. Lang. 1968. *Politics and Television.* Chicago: Quadrangle.

——— 1983. "The 'New' Rhetoric of Mass Communication Research: A Larger View." *Journal of Communication* 33:128–140.

Lapham, Lewis H. 1988. "Politics Noveau." *Harper's Magazine* December:12–14.

Lasch, Christopher. 1979. *The Culture of Narcissism: American Life in an Age of Diminishing Expectations.* New York: Norton.

Lasica, J. D. 1989. "Photographs That Lie: The Ethical Dilemma of Digital Retouching." *Washington Journalism Review* June:22–25.

Lave, Jean. 1988. *Cognition in Practice: Mind, Mathematics, and Culture in Everyday Life.* New York: Cambridge University Press.

Lee, C. 1980. *Media Imperialism Reconsidered: The Homogenizing of Television Culture.* Beverly Hills, CA: Sage.

Lehman-Haupt, Christopher. 1988. " 'Unmaking' Unmasks a Hollow Office." (New York Times) p. F12 in the Arizona Republic, October 2, 1988.

Lehnerer, Melodye 1990. "Bestiality: Was Prime Time Simply Not Ready?" Presented at the Popular Culture Association Meetings, Toronto, Ontario, Canada, March 9, 1990.

Levine, Donald N. 1971. *Georg Simmel: On Individuality and Social Forms.* Chicago, IL: University of Chicago Press. 187–198.

Levy, Mark R. 1979. "Watching TV News as Para-Social Interaction." *Journal of Broadcasting* 23:69–80.

Levy, Mark R. (ed.). 1989. *The VCR Age: Home Video and Mass Communication.* Newbury Park, CA: Sage.

———— and S. Windahl. 1984. "Audience Activity and Gratifications: A Conceptual Clarification and Exploration." *Communication Research* 11:51–78.

Lichter, S. Robert, Daniel Amundson, and Richard Noyes. 1988. *The Video Campaign: Network Coverage of the 1988 Primaries*. Washington, D.C.: American Enterprise Institute.

Lindlof, Thomas R. 1987. *Natural Audiences: Qualitative Research on Media Uses and Effects*. Norwood, NJ: Ablex.

Lipset, Seymour Martin. 1989. "The US Elections: The Status Quo Re-affirmed." *International Journal of Public Opinion Research* 1:45–77.

Littlejohn, D. 1975. "Communicating Ideas by Television." Pp. 63–79 in *Television as a Social Force,* edited by D. Carter and R. Adlen. New York: Praeger.

Luckmann, Thomas. 1989. "On Meaning in Everyday Life and in Sociology." *Current Sociology* 39:17–29.

Lull, James. 1982. "The Social Uses of Television." Pp. 397–409 in *Mass Communication Review Yearbook,* Vol. 3 edited by D. C. Whitney et al. Beverley Hills, CA: Sage.

————. (ed.). 1988. *World Families Watch Television*. Newbury, Park, CA: Sage.

Luschen, Gunther. 1967. "The Interdependence of Sport and Culture." *International Review of Sport Sociology* 2:127–139.

Lyman, Stanford M. 1978. *The Drama of Social Reality*. New York: Oxford University Press.

———— and M. B. Scott. 1970. *A Sociology of the Absurd*. New York: Appleton Century Crofts.

———— and Arthur J. Vidich. 1988. *Social Order and the Public Philosphy: An Analysis and Interpretation of the Work of Herbert Blumer*. Fayetteville, AK: The University of Arkansas Press.

McDonald, J. Fred. 1990. *One Nation Under Television: The Rise and Decline of Network TV*. New York: Pantheon.

McLuhan, Marshall. 1962. *The Gutenberg Galaxy: The Making of Typographical Man*. Toronto: University of Toronto Press.

————.1964. *Understanding Media: The Extensions of Man*. New York: McGraw-Hill.

———— and Q. Fiore. 1967. *The Medium Is the Message: An Inventory of Effects*. New York: Random House.

McQuail, Denis. 1983. *Mass Communication Theory*. Newbury Park, CA: Sage.

Maines, David. 1982. "In Search of Mesostructure." *Urban Life* 11:267–279.

———— 1987. "The Significance of Temporality for the Development of Sociological Theory." *The Sociological Quarterly* 28:303–311.

———— and Carl Couch (eds.). 1988. *Communication and Social Structure*. Springfield, IL: Charles C Thomas

Mannheim, Karl. 1936. *Ideology and Utopia*. New York: Harcourt, Brace Jovanovich.

Manning, Peter K. 1988. *Symbolic Communication: Signifying Calls and the Police Response*. Cambridge, Mass: MIT Press.

Martin, William. 1981. "The Birth of a Media Myth." *The Atlantic*. June:9–16.

Marx, Gary T. 1988. *Undercover: Police Surveillance in America.* Berkeley, CA: University of California Press.

Mayer, Jane and Doyle McManus. 1988. *Landslide: The Unmaking of the President, 1984–1988.* New York: Houghton Mifflin.

Mendelsohn, H. 1964. "Listening to Radio." Pp. 239–248 in *People, Society and Mass Communication,* edited by A. Dexter and D. M. White. New York: Free Press.

Merrill, John C. 1977. *Existential Journalism.* New York: Hastings House.

Meyrowitz, Josuha. 1985. *No Sense of Place: The Impact of Electronic Media on Social Behavior.* New York: Oxford University Press.

Mickelson, Sig. 1989. *From Whistle Stop to Sound Bite: Four Decades of Politics and Television.* New York: Praeger.

Miller, Mark Crispin. 1988. *Boxed In: The Culture of TV.* Chicago, IL: Northwestern University Press.

Minow, N. N., J. B. Martin, and L. M. Mitchell. 1973. *Presidential Television.* New York: Basic Books.

Mitroff, Ian I. and Warren Bennis. 1990. *The Unreality Industry.* Seacaucus, NJ: Carol Publishing Group.

Molotch, H. and M. Lester. 1974. "News as a Purposive Behavior." *American Sociological Review* 39:101–112.

———. 1975. "Accidental News: The Great Oil Spill." *American Journal of Sociology* 81d:235–260.

Monaco, J. 1978. *Media Culture.* New York: Dell.

Morris, Colin. 1984. *God-in-a-Box.* London: Hodder & Stoughton.

Morrison, David E. and Howard Tumber. 1988. *Journalists at War: The Dynamics of News Reporting During the Falklands Conflict.* Newbury Park, CA: Sage.

Murphy, M. 1978. "The Next Billy Graham." *Esquire* October 10:25–32.

Nesbit, Dorothy Davidson. 1988. *Videostyle in Senate Campaigns.* Knosville, TN: The University of Tennessee Press.

Nessen, R. 1978. *It Sure Looks Different from the Inside.* Chicago: Playboy Press.

Newcomb, Horace. 1974. *TV: The Most Popular Art.* Garden City, NY: Anchor Press.

Nimmo, D. 1976. "Political Image and the Mass Media." *Annals* 427:33–44.

——— and James E. Combs. 1983. *Mediated Political Realities.* New York: Longman.

Nisbet, R. 1976. *Sociology as an Art Form.* London: Oxford University Press.

Noble G. 1975. *Children in Front of the Small Screen.* Beverly Hills, CA: Sage.

Noelle-Neumann, E. 1973. "Return to the Concept of Powerful Mass Media." *Studies of Broadcasting* 9:67–112.

Oberdorfer, Donald. 1982. *Electronic Christianity: Myth or Ministry.* Taylors Falls, MN.: John L. Brekke & Sons.

O'Connor, Ann-Marie. 1987. "Dateline: Honduras. Subject: the Contras." *Columbia Journalism Review* May/June:38–41.

Oudes, Bruce. 1989. *From the President: President Nixon's Secret Files.* New York: Harper & Row.

Park, Robert. E. 1940. "News as a Form of Knowledge." *American Journal of Sociology* 45:669–686.

Patterson, Thomas E. 1980. *The Mass Media Election*. New York: Praeger.

Patterson, T. E. and R. D. McClure 1976. *The Unseeing Eye*. New York: Putnam.

Peterzell, Jay. 1990. "Betraying the Source: How the U.S. Press Helps Finger Protestors Abroad: Ignoring the Leson of Xiao Bin." *Columbia Journalism Review* March/April:6–8.

Phillips, E. B. 1977. "Approaches to Objectivity: Journalistic vs. Social Science Perspectives." Pp. 63–78 in *Strategies for Communication Research*, edited by P. M. Hirsch, P. V. Miller and F. G. Kline. Beverly Hills, CA: Sage.

Porter, Bruce. 1989. "The Scanlon Spin: How P. R. Pro John Scanlon Befriends and Bewitches the Media." *Columbia Journalism Review* September/Octo-

Postman, Neil. 1984. *Amusing Ourselves to Death*. NY: Viking.

Raphel, Arnold. 1980–81. "Media Coverage of the Hostage Netgotiations—from Fact to Fiction." Presented at the 24th Session of the Executive Seminar in National and International Affairs, Foreign Service Institute, Washington, D.C.

Raymond, Paul Bradford. 1987. "Shaping the News: An Analysis of House Candidates' Campaign Communications," Pp. 13–30 in *Campaigns in the News: Mass Media and Congressional Elections*, edited by Vermeer, Jan Pons. New York: Greenwood Press.

Real, Michael R. 1989. *Super Media: A Cultural Studies Approach*. Newbury Park, CA: Sage.

Reeves, R. 1978. "The Dangers of Television in the Fred Silverman Era." *Esquire* April 25:45–57.

Regent-Lee, Denise. 1990. "The Television Situation Comedy: Development and Change." Unpublished Masters Thesis. Arizona State University.

Riesman, D., R. Denny, and N. Glazer. 1950. *The Lonely Crowd*. New Haven, CT: Yale University Press.

Robinson, Gertrude. 1984. Television News and the Claim to Facticity: Quebec's Referendum Coverage." Pp. 199–221 in *Interpreting Television: Current Research Perspectives*, edited by Willard D. Rowland, Jr. and Bruce Watkins. Newbury Park, CA: Sage.

Robinson, Michael J. 1977. "Television and American Politics: 1956–1976." *The Public Interest* Spring:1–39.

Robinson, Michael J., and M. A. Sheehan. 1983. *Over the Wire and on TV*. New York: Russell Sage.

Roshco, B. 1975. *Newsmaking*. Chicago: University of Chicago Press.

Rose, Tom. 1990. *Freeing the Whales: How the Media Created the World's Greatest Non-Event*. Secaucus, NJ: Carol Publishing Group.

Rosellini, Lynn. 1990. "The Changing Voice of Talk Radio." *U.S. News and World Report* January 15:51–55.

Rosenblum, B. 1978. *Photographers and Their Photographs*. New York: Holmes/Meier.

Rosengren, K. E., P. Arvidson, and D. Sturesson 1978. "The Barseback "Panic": A Case Study of Deviance." Pp. 131–152 in *Deviance and Mass Media*, edited by C. Winick Beverly Hills, CA: Sage.

———. 1983. "Communication Research: One Paradigm or Four." *Journal of Communication* 33:185–207.

Rourke, F. F. 1961. *Secrecy and Publicity: Dilemmas of Democracy.* Baltimore, MD: Johns Hopkins University Press.

Roszak, T. 1969. *The Making of a Counter-Culture.* New York: Anchor.

Michael Ryan & Douglas Kellner 1988. *Camera Politica: The Politics and Ideology of Contemporary Hollywood Film.* Bloomington, Ind: Indiana University Press.

Sachs, C. 1963. *World History of the Dance.* New York: W. W. Norton.

Sage, George H. 1970. *Sport and American Society: Selected Readings.* Reading, MA: Addison-Wesley Publishing.

Said, Edward. 1981. *Covering Islam.* New York: Pantheon.

Schanche, D. 1978. "Thorny Reality Slows the Drive for Mideast Peace." *Los Angeles Times* January 1.

Schandler H. Y. 1977. *The Unmaking of a President: Lyndon Johnson and Vietnam.* Princeton, NJ: Princeton University Press.

Schidlovsky, John. 1989. "Euphoria and Wu'er Kaixi . . . And Then the Killing." *Washington Journalism Review* September:20–24.

Philip Schlesinger and Bob Lumley. 1985. "Two Debates on Political Violence and the Mass Media." Pp. 324–349 in Teun A. van Dyk (ed.) *Discourse & Communication.* N.Y. Walter de Gruyter.

Schlesinger, Philip, G. Murdock, and P. Elliott. 1983. *Televising 'Terrorism': Political Violence in Popular Culture.* London: Comedia Publishing Group.

Schneider, Fred. 1985. *The Substance and Structure of Network Television News: An Analysis of Content Features, Format Features, and Formal Interviews.* Unpublished doctoral dissertation, Syracuse University.

Schorr, Daniel. 1977. *Clearing the Air.* Boston: Houghton Mifflin.

Schudson, Michael. 1978. *Discovering the News: A Social History of American Newspapers.* New York: Basic Books.

Schultze, Quentin J. 1988. "The Wireless Gospel." *Christianity Today* January 15, 32(1):18–23.

Schutz, Alfred. 1967. *The Phenomenology of the Social World* (trans. by G. Walsh and F. Lenhert). Evanston, IL: Northwestern University.

Schwartz, T. 1974. *The Responsive Chord.* New York: Anchor.

Seeger, Arthur A. 1983. *The Berkeley Barb: Social Control of an Underground Newsroom.* New York: Irvington.

Seymour-Ure, C. 1974. *The Political Impact of Mass Media.* London: Constable.

Shaw, D. L. and M. E. McCombs. 1977. *The Emergence of American Political Issues: The Agenda-Setting Function of the Press.* St. Paul, MN: West.

Sick, Gary. 1985. *All Fall Down: America's Tragic Encounter with Iran.* New York: Random House.

Simmel, Georg. 1950. *The Sociology of Georg Simmel.* Trans. & ed. by Kurt H. Wolff. NY: Free Press.

Simmons, Robert O., Jr. 1987. "Why Some Constituencies Are Better Informed than Most About the Positions of House Incumbents." Pp. 51–75 in *Campaigns in the News: Mass Media and Congressional Elections,* edited by Vermeer, Jan Pons New York: Greenwood Press.

Simpler, Steven. 1986. "Pastor's Animated Sermons Fuel 'Sunday Super Bowl.' " *Arizona Republic* September 20:F2.

Slater, P. 1970. *The Pursuit of Loneliness.* Boston: Beacon.

Snow, Robert P. 1983. *Media Culture*. Newbury Park, CA: Sage.

———. 1984. "Crime and Justice in Prime-Time News: The John Hinckley Jr., Case." Pp. 212–232 in *Justice and the Media*, edited by Ray Surette. Springfield, IL: Charles C. Thomas.

Speier, M. 1973, *How to Observe Face to Face Communication*. Santa Monica, CA: Goodyear.

Stabler, K. and D. O'Connor. 1977. *Super Bowl Diary*. Los Angeles: Pinnacle.

Stephenson, W. 1967. *The Play Theory of Mass Communication*. Chicago: University of Chicago Press.

Stone G. P. 1971. "American Sports: Play and Display." Pp. 46–65 in E. Dunning (ed.), *The Sociology of Sports*. London: Frank Cass.

Stone, Gregory P. 1972. *Games Sport and Power*. New Brunswick, NJ: Transaction Books.

Toffler, A. 1970. *Future Shock*. New York: Random House.

Tracey, M. 1977. *The Production of Political Television*. London: Routledge & Kegan Paul.

Tuchman, G. 1972. "Objectivity as Strategic Ritual." *American Journal of Sociology* 77:660–679.

———. (ed.). 1974. *The TV Establishment: Programming for Power and Profit*. Englewood Cliffs, NJ: Prentice-Hall.

———. 1976. "What Is news? Tell Stories." *Journal of Communication* Autumn:94–97.

———. 1978. *Making News: A Study in the Construction of Reality*. New York: Free Press.

———, A. K. Daniels, and J. Benet. (eds.). 1978. *Hearth and Home: Images of Women in the Mass Media*. New York: Oxford University Press.

Tunstall, J. 1977. *The Media Are American*. New York: Columbia University Press.

Vermeer, Jan Pons. (ed.). 1987. *Campaigns in the News: Mass Media and Congressional Elections*. New York: Greenwood Press.

Vidich, Arthur J. 1990. "The American Democracy: An Analysis of the 1988 Presidential Campaign." Presented at the 1990 Stone Symposium, St. Petersburg, FL, January 25–28.

——— and Stanford M. Lyman. 1984. *American Sociology: Worldly Rejections of Religion and Their Directions*. New Haven, CT: Yale University Press.

Von Hoffman, N. 1977. "The Breaking of a President: Shattering the Watergate Myth." *Penthouse* March:46ff.

Weaver, Paul. 1972. "Is Television News Biased?" *Public Interest* 26:57–74.

Weiss, Philip. 1988. "Party Time in Atlanta." *Columbia Journalism Review* September/October:27–34.

Weschler, Lawrence. 1990. "The Media's One and Only Freedom Story." *Columbia Journalism Review* March/April:26–31.

Wenner, Lawrence A. (ed.). 1989. *Media, Sports and Society*. Newbury Park, CA: Sage.

Wheeler, M. 1976. *Lies, Damn Lies, and Statistics*. New York: Liveright.

Williams, Frederick R. 1982. *The Sociology of Culture*. Newbury Park, CA: Sage.

Witcover, J. 1977. *Marathon: The Pursuit of the Presidency, 1972–1976*. New York: Signet.

Wolfe, T. 1976. The Me Decade and the Third Great Awakening." Pp. 94–110 in *Mauve Gloves and Madmen, Clutter and Vine*, edited by Tom Wolfe. New York: Farrar, Strauss & Giroux.

Woodward, Kenneth. 1980. "A One Million Dollar Habit." *Newsweek*. September 15:35.

Zerubavel, E. 1977. "The French Republican Calendar: A Case Study in the Sociology of Time." *American Sociological Review* 42:868–876.

———. 1981. *Hidden Rhythms*. Chicago, IL: University of Chicago Press.

Zoglin, Richard. 1990. "The Great TV Takeover." *Time* March 26:66–68.

Name Index

Adams, William, 55, 57, 85–87, 101, 102, 105, 177, 255
Ailes, Roger, 85–87, 101, 102, 105, 177, 255
Alexander, Jeffrey C., 244, 255
Altheide, David L., 2, 4, 10, 23, 52, 56, 60, 62–67, 70, 75–78, 89, 94, 101, 103, 107, 109, 135, 136, 141, 164, 166, 167, 176, 212, 247, 249, 250, 255, 256
Anderson, James A., 6, 7, 249, 256
Anson, R. S., 101, 256
Arledge, Roone, 46, 217
Aronson, James, 164, 256

Babbitt, Bruce, 182, 183
Bakker, James, 14, 206, 209, 213 ff
Ball-Rokeach, Sandra, 1, 258
Bantz, Charles R., 55, 257
Baran, S. J., 1, 258
Barnouw, Erik, 60, 256
Barrett, M., 259
Batscha, Robert M., 164, 256
Beccheloni, G., 82, 256
Bell, Quentin, 11, 256
Bennett, W. Lance, 55, 135, 256
Bennis, Warren, 55, 248, 263
Bensman, Joseph, 55, 256
Berger, Peter, 249, 256
Berman, Ronald, 249, 256
Blanchard, R. O., 84, 257
Bloom, Allan, 215, 230, 242, 257
Blumer, Herbert, 4, 80, 250, 257
Bogart, Leo, 217, 257
Bonafede, D., 105, 257
Boorstin, D. J., 101, 257
Boot, William, 74, 257
Bourdieu, Pierre, 249, 257
Braestrup, Peter, 78, 141, 257

Brissett, Dennis, 6, 257
Brittan, Arthur, 205, 257
Bronk, C. Anthony, 177, 257
Brummett, B., 217, 258
Burns, Tom, 59–61, 68, 80, 85, 92, 257
Bush, George, 14, 40, 187 ff

Cantor, Muriel, 17, 257
Carey, James, xi, i, 54
Carlson, Timothy, 36, 257
Carson, Johnny, 39, 207
Carter, Hodding, 169, 172
Carter, Jimmy, 84, 90, 95, 98, 106, 109 ff, 161, 175
Chesebro, James, 45, 257
Chomsky, Noam, 55, 266
Cicourel, Aaron, 80, 257
Clift, Eleanor, 82, 257
Cohen, Akiba, 55, 257
Cohen, Bob, 231, 257
Cohen, Stanley, 164, 257
Combs, James, 83, 257, 263
Comstrock, George, 1, 257
Cook, Timothy, 188, 258
Cosell, Howard, 223, 234, 235, 258
Couch, Carl, xiii, 10, 57, 81, 82, 87, 258
Cox, Harvey, 215, 258
Csikszentmihalya, M., 6

Daguerre, Louis, 66
Daley, Richard, 91, 92
Darman, Richard, 85, 111, 186
Davis, D. E., 1, 258
Deaver, Michael, 85, 87–89, 111, 186
DeFleur, M. L., 1, 258
Denisoff, R. S., 26, 258

268

Subject Index